W. C. Handy

W. C. Handy

The Life and Times of the Man Who Made the Blues

David Robertson

ALFRED A. KNOPF   NEW YORK   2009

THIS IS A BORZOI BOOK
PUBLISHED BY ALFRED A. KNOPF

Grateful acknowledgment is made to the following for permission
to reprint previously published material:
Handy Brothers Music Co., Inc.: Excerpts from "Atlanta Blues
(Make Me One Pallet on the Floor)" by William C. Handy; "Aunt
Hagar's Children Blues" by William C. Handy and J. Tim Brymn;
"Beale Street Blues" by William C. Handy; "The Hestitating Blues"
by William C. Handy; "Joe Turner Blues" by William C. Handy and
Walter Hirsch; "Mr. Crump" by William C. Handy; "St. Louis
Blues" by William C. Handy; and "Yellow Dog Blues" by William C.
Handy. All rights reserved. Reprinted by permission of Handy
Brothers Music Co., Inc.
Handy Brothers Music Co., Inc. and Jerry Vogel Music Company,
Inc.: "The Memphis Blues" by William C. Handy and George A.
Norton. All rights reserved. Reprinted by permission of Handy
Brothers Music Co., Inc. and Jerry Vogel Music Company, Inc.

Library of Congress Cataloging-in-Publication Data

Robertson, David.
W. C. Handy : the life and times of the man who made the blues /
by David Robertson.—1st ed.
p.   cm.
Includes bibliographical references.
ISBN 978-0-307-26609-5
1. Handy, W. C. (William Christopher), 1873–1958.
2. Composers—United States—Biography.
I. Title.
ML410.H18R63 2009
782.421643092—dc22
[B]   2008045983

Manufactured in the United States of America
First Edition

This book is for Andrew Jackson Sellers and Melinda Neal

All night the saxophones wailed the hopeless comment of "Beale Street Blues," while a hundred pairs of golden and silver slippers shuffled the shining dust.

—F. Scott Fitzgerald,
on a song by W. C. Handy,
in *The Great Gatsby,* 1925

Contents

W. C. Handy

PROLOGUE

——

A View of Mr. Handy

ONE AFTERNOON IN MEMPHIS, 1918

> Beale Street is where the blues began.
>
> —George William Lee, black civic
> leader of Memphis, social
> historian, and friend of W. C.
> Handy, in *Beale Street,* 1934

Early afternoons would have been the best time to see William Christopher Handy walking along Beale Avenue. The leader of a cabaret dance band tends to be a late-morning riser, particularly when, like Handy, he has a regular late-night engagement at the Alaskan Roof Garden. This was the most prestigious supper club in Memphis, Tennessee, on the top floor of the Falls Building downtown. There until well into the night W. C. Handy and his orchestra played his new blues music for the affluent white patrons.

How gracefully had the young white ladies' dance slippers the night before shuffled in and out of the rhythms of two-four beats of his blues song "Beale Street"—*If Beale Street could talk / If Beale Street could talk / Married men would have to take their beds and walk*—while on the bandstand he had played cornet, occasionally along with Charles Hillman on piano, Sylvester V. Bevard on trombone, and Jasper Taylor on drums. Then, at some time in the evening's entertainment, the musicians in Handy's band would introduce in their songs what he called his "Tangana" rhythm, also known as the tango. The stocky, light-skinned bandleader and his musicians played it as if for no other reason than to see if these pale, lovely young dancers before them could match their privileged footsteps against the Latin rhythms, which Handy now hears in his mind playing alongside African American blue notes as he walks down the sidewalks of Beale.

"The Main Street of Negro America" is what his friend George Lee calls this thoroughfare, known officially in Handy's day as Beale Avenue. The avenue stretches in an almost straight east-west line for one mile through the African American neighborhood of a city that in 1918 has the largest urban black population in the South. The possibilities of a better economic life here have drawn thousands of people of color from the neighboring rural states of Mississippi, Arkansas, and Alabama to the Beale Avenue neighborhood. A significant number have become comparatively prosperous business owners and professionals, such as Lee, who has his own insurance company on Beale and is prominent in the local Republican Party. Unlike in most of the South, the political franchise is available in this Tennessee city to men of color. Black males are permitted to vote in the Beale wards, albeit under the watchful eye of E. H. "Boss" Crump, the white arbiter of Memphis politics. Handy, shortly after his arrival in Memphis in 1905 with his family from Clarksdale, Mississippi, even had been commissioned by the Crump political machine to write a campaign song for their leader. His composition "Mister Crump," later reworked and published as "The Memphis Blues," had helped gain him his first national notice, and by 1918 he is not only a hardworking performer but also the most celebrated composer and publisher in Memphis of the increasingly popular blues songs.

Handy this day continues his progress down Beale Avenue. People of color are everywhere about him on the street, coming in and out of the barbershops, law offices, dry goods stores, and groceries. Many greet him. He returns their handshakes—"ebony hands, brown hands, yellow hands, ivory hands" as he later lyrically recalled the population on Beale Avenue in the first decades of the century—or he tips his hat genteelly to the ladies. He is, after all, the man who has celebrated this avenue and its inhabitants in his most popular song for the uptown white audiences.

At this hour in the early afternoon, the sun is high overhead behind him, having risen over the eastern, or residential, blocks of Beale, near where Handy and his wife own a small house. The sun is now beating down on the westward blocks between the intersections of Beale with Fourth Street and with Hernando Street, the vice and entertainment center of Beale Avenue. In addition to being a thoroughfare of respectable vocations and middle-class residences, Beale at its western end near the Mississippi River is also the weekend destination for African American lumber camp workers and plantation hands from Tennessee, Arkansas, and Mississippi. They seek out the pleasures of the avenue's well-known blocks of Jim Crow vaudeville theaters, saloons, cafés, brothels, and gambling dens. George Lee spoke for both the assumptions of Memphis blacks and the paternalistic conditions of the avenue when he characterized the western end of Beale as being "owned largely by Jews, policed by the whites, and enjoyed by the Negroes." Lee omitted only the omnipresent political influence of Boss Crump and the recently arrived Italian entrepreneurs who operate many of the avenue's black vaudeville halls. It is toward that district of theaters and saloons that Handy is purposefully walking.

Here the middle-aged and dignified-looking composer is also greeted by the African American grifters, professional gamblers, and pimps, the "easy riders" who make their living off the rural weekend visitors. Handy is a frequent customer at the sometimes dangerous saloons where they congregate, and to a degree he enjoys these associates. *You'll meet honest men, and pickpockets skilled,* he had praised the inhabitants of the avenue in his lyrics to "Beale Street," and then he realistically concluded his couplet with *You'll find that business never closes 'til somebody gets killed.* He is proud that he is regarded on this rough section of Beale as sufficiently "jogo"— a term then used by urban African Americans meaning, among other things, authentically and nonapologetically a person of color, cannily streetwise. As before, he genially returns all greetings, even from the easy riders who too-familiarly call him "'Fess Handy," in their ironic or mocking recognition that he once had been an instructor of music at a black college in Alabama.

As he continues on his way, Handy perhaps briefly steps inside the dark interior of Pee Wee's Saloon, at 317 Beale, one of his favorite drinking establishments and the acknowledged gathering place for the city's African American musicians. Handy and other musicians are allowed privileges here by the white owner, storing their instruments in the back room and making bookings on the saloon's single telephone with its four-digit number—Memphis Exchange 2893—so long as between their telephone calls they spend a reasonable amount on whiskey or at the dice and pool tables. Handy appreciates the well-stocked inventory of bottles behind the long mahogany bar, and he is fond of the cigar stand near the front door, but this is a stop for business as well as pleasure. In addition to composing and publishing new blues music, he also manages and makes bookings for as many as twelve regional dance bands performing under his name, but he cannot yet afford a telephone at his office.

Now, as Handy walks outside, the light plays upon the multistoried concrete and brick façades of Beale Avenue's vaudeville theaters: the Lincoln, the Grand, the Daisy, and, a few blocks north of the avenue and the most opulent of all in the city, the Savoy Theatre. The latter is operated by Anselmo Barrasso and his extended family of Italian immigrants. Handy sees the vaudeville theaters and specifically the Barrasso-managed black performers both as a source for his material and as his competition.

"A first-class house for colored people only in the heart of the town," the Barrasso family advertises their Savoy Theatre, where interspersed between black comedians, female dancers with "snake hips," and the opening "dumb act" of nonspeaking jugglers and acrobats, African American singers perform songs of their own composition. The multicity syndicates of variety theaters, operated by New York City and Boston entrepreneurs and known collectively as vaudeville, are in 1918 the dominant venue in which Americans in smaller cities hear popular music, much more so than by Handy's twelve blues bands. Vaudevillian impresarios in the East such as Benjamin Keith, Edward F. Albee, and the future motion picture executive Marcus Lowe controlled among them the bookings of at least 2,973 variety theaters that they either owned or had under exclusive contract, with their signed musicians and singers weekly traveling a national circuit. But the Savoy vaudeville theater in Memphis is unique in the race of both its performers and its patrons.

By tacit agreement, the national vaudeville booking companies allow no more than one black performer—or "unbleached American," as sometimes advertised—to appear at local performances, usually singing a minstrelsy song from the last century. The Barrassos, however, astutely realize that Memphis, with its black majority and availability of cheaply employed black entertainers, offers a profitable opportunity to fill the theaters the family owns. By independently booking black entertainers, they avoid the 5 to 10 percent commission on ticket sales charged to theater owners by the Keith or Lowe syndicates, and the Savoy is filled to capacity almost every night with African American audiences eager to hear and see black vaudevillians. Some of the Savoy singers perform the new twelve-bar songs with their distinctively inflected African American notes and lyrics known as the blues. The Barrassos themselves consider these songs as no more than just another novelty act for their theater, limited in appeal to African American patrons, but the songs certainly sell tickets. In competition with the national chains, the Barrassos have enlarged their theatrical business from the Savoy to include a booking agency exclusively for African American vaudeville entertainers playing to black audiences. Eventually including more than forty theaters regionally, it is called the Theater Owners Booking Association, or TOBA. (Because of this vaudeville circuit's notoriously low pay, dingy dressing rooms, and grueling traveling, the agency's acronym is also known by its performers as "Tough on Black Asses.")

Handy's relation with TOBA and its featured musicians is ambiguous. He occasionally buys or simply appropriates for his own the blues compositions originally composed and sung by black vaudevillians that he has heard on the TOBA circuit. In his history of Beale Street, George Lee later wrote diplomatically that the signature blues song "Early Every Morning," performed on the Savoy stage by Viola McCoy, made Handy "a great deal of money when he later sold his copyrighted rescorings of her song to Paramount and other recording companies." And whether by chance or not, the slide trombone glissando often played by Memphis vaudevillian orchestras in an unconventional or "laughing" manner to introduce a blues singer is beginning to make its appearance in Handy's compositions, such as the brassy, up-tempo measures at the beginning of "Beale Street."

Yet on this day in the entertainment district, Handy wants more for the blues than the novelty of a black vaudeville act, just as he wants more for himself than his local reputation as a hot horn player and clever composer. Despite his jogo street status, he is a businessman, unswervingly Republican in his politics and always with an awareness of the potential for creating a new national market for his version of the blues, including among white listeners. This ambition was why, after so many late nights at the Alaskan Roof Garden, he had "made up my mind to endure it cheerfully" whenever he was "commanded to play two extra hours" by his white patrons. "Every dime added to what you had made the going easier," he now tells himself. And this ambition to become a nationally known composer and publisher of the blues is why he had moved with his family to Memphis from the agricultural delta of Mississippi after overhearing the black folk blues played by a trio of African Americans.

The "weirdest music I ever heard," Handy later wrote of this chance encounter, sometime in 1903–04, in Cleveland, Mississippi. He was then the leader of a local brass band, ambitious to become "the colored Sousa," in emulation of the famous white composer of marches, John Philip Sousa. But nothing in his formal training had prepared him for the experience of hearing this group playing for tips on a battered guitar, mandolin, and bass. Their efforts at first sounded like a mistake to Handy, a performer trained in the European harmonic scale. The three musicians deliberately played minor notes where majors were expected, "worrying" the flat notes with their fingers on the strings in a strange vibrato, and filling out the rest of their song's short measures with improvised keening lyrics like "Oh, lawdy" and "Oh, baby." The musical effect was, surprisingly, an artistic success, strangely expressive of both deep melancholy and joy. Even more astonishing to Handy was the "rain of silver dollars" he saw gladly thrown down at the performers' feet by a crowd of wildly enthusiastic white listeners, for the music they called "the blues."

"Then I saw the beauty of primitive music," Handy recalled in his memoir of the encounter with these unnamed black folk blues performers. "Their music wanted polishing, but it contained the essence. Folks would pay good money for it." The genius of Handy over the years between 1904 and 1920 was his realizing the commercial potential of the Mississippi Delta blues music to reach beyond a regional and racial folk song and become part of mainstream American music. Handy "polished" the folk blues into a new, sophisticated popular music that delighted hundreds of listeners in Memphis and nearby southern states; he was confident it would also delight tens of thousands of listeners elsewhere in the United States. "That night a composer was born," Handy later proudly recalled, "an *American* composer."

Handy's emphatically describing himself as an *American* composer asserted his lifelong faith that the African American blues were the fulfillment of what had been known since the late nineteenth century as the "Dvořák Manifesto." This was the prediction by the Czech composer Antonín Dvořák that the great national music of the United States would be based upon African American spirituals and other folk music of the nation's black people. Indeed, Handy would be interested throughout his life in the symphonic possibilities of the blues, with their uniquely played minor notes and folk melodies. But he also saw himself as an American composer in the sense of no longer being just another unknown provincial person of color who played European-inspired marches and waltzes. "I let no grass grow under my feet," Handy later wrote of first hearing the Mississippi blues; shortly thereafter he moved his family to Memphis and organized his blues orchestras and music publishing business. The blues performed as commercial entertainment and sold as sheet music to a national audience promised to make William Christopher Handy, as an *American* composer, a rich man.

This day on Beale Avenue he is not yet wealthy or nationally famous. But, ever optimistic, Handy perceives as tantalizingly close

the possibilities of his becoming both. Whenever his orchestra strikes up one of his blues compositions at the Alaskan Roof Garden, he can see how, on the opening bars, his white audiences become enthralled with his music. To his mind, their reactions are almost as if they are hearing the passionate first notes to a great romantic symphony: "Something within them suddenly comes to life. An instinct that wanted so much to live, to fling its arms and to spread joy, took them by the heels," he later recalled.

Handy's latest song, "Beale Street," has been recorded by the white "laughing trombone man," Harry Raderman, and later will also be recorded by the white Wadsworth's Novelty Orchestra for the Pathé company. However, despite his growing popularity and Handy's own increasingly sophisticated scoring of the original black folk melodies, the blues are still regarded by most white listeners as no more than an amusing racial novelty, a primitive music best appreciated and performed by African Americans. His most frequent press notices so far have been limited to the nationally circulated African American newspaper the Indianapolis *Freeman*, which in a review of a twenty-four-year-old vocalist on the TOBA circuit reported that "Miss Bessie Smith is a riot" singing "Yellow Dog Blues" and other Handy-composed blues songs. In 1918 none of his songs has yet been recorded by a white female vocalist. Until such a major crossover acceptance of his music occurs, Handy's financial position in Memphis is perilous, whatever his dreams of future prosperity.

As if a signifier of his financial circumstances, the afternoon sun now reflects off the gilded pawnshop balls of Morris Lippman's Loan Office, at 174 Beale, as Handy continues down the avenue. Many times in the past he has found it necessary to pawn his cornet there for household expenses. Acting both out of friendship and artistic admiration, the Jewish pawnbroker frequently allows his black customer temporarily to redeem the instrument without cash in order to play a night's engagement—with the understanding that the cornet the next morning will be returned. The generosity is always appreciated. But this afternoon, Handy finds himself not quite so insolvent as on others, and his horn is safely at his home. He passes by Lippman's pawnshop without acquiring any new debts.

The hard fact is that, despite his personal popularity on the street and thirteen years' residency in Memphis, Handy in 1918 is not fully accepted as a creditworthy businessman at the respectable upper end of Beale Avenue. His requests to cash checks have been refused at several Beale businesses owned by blacks, and he is well aware of what he calls the other "little digs" directed against him by the city's more prosperous African Americans. "They had a strange way of rating artistic work and worth," Handy wrote two decades later, with some resentment over the disregard given him by Memphis's class of black bourgeois. "If anyone owned a dozen cans and piled them on a couple of shelves behind a printed sign, he was a grocer and a businessman, if you please, but one who contracted for musicians and played for parties over a dozen states was a good timer and rounder, if not worse."

Ambitious for respect from both blacks and whites, but at the same time making his living from a raw music associated with the uneducated or the criminal among people of color, W. C. Handy in his life and in his musical compositions personified the "two souls" that W. E. B. Du Bois in *The Souls of Black Folk* had written marked the black experience in America. "One ever feels this two-ness," Du Bois had observed in 1903, the same year that Handy first heard the blues in the Mississippi Delta town—"an American, a Negro: two souls, two thoughts. Two unreconciled strivings; two warring ideals in one dark body, whose dogged strength alone keeps it from being torn asunder."

Handy was well familiar with this conflicted striving. He was born in 1873 the son of an accomodationist minister and farmer in Alabama, a former slave who had led his life as Booker T. Washington, the great opponent of Du Bois, had urged black people to do: that African Americans must emphasize the mechanical and agricultural skills and limit their intellectual aspirations to education and the ministry. Desiring more than his father's choices, Handy had become a professional musician and entertainer, the first male in two generations of his family not to pastor a church. As a black entertainer, he had recognized and promoted in the blues a distinctively jogo form of black music, just as Du Bois in the first decades of the twentieth century had urged the members of the new National Association of Colored People to develop their race's intellectual and artistic potentials. However, Handy had not hesitated a beat in "polishing" what he called "primitive music" for his personal success with regional white audiences and with what he hoped would become national audiences.

To frame Handy's life and his musical talents and ambitions at this time between the racial inner conflicts perceived in 1903 by Du Bois is not so remote. Handy by the second decade of the twentieth century very likely had heard in some detail of Du Bois's ideas and writings from his business partner, Harry H. Pace, a former student of Du Bois's at Atlanta University. Pace, before his partnership with Handy, had published in association with Du Bois a short-lived newspaper for an exclusively black readership along Beale Avenue. In fact, the office door of the music publishing business toward which Handy walks is lettered on its glass front "Pace & Handy," and Harry Pace makes most of the financial and marketing decisions in their partnership. At times they disagree on the correctness of Handy's marketing the blues to white audiences.

Maybe Professor Du Bois down in Atlanta and those top-rail Negroes here in Memphis simply disrespect or distrust me because I once was a blackened-cork minstrel, Handy perhaps now thinks. In the last years of the nineteenth century, before he became a regional performer of the blues, a young W. C. Handy had toured successfully as a featured cornet performer in the final decades of the traveling black minstrel shows. It was a vocational decision that had deeply disappointed both his parents and his in-laws, who associated black minstrelsy with what Handy sometimes called "this or that monkey business," which he was willing to endure for financial rewards. Their disapproval came despite Handy's protestations that he earned far more money for his wife and children as a minstrel musician than he would have made as a black man from any other form of musical performance or teaching, and that he maintained his dignity as a black individual through the professionalism of his performances. Now, holding his head high under his fedora and walking at a jaunty, brisk step, Handy continues his purposeful walk down the avenue.

The sun has risen higher on this day in Memphis, sometime before mid-July 1918, beating down in its afternoon heat upon the furthermost limits of Beale, at its swarming cotton docks, fish markets, houses of ill repute, and cocaine parlors. There the street meets the enormous mud-colored river, and both the street and the city terminate. Farther southward, by the mile-wide breadth of the river into the neighboring state of Mississippi, the sun is incubating the late-season crops along the plantations and farms of the Mississippi Delta.

Handy, however, has stopped well before the river. He has reached his destination, the redbrick Solvent Savings Bank building at 386 Beale Avenue, an African American–owned bank where he has his office on the second floor. This serious and proud brown-skinned man enters by the door marked "Pace & Handy" and begins the main business of his daylight hours, the receiving and fulfilling of sheet music orders for his blues music, now placed in bulk by music and five-and-dime stores nationally for their black customers, as well as by individuals. "Yellow Dog Blues," "Joe Turner Blues," "The Hesitating Blues," and "Beale Street" all were composed by Handy and performed commercially in 1918 by him with his various Memphis bands—and all were published by his company with brightly colored covers to attract the eye. It is the hope of Pace & Handy that these copyrighted songs in printed stacks on Handy's desk might continue to return money to the partners with repeated sales.

"All leaders will do well to get in touch with the Pace-Handy music company, as no repertoire can be completed without some of Handy's 'blues,'" the *Freeman* had enthused to black bandleaders and would-be blues bandleaders in June 1917. But despite this publicity and the occasional big orders from the Woolworth chain of stores to stock their music counters, Pace & Handy sustains itself in 1918 as a nickel-and-dime business: fifty to sixty cents received from a customer for each ordered score, minus three cents for return postage paid by the company.

Memphis may not be a fast enough city for him, Handy now thinks. Perhaps he should relocate his various blues bands, his family, and his share of the publishing firm somewhere closer to the big national audiences, Chicago, perhaps, or even New York City.

African American artists and businessmen in New York were beginning to make national reputations for themselves in the uptown neighborhood of Harlem. Harry Pace could come with him or not, just as his partner wished, for after the move he might be able to buy out Pace's interest. Handy, always a believer in better fortune to be found down the road, is confident that he can make a name for himself in New York City. He might even be able to promote that song with the haunting tango melody that was such a favorite of his but that had been such a disappointingly slow seller in Memphis in 1914: the "St. Louis Blues." His national time is coming, W. C. Handy is certain of that.

In fact, Handy did permanently move in late 1918 to New York City, for a while owning a house along the prestigious residential street of black professionals known as Strivers' Row in Harlem. He continued his partnership there with Pace for a few years, and then he found greater fame on his own. From his offices at the Gaiety Theater Building, 1547 Broadway, and then at various locations in the city, Handy over the decades composed or successfully marketed the blues songs that became much of the American soundtrack of the 1920s, 1930s, and 1940s. These included not only such unjustly forgotten compositions as "A Good Man Is Hard to Find," "Loveless Love," and "Aunt Hagar's Children Blues" but also his favorite, the classic of American popular music, the "St. Louis Blues."

In New York City, Handy discovered a prominent white female vocalist willing to take a risk by recording "St. Louis Blues." In its sales of phonograph records and sheet music, and on the musical stage, the song quickly became a perennial success. Its unique combination of black folk rhythms and Latin-inspired tango, bridged by early jazz measures, made it equally adaptable to the single guitarist or pianist or to the symphony orchestra. Over the decades of Handy's life, his favorite song was sung, conducted, or played at cabarets, symphonic concert halls, movie theaters, political rallies, and churches. The performers would include, among others, Pearl Bailey, Count Basie, Cab Calloway, Leonard Bernstein, Nat "King" Cole, Ella Fitzgerald, Thomas "Fats" Waller, Pete Seeger, Dizzy

Gillespie, Benny Goodman, Earl "Fatha" Hines, Billie Holiday, Eartha Kitt, Dave Brubeck, Peggy Lee, and Bob Wills and His Texas Playboys.

If he had written no more than this composition, the song alone would justify Handy's title as a great blues composer. Was there ever any more distinctly "American" song played throughout much of the twentieth century than the "St. Louis Blues"? It is instantly recognizable to millions both within and outside the United States, its score adapted as a fast-time marching tune by the American military and a line of its lyrics taken as the title of a short story by William Faulkner. Who has not heard, or hummed, or played the anonymous lamentation of a blues-filled lover who has been jilted by her man in favor of that femme fatale, the infamous St. Louis woman with her diamonds and her "powder an' her store-bought hair"? The Library of Congress in its online catalog currently lists 1,605 separate musical recordings internationally and in the United States of the "St. Louis Blues."

Handy's success with "St. Louis Blues" and other hits made his sheet music company on Broadway perhaps the largest black-owned business throughout the 1920s and early 1930s in New York City, and he was the foremost African American competitor there among the prolific and mostly white song composers and sheet music marketers whose offices were known collectively as Tin Pan Alley. Handy also provided employment to such talented African American musicians and arrangers as Fletcher Henderson and Avis Blake (the wife of Eubie Blake), and he contributed with his published writings on the blues to the cultural revival in the 1920s known as the Harlem Renaissance. His studies of blues and later spirituals began to attract the attention of intellectuals such as Edmund Wilson and Carl Van Vechten.

In 1931 Handy was invited back to Memphis by the political and economic elite of both races as the honored guest at Handy Park, a small plot dedicated in his honor on what was now renamed Beale Street in honor of his early song. A near-life-size statue of Handy holding his cornet and identifying him as the Father of the Blues was later raised on a stone platform at the park's center. The bronze statue portrays him as he was when he walked Beale Avenue in the first decades of the twentieth century. His cornet is not raised to his lips, but rather the sculptor portrayed Handy holding it at shoulder level, as if he has just finished playing, or is just commencing to play, his instrument.

But times, and musical styles, change. By Handy's death in 1958, he was seen as iconic, distant, more of a figure from the nineteenth than the twentieth century, and not specifically remembered as a striving and conflicted African American performer and composer. With the exception of the "St. Louis Blues," his songs were then unfashionable. That same first week of April 1958, as Handy's funeral was taking place in New York City, the top-selling single records, according to *Billboard* magazine, included among their number "Breathless," by Jerry Lee Lewis, "Maybe Baby," by Buddy Holly and the Crickets, and "Rock and Roll Is Here to Stay," by Danny and the Juniors.

Like the reputation of W. C. Handy with his statue in the park, Beale Street itself was also beginning to decline. By the early 1960s, pawnshops and liquor stores had begun to outnumber the offices of black professionals and even the once-celebrated saloons, cafés, and cabarets. The worst week for Beale and its residents began on March 29, 1968, on the tenth anniversary of the date of Handy's death. On that day, Dr. Martin Luther King Jr. attempted to lead six thousand demonstrators in a march down Beale Street to the Memphis city hall in support of the city's striking garbage workers, predominantly African Americans, who were seeking a pay increase and union representation. Young black men who were following the marchers but were not part of King's organization began breaking windows and snatching merchandise from stores along Beale. Memphis police responded by dispersing the demonstrators with tear gas and truncheons, injuring about fifty marchers and looters, and a young black man who the police said had menaced them with a knife was shot dead by officers. King was forced to cancel the day's march and retreated to his motel room headquarters about five blocks south of Beale. "Placards, apparently dropped by the marchers, were scattered across the small park named for W. C. Handy, the famous jazz musician," *The New York Times* reported the next day. At the end of the week, before he could reattempt his Beale Street march, King was assassinated on April 4, 1968, as he stood on the balcony of his room at the Lorraine Motel.

Riots in Memphis and other American cities quickly followed King's murder. As part of an "urban development scheme," the Memphis Housing Authority began in 1970 to raze many of the buildings along Beale Street, as well as the apartments and small houses on adjacent streets. Should it now be possible for W. C. Handy for a few animated moments to step down from his pedestal in his park and again walk on Beale, he would not recognize the street. The historic Pee Wee's Saloon, where Handy finished the "St. Louis Blues" while leaning against a cigar counter, had become a laundry and then finally a vacant lot, as dead and gone in popular memory as "Joe Turner Blues," another of his once most-played national hits. Also razed and absent were the Monarch, the Panama, and the Hole in the Wall saloons, as well as the Savoy Theatre with its TOBA blues singers like Bessie Smith. A neon-lit Hard Rock Cafe was built in 1997 on the former site of a saloon across from Handy Park, and Beale Street in the early twenty-first century had become a franchised bar district catering largely to white college youths and tourists. The few buildings remaining from Handy's time are now only brick façades supported by iron girders with literally nothing behind them, to give tourists the illusion of storefronts as they stroll on Beale. Handy would also find that his statue was no longer the most unique personal memorial to be found on Beale Street. A recently installed and much more frequently visited sculpture is the one representing a teenaged Elvis Presley, hips thrust forward and his guitar at a ready angle, at Second Street and Beale. The King of Rock and Roll, who successfully amalgamated white country music with black rhythm and blues, was a frequent visitor in his adolescent years to Beale Street's clothing stores and concerts during Handy's final decade.

Forty years before the racially mixed music of rock and roll was the shock of the new, W. C. Handy had been the first nationally acclaimed composer to have combined white dance music with distinctively African American styles of playing. His perfection at scor-

ing the "blue note"—the mood-shifting note based on African har-
monics that Handy had first heard in Mississippi black folk music—
brought the blues to the attention of Tin Pan Alley. His use of folk
blues measures in three short bars—leaving space for an improvised
lyric or solo—also led directly to the playing and singing of jazz.
What the *Freeman* in 1917 had hailed as "Handy's blues," played
either as jazz or big band performances, became the favorite popular
music of both black and white Americans from the 1920s through
the 1940s. Handy thereby brought African American music into the
mainstream of commercial culture and changed the direction of
American popular song. He was not properly the Father of the
Blues, as he was later acclaimed, but he was certainly the *maker* of
the blues in the early twentieth century. He made the blues as a consciously composed art—working as an "*American* composer"—and
he also *made* them in that word's sense of guaranteeing their success
and of commercially promoting this music.

To a current generation who associates the blues exclusively with
rural Delta musicians such as Robert Johnson, or with New Orleans–
based performers such as Jelly Roll Morton, Handy reminds listeners of the comparatively unexamined origins of "published blues"
as dance music coming from other cities where the urban blues
were performed by small orchestras. The blues as we know them
were also created in part by the commercial songwriters of Memphis and Tin Pan Alley, and from the now little-remembered stage
performances of African American musicians on the TOBA vaudeville circuit of black theaters. And, it must be remembered, Handy's
professional life reaches back to a national entertainment by African
American performers that is older than vaudeville, ragtime, or even
the blues themselves: blackfaced minstrelsy.

The image of the young W. C. Handy playing his cornet on the
stage surrounded by African American comedians dressed as minstrels in garish costumes and burnt cork makeup is disturbing. But,
in obverse, it is also a token of Handy as an African American artist
determined to perform his music with skill and dignity even in a
show of caricature and crude racial humor. He was, despite a natural geniality, willing "to fight it out," in his later words, to bring
African American music into national acceptance as art. To do so, he

played his horn in the Jim Crow minstrelsy entertainment of the 1890s, at Carnegie Hall in the 1930s, and in television studios of the late 1940s.

Born just eight years after the end of the Civil War, and living into the year that Memphis resident Elvis Presley was inducted into the U.S. Army, Handy in his life and career embodied both the popular culture and particularly the popular music of the United States from the late nineteenth century until the mid-twentieth century. As an American composer, and as an African American individual, he had memories spanning from the experience of his parents talking about their slavery in pre–Civil War Alabama to the triumph of his own prosperous old age. Loaded with honors and a social acquaintance with U.S. presidents such as Dwight D. Eisenhower, Handy finally came to a benign neglect. It was, like Handy's typical day of stately promenading toward his office on Beale Avenue, a remarkable walk through American history and culture. And it began with his birth inside a log cabin on November 16, 1873, in Florence, Alabama, on a small black-owned farm locally known as Handy's Hill.

CHAPTER ONE

———

Slavery, the AME Church, and Emancipation

THE HANDY FAMILY OF ALABAMA, 1811–1873

Resolved. An ordinance acknowledging the abolition of slavery in this State by the military power of the United States and prohibiting its future introduction in this State.

> —Resolution passed at the Alabama
> State Constitutional Convention
> for readmission to the Union,
> meeting five months after the
> end of the Civil War, on
> September 15, 1865

As a boy growing up in northern Alabama, Handy later wrote, he had learned melody by listening to the birds and other small creatures around his father's farm on the deceptively peaceful hills overlooking the small town of Florence. "There was a French horn concealed in the breast of the blue jay," he later recalled. "The tappings of the woodpecker were to me the reverberations of the snare drum. The bullfrog supplied an effective bass. In the raucous call of the distant crow I would hear the jazz motif." Near this family farm were deep woods where, as a solitary boy, he would ramble for pleasure or practice the oratory he had learned in school to what he felt was a sympathetic audience of pine trees and chinkapin oaks.

The Tennessee River marked the boundary of his known world, the river flowing to the south of his hometown of Florence and then turning northwestward into the state of Tennessee and toward the big city of Memphis. The river at this point appeared inviting to a small boy, several miles safely downstream from the lethal currents known as the Muscle Shoals. As an adult, he recalled this nineteenth-century world of his rural Alabama childhood growing up as the son and grandson of respected ministers as at times bucolic, and seemingly paradisiacal.

But this peaceful-appearing landscape, like the Tennessee River with its treacherous undertows and dangerous shoals, could easily be a place of risk and death. The northern Alabama hills and the small river town of Florence only a few years before his birth had been among the most contested landscapes of the Civil War. At its conclusion, the war had delivered his parents from their slavery and the young Handy himself into a perilous semifreedom.

William Christopher Handy was born "eight years after the surrender," in the words his mother and father always used to date every important event in their lives. The "surrender" was, of course, that of Confederate military forces in 1865. Emancipation had come to all of the area's former slaves—including Handy's parents—with the arrival of federal occupation troops in what was no longer Alabama but U.S. Military District Number Three. Handy thus was the first generation of his family to be born out of bondage and with the possibilities of some civil liberties. But by 1873, federal occupation troops had been five years withdrawn from what was now the white-Reconstructed state of Alabama. This black child and his parents were left at the northernmost edge of a Deep South state where they were no longer human property to be bought or sold, but nonetheless they were by no means fully free citizens.

The town of Florence since its founding always had been at a debatable and sometimes contested boundary. Named by a hopeful frontier surveyor after the Tuscany hill city of Italy, Florence was sited not in the flat coastal plains or delta areas of southern Alabama, with their great slave-worked plantations and white oligarchies, but upon an extension of the Appalachian foothills into the northern part of that state, along the narrow east-west valley of the Tennessee River. The white townspeople of antebellum Florence and the surrounding Lauderdale County were small-acreage farmers and independent merchants who had little economic need for black field hands and who were profoundly distrustful of the wealth and political interests of the white plantation owners farther south in their state. In the U.S. Census of 1860, five years "before the surrender," Lauderdale County reported 38.7 percent of its population enslaved, compared with rates as high as 78 percent and 76 percent of the population in the state's lower counties.

Although remote and not economically or demographically linked to the plantations farther south, this town in the years before Handy's birth had also been at the divisive and changing currents of American national history. Andrew Jackson, slave owner and future president, speculated from his Tennessee home in land and slaves at Florence. A generation later, Dred Scott, who gave his name to the U.S. Supreme Court decision in 1857 upholding the permanence of black slavery, had labored in Florence as a hostler at the town's finest tavern, on Tennessee Street, where Jackson had stayed during his business transactions. Practically everyone, obscure or prominent, slave or free man, who traveled through the Tennessee Valley early in the nineteenth century or later in Handy's boyhood, had to tarry at least temporarily in Florence. Just a few miles upriver from the town was the almost unnavigable impediment of the Muscle Shoals, where the low water and rocky projections could rip the bottom out of any riverboat, and the dreaded whirlpools could easily drown any capsized boatman. Passengers and their freight traveling along either the upper or lower Tennessee River therefore had to disembark before the Shoals and make arrangements in Florence to travel around them by land or continue on low-draught river barges. These were propelled usually by black roustabouts, who traditionally were considered to have put the "muscle" into the name of Muscle Shoals. (Handy as a boy in the 1870s and early 1880s would be fascinated by the work songs of these river men, and one of the few songs he recorded as an adult would be the "Muscle Shoals Blues.")

Its remoteness had not spared Florence and Lauderdale County from the violence of the Civil War. Anti-Confederate sentiment had been strong there among some white residents. These white males of Appalachia derided the wealthy secessionists located on plantations farther south as wanting "a rich man's war and a poor man's fight." In 1861 they had chosen to shoot accordingly. Throughout the national conflict, irregular partisan bands of Union sympathizers and Confederate loyalists had waged a savage guerrilla battle against one another at the river fords or mountain passes of Lauderdale County, sometimes for reasons of personal gain or family feuds. Generals on both sides also had been quick to see the importance of Florence as a choke point on the Tennessee River. The town experienced military occupations by both the Union and Confederate armies a total of thirty times during the war. Florence had also been visited, if that is the proper word, by the horse-mounted forces of perhaps the most feared of the Confederate generals, Nathan Bedford Forrest. He later would endorse the Ku Klux Klan and in 1863 scoured the Tennessee River valley of northern Alabama, killing or intimidating into surrender all of a luckless Union force who had been foolish enough to try to invade these hills.

But the color of a battle flag, or of one's own skin, was not enough to guarantee humane treatment by either side's partisans. Neither was one's status as a noncombatant, as Handy was told by his parents in a family story. Handy's maternal grandfather, a freed slave, had been shot and left for dead at his former master's farm after a gang of Union and Confederate deserters, seeking money, had tortured his white former owner, demanding to know where this prosperous farmer had hidden his cash. Both the farmer and Handy's grandfather refused to tell them, and both were shot by the deserters. Handy's grandfather, Christopher Brewer, survived his gunshot wound. His former master did not.

This was the post–Civil War Alabama into which the future blues composer was born, and where he first began to hear his melodies in the natural world around him. But, in a sense, Handy was lucky in the fate of his northern Alabama hometown. Had he been born more southward, perhaps in the town of Selma along the southern-flowing Alabama River or even farther into the plantation area of the state known as the Black Belt, he would have had fewer opportunities for education and economic security. "Educate a Negro and you spoil a field hand," the Montgomery *Advertiser* newspaper asserted for its white readership in the second decade of Handy's boyhood, after the surrender at Appomattox Court House.

The Handy family were not illiterate field hands. William Wise

Handy, the composer's paternal grandfather and the patriarch of the Alabama Handys, like the composer's maternal grandfather, had been a slave; but he secretly had learned to read and write during his slavery, and both before and after his emancipation he was a skilled artisan. The first U.S. Census after the Civil War lists the elder Handy's occupation as "shoe mechanic." He was also—before the surrender—a lay preacher to Lauderdale County's other slaves, and, in the decades before his grandson's birth, had been fiercely desirous of his and his family's freedom.

Born in 1811 into bondage in Princess Anne, Maryland, William Wise Handy and two of his brothers had plotted their escape from slavery with the aid, as W. C. Handy was later told in a family tradition, of the Underground Railroad. One of the brothers succeeded in traveling unapprehended to Canada, where he was a free man, and another brother escaped to freedom "somewhere in the East," but William Wise Handy had been overtaken. As was customary with recalcitrant slaves, he had been sold farther south, in this instance to the plantation of a prosperous merchant and planter, Bernard McKiernan, near Florence. There, as W. C. Handy later recollected in his memoir, his grandfather "started an insurrection for escape, and was shot but not killed." The year is not specified in the memoir, but William Wise Handy's attempted revolt may have been among those "reports of an incomplete and indefinite nature of plots among slaves in Madison County, Tennessee, and in the northern section of Alabama," published in the Nashville *Union* on June 28, 1842. (Madison County is across the Tennessee state line, close to Florence.) If so, William Wise Handy was then thirty-one years old when he received a lead ball into his body in a risk for his freedom.

His master, Bernard McKiernan, was not a forgiving man, but the elder Handy was not summarily killed or "transported"—sold to another master even farther south—most probably because he was a skilled laborer. Nor did the gunshot wound stop his later efforts for freedom or his continued involvement with the Underground Railroad. In 1850, he covertly assisted in another attempt at freeing his fellow slaves on the McKiernan plantation. That year, a white abolitionist and member of the Underground Railroad from Cincinnati,

Seth Concklin, met with an escaped slave in Philadelphia who pleaded for Concklin to travel to Alabama and rescue this former slave's wife and three sons, owned by McKiernan at his plantation. Concklin agreed to make this dangerous attempt. He traveled south alone, but apparently he had been informed in advance of a daring and willing accomplice among the plantation's slaves, W. C. Handy's grandfather. In a letter covertly and anxiously sent to other abolitionists from aboard a steamboat headed north on the Mississippi River, Concklin wrote how he casually had reconnoitered the McKiernan plantation, where he saw a black man identified only as "William" making shoes in his shop assisted by two young boys:

> I immediately gave the first signal, anxiously waiting thirty minutes to give the second and main signal. . . . William appeared unmoved; soon sent out the boys; instantly sociable. . . . Our interview only four minutes; I left, appeared by night; dark and cloudy; at ten o'clock appeared William; exchanged signals. . . . During our interview William prostrated on his knees and face to the ground, head cocked back, watching for wolves [slave patrols], by which position a man can see better in the dark. . . . I thought of William, who is a Christian preacher, and of the Christian preachers in Pennsylvania. One watching for wolves by night, to rescue Vena and her three children from Christian licentiousness; the other standing erect in the open day, seeking the praise of men.

Such was the composer's grandfather. In fact, Seth Concklin did succeed in freeing two slaves from the McKiernan plantation and escaped with them by steamboat on the Ohio River as far north as Evansville, Indiana, a town that would later figure significantly in W. C. Handy's first success as a musician. There the abolitionist and the two slaves were recognized and seized by the local sheriff in accordance with the legal authority of the Fugitive Slave Law. McKiernan subsequently traveled by steamboat from Florence to Evansville to recover his human property and to bring back Concklin for trial in Alabama. During the return down the Ohio River,

however, Concklin was reported as having attempted to escape
while in McKiernan's company. The abolitionist's body, his hands
and feet in iron manacles, was later recovered from the river, his
head showing signs of severe blunt trauma. William Wise Handy
apparently escaped the wrath of his owner for his participation in
this attempted escape. He remained a slave on the McKiernan plantation for the next fifteen years.

After the emancipation of 1865, W. W. Handy became a property
owner, buying in 1868, probably with wages concealed from his former owner, the tract of land in Florence later known as Handy's
Hill. He also became the most revered local minister among the
now-freed blacks; in 1865 he was licensed to preach by the Methodist
communion, and he helped in 1867 and 1868 to fashion a chapel
from an old brick building that previously had been used as a cowshed. There he preached to Florence's first post–Civil War congregation of the African Methodist Episcopal Church (AME). This
national communion of both whites opposed to slavery and people
of color, established in the eighteenth century by black freedmen
in Philadelphia, had been banned from antebellum Alabama since
1820. But two years "after the surrender," in 1867, the church had
begun to send "missionaries to Alabama," in its description, eventually establishing thirty missions, or chapels, in Reconstructed
Alabama. Among the number was W. W. Handy's new chapel built
in Florence. The elder Handy, who was fifty-seven years of age in
1868, was aided in his work by his adult son, Charles Bernard Handy,
who had also been born a slave at the McKiernan plantation and
would become the future composer's father. This northern Alabama
congregation, which still worships at the Greater St. Paul AME
Church of Florence, played a significant part in the violent history of
Reconstruction.

On the evening of April 24, 1867, the first political meeting of
Lauderdale County's black freedmen was held at the AME chapel
built by Handy's grandfather. By the light of oil lamps, James T.
Rapier, a prosperous local black farmer who had obtained his education before the Civil War and who would later become this Alabama
district's first black congressman, explained to the gathering of one
hundred and fifty freedmen the proposed Fourteenth Amendment

to the U.S. Constitution, which would grant them full civil liberties. Rapier then urged their registration as voters, under military protection, for Alabama to seek readmission to the Union under ratification of that amendment. The proceedings of that meeting, as well as a later declaration by the black freedmen of their political loyalty to the national Republican Party, were subsequently published for the predominantly white readership of the Florence *Journal* newspaper.

Consequences of that night at the AME chapel followed. A school for black children seven miles outside of Florence was burned to the ground, and in November 1868, one hundred and twenty-five hooded white horsemen rode through the town square of Florence, shooting one black man and hanging three others. Rapier was forced temporarily to flee for his life. Charles B. Handy, who was then twenty years old, at considerable risk to his own physical well-being helped the black Republican congressman to safety. This was a historical fact that his son, W. C. Handy, a self-described "Republican by tradition," later recounted to his friends with great pride. As he recalled to a friend in the presidential election year of 1952, explaining his lifelong loyalty to the Republican Party, "Many times my father has told me how he helped hide Rapier from the Ku Klux on an island in the Tennessee River until they could spirit him away to Washington."

Charles Handy in his own emancipation carefully followed in his father's footsteps. In March 1872 he married an educated local woman of color, Elizabeth Brewer, and in addition to his now farming a section of Handy's Hill, he eventually assumed his father's position as the minister of the Florence AME chapel when W. W. Handy's health declined. The histories of at least two generations of the Handy family—and the history of their Alabama slavery—were thus intimately involved with this place of black worship. The Reverend C. B. Handy, as he eventually became known, was contemporarily described by his national church superiors as "a good teacher as well as a good preacher," perhaps implying that, in addition to preaching AME church orthodoxy, Charles Handy like his own father urged his fellow blacks to acquire literacy and political power. In addition to farming and ministering to his congregation,

Handy also briefly edited and managed the business affairs of an African American newspaper in Florence, the *Watcher*. For a few short years after the Civil War, small-property-owning black men like Charles Handy—known locally and politically as the "black and tan Republicans"—enjoyed an unaccustomed freedom of expression and liberty to vote in the general elections of Reconstruction Alabama.

This freedom was dramatically curtailed the year before W. C. Handy's birth in 1873, after the removal of federal occupation troops in 1868 and the restoration of former slave owners to political power in 1872. Thereafter, congressional representation by such men of color as James Rapier was a thing of the past, and the political and social fortunes for African Americans living in Alabama were, at best, uncertain. Whites in large numbers, whether former Confederates or Unionists, united behind the state Democratic Party, and black males in Alabama were allowed to vote in primaries and general elections only in diminishing numbers, until their ultimate disenfranchisement early in the twentieth century. A white resident of W. C. Handy's hometown and a near contemporary of the composer, the now-forgotten novelist Thomas S. Stribling, provided a remarkable historical portrait in a Pulitzer Prize–winning novel of 1932 about turn-of-the-century Florence. Stribling remembered this Alabama community in the late 1870s as having been a pleasant, usually placid, river town for its ruling white residents; however, a strict political conformity and racial segregation was enforced. As one of Stribling's white merchants agreeably confirms to another after a Democratic Party political rally, "It's social suicide to vote the Republican ticket here in Florence, much less bob-bashiely with niggers."

The Handy family outwardly accommodated themselves to their political reversals in the years after Reconstruction. Charles Handy on occasion invited prominent white ministers as guests to his congregation's worship at the AME chapel, where they heard sermons more religiously evangelical than Republican. His family also industriously cultivated the fields of Handy's Hill to a degree that was approvingly noticed by both Florence's white and black residents. The Reverend Handy, or a reasonable roman à clef resemblance to

him, even makes a brief appearance in Stribling's fiction as Bishop
Sinton of the local AME church, "a heavy black man who used correct and moving if rather florid English," as he appears to a white
minister at their awkward first social meeting. The minister was
known by the town's whites to have urged his black congregation to
have "patience and love, not rifles," in the face of their changed circumstances.

Yet concealed from the white minister who perceives him so
benevolently, Bishop Sinton, in Stribling's unblinking account, is
also covertly associated with a Dr. Greenup, a local black physician
who not "more than fifty or a hundred white persons in Florence"
knew existed, and who urged his rural patients at times of threatened local lynchings to stock up on guns and ammunition. These
two educated black professionals in the "colored," or West Florence,
section, were longtime political and social allies in Lauderdale
County. As Stribling further explains:

> The two had always worked together. They had planned
> and introduced into the black settlements negro [sic] dolls
> with black curly hair to be given to little negro girls
> instead of the usual blond dolls. They introduced especial
> books into the negro public schools with stories of negro
> social leaders, negro warriors, negro poets, negro scien-
> tists. . . . But the two men differed with each other on the
> matter of guns.

The historical Charles B. Handy, who lived from 1848 into the first
decade of the twentieth century, embodied these same racial contradictions between a Dr. Greenup and a Bishop Sinton. On the
one hand, Charles Handy had been the physical defender of Congressman Rapier against the Ku Klux Klan, and in fact, as his blues
composer son later pointedly remembered, the minister had discreetly hidden a gun in his cabin on Handy's Hill during the post-
Reconstruction years for the defense of his family. (It was a
smooth-bore musket kept from the Civil War.) But on the other consideration, William Handy was also the chosen pastor of his local
AME church, who was known by whites to urge "patience and love,

not rifles" to his congregation, and who was also recognized by the Florence white majority as a prudent and economically successful tiller of the soil. The Handy family, as the Florence *Times-Journal* in 1873 observed in printing its notice of the death of the "colored preacher" William Wise Handy, "retained the good will of all persons, white and black," and the newspaper particularly praised his "humble" character. (Presumably the newspaper's correspondent was unaware of W. W. Handy's assistance to the Underground Railroad a little more than two decades earlier.)

Here both the composer's father and grandfather were following the admonitions of Booker T. Washington, their fellow Alabamian, whose Negro Normal School in Tuskegee was to be partially funded in 1880 by the state of Alabama to educate blacks in the mechanical and agricultural skills. B. T. Washington's state-approved ideology and pedagogy assumed that southern African Americans after emancipation and Reconstruction were to remain politically accepting of white rule and to aspire no higher in their professions than to become educators, physicians, or ministers to their race. To those southern blacks in agreement with Washington's practical ideas, such as Charles B. Handy, the ambition for a black male to become a serious composer was presumptuous, and the art of music for educated African Americans was to be, at most, limited to the hymnology of folk spirituals or to the racially uplifting performances of western European classical compositions.

The minister's future son, William Christopher Handy, was also to embody these same racial contradictions in his own life. Well into his sixties, he reflected how he bore in his middle name the memory of his maternal grandfather, Christopher Brewer, the slave who, voluntarily freed by his owner, had been shot for refusing to reveal to Union and Confederate guerrillas where his former master had hidden his money. (After the Civil War, Brewer loyally had sought out members of his former master's family and shown them where their family money was hidden.) Yet the composer equally reflected upon the personal motivations contained within his first name, prompted by the example of his paternal grandfather, William Wise Handy, emancipated only after a bloody national war and who also had been shot, in this instance for having attempted a slave revolt. As W. C. Handy later wrote:

It is probably my inheritance from these two characters that enabled me to submit to certain hard conditions long enough to fight my way out and yet be considered sufficiently "submissive" by those who held the whip hand.

The future composer who would "fight it out" in both his life and his blues art was born the first son to Charles and Elizabeth Handy in the rainy early winter on November 16, 1873, in his paternal grandfather's log cabin on Handy's Hill. This was the same year that the family patriarch, William Wise Handy, the former slave shoemaker who had watched so carefully for "wolves," died. The new baby was a colicky infant, sick for the first six months of his life. He was also troubled by weak eyesight. But the child named William Christopher Handy eventually grew into a stout and healthy boy, heavily built like his father. He additionally would soon display, unique among all his family, a preternatural talent for composing and playing the music he heard in the separate worlds of blacks and whites on Handy's Hill and in Florence.

CHAPTER TWO

W. C. Handy and the Music of Black and White America, 1873–1896

In the military camp, in the crowded streets of the city where the troops march to the front, in the ballroom, in the concert hall, at the seaside and in the mountains, go where you may, you hear Sousa, always Sousa.

—*Musical Courier,* on the popularity of John Philip Sousa, the "March King," July 4, 1898

The innate love of harmony and beauty that set the ruder souls of his people a-dancing and a-singing raised but confusion and doubt in the soul of the black artist; the beauty revealed to him was the soul-beauty of a race which his larger audience despised, and he could not articulate the message of another people.

—W. E. B. Du Bois, *The Souls of Black Folk,* 1903

With all their differences, most of my forebears had one thing in common: if they had any musical talent, it remained buried." So did W. C. Handy, in the middle of his life as a distinguished blues composer, look back in his memoir to his family's experience of Reconstruction Alabama. He had been born into a family in which the church, not the dance floor, was of importance, and music was shunned for all purposes except the religious and the educational. Among the earliest memories of his childhood in the early 1870s, the composer recalled a corner fireplace in the family cabin where his grandmother and mother would bake corn cakes, or ash cakes, and a trundle bed in the attic where he slept. But there were no childhood memories of any musical instruments in the Reverend Charles Handy's home.

The AME Church, and the work to support it, always came first. Schooling for his firstborn son was important to Charles Handy, but so was his son's earning wages in order to tithe a portion of his weekly income—a nickel for Sunday school and a dime for the church collection. As soon as he was big enough to be hired outside the family farm, the boy "pulled fodder, picked cotton, cradled oats, clover, millet and wheat, and even operated a printing press" for various Florence employers, all to meet his father's expectations and to contribute to the upkeep of the church where his father preached. The young Handy was also a willing attendant at his father's church on Sundays, where he was a careful listener to the folk spirituals sung by the congregation unaccompanied by organ or piano. The boy particularly liked the pleasing melancholy he heard in the black spiritual "Cheer the Weary Traveler" and the fast-tempo excitement of "Gospel Train's A-Comin'."

His mother, Elizabeth Brewer Handy, was just as pious as his father but not as exacting toward her child. She indulged her firstborn son as far as her domestic skills and the family economics would allow. As a middle-aged man, W. C. Handy still recalled with pleasure how his mother had carefully stitched for him a fluted waistcoat embroidered with lace, to be worn with his best going-to-church outfit, a small boy's sailor suit and red-topped brass-toed boots. "Despite my tender years," Handy recalled humorously, "I was something of a [lady]killer."

Between chores and church attendance, the young Handy also attended classes at the racially segregated Florence District School for Negroes. He was soon praised there by his teachers for his good grades and skill at public speaking. After his school day ended, he would continue his education by entering, unnoticed, into the lobby of the Exchange Hotel. This was the finest commercial establishment of its kind in the town for whites, where the then-current Alabama governor and Florence attorney, Edward A. O'Neal, held sway over a circle of admirers whenever he returned from the state capital. The boy would eavesdrop unseen from a corner while the governor, a former Confederate general, sonorously read aloud from regional newspapers and then solemnly pronounced his judgments on the day's events. These surreptitious visits became "my daily custom," Handy recalled. As an adult he subsequently would acquire a poet's gift for writing song lyrics with African American dialect and colloquialisms, but Handy's later personal manner of public speaking was indelibly set by this boyhood experience. What he learned at the Exchange Hotel was a rhetoric that was orotund, formally cordial, and, even by the late nineteenth century, a little old-fashioned. Almost as if having mastered a second language, Handy as a boy found that "whatever credit I may have received in school for elocution" came from his successfully "emulating" this received standard of another race.

Surprisingly, the Florence District School for Negroes also offered the opportunity for Handy's first musical instruction, despite the fact that Lauderdale County provided no instruments for the black school. This advantage for the students was provided by Young A. Wallace, a remarkable scholar and a newly arrived schoolmaster from Fisk University at Nashville. A tall, thin, ascetic-looking man with a goatee, Wallace was determined that his African American pupils receive a sound musical instruction. The early-morning hour at the Florence school was nominally reserved for religious devotions, but Wallace began the day by having the boys hold open copies of *Gospel Hymns* in their left hands and then, following his lead, sing and mark out the printed musical notes into imaginary scales in the air with their right hands. By this practice, similar to the Sacred Harp shape note style of singing then taught in the white and black churches of Alabama, Handy learned his musical scales. It remained a point of pride to the composer, who apparently had perfect pitch even as a child, that "by the time I was ten, I could catalogue almost any sound that came to my ears." He and the other boys eventually could sing melodies that Wallace provided them from the scores of Bizet or Verdi, and Handy found he could transcribe into musical notes even the birdsongs he heard on Handy's Hill or the whistles of the steamboats along the Tennessee River.

Yet despite his dedication as a teacher, the schoolmaster, known honorifically by both whites and blacks in Florence as Professor Wallace, considered his instruction to be no more than a utilitarian means of racial uplift. "Southern white gentlemen," Handy recalled him telling his classes, "looked upon music as a parlor accomplishment." The pupils were expected to act accordingly. "Such men should be our example," Professor Wallace told them. He limited their advanced musical instruction to learning only scores by European classical composers. The hymnal previously used by Wallace as the school's elementary musical text, *Gospel Hymns,* was also strictly proscriptive in its selection of scores and lyrics. This hymnal, the standard Protestant text of white congregations, drew heavily upon the sacred songs of eighteenth-century composers such as Charles Wesley and Isaac Watts, with a few mid-nineteenth-century additions, including "Where Hast Thou Gleaned Today?" Handy, as a minister's son, noticed that the black spirituals he heard in his father's church, and which were then being performed nationally with great success by the Fisk Jubilee Singers, were excluded from their lessons by this Fisk alumnus. The schoolmaster, Handy later pointedly recalled, "made no attempt to instruct us in this remarkable folk music."

Thus by the time he was twelve, in 1885, Handy in his own way had begun to reflect upon the "two-soulness" of language and music that W. E. B. Du Bois later would find so inescapable for the African American. On other occasions, Handy heard a secular music that was not part of the white world of Florence. One sweltering spring day, when the doors of the Florence school had been thrown open to catch any breeze and while Handy was worrying over his lessons, his attention was caught by the overheard song of a black plowman working on a field.

A-o—oo-A-o— / *I wouldn't live in Cai-ro-oo* / *A-o, A-oo-o,* the plowman sang as he followed his mule across the soil of McFarland's Bottoms. The simple four bars of this folk song, with its melancholy lyrics and keening tones, continued "ringing in my ears," Handy wrote, long after the man had finished his labors. And the singer's musical complaint about the mysterious river town farther up the Mississippi and Ohio rivers raised the young Handy's curiosity about the larger world outside northern Alabama: "What was wrong with Cairo?" he wondered silently at his desk. "Was Cairo too far south in Illinois to be 'up North,' or too far North to be considered 'down South'?"

The distinction between "up North" and "down South"—and between the two worlds of black and white residents of Florence—was made unforgettably distinct to Handy as a schoolboy one day when he passed through the town square. There he saw an enthusiastic crowd of white listeners gathered around a political candidate delivering a stump speech. Handy stopped to eavesdrop, and to his shock he heard the speaker loudly promise to cheers that, if elected, "I won't spend one dollar for nigger education." The "uneducated nigger," this man reminded his admirers, had served their former masters of the Confederacy well, "like so many faithful watchdogs." Handy reacted as if slapped.

Surprisingly, this incident appears to have been his first memorable and personal experience of prejudice in Alabama. In the neighborhood of Handy's Hill, his family had always been regarded with respect by their black neighbors. Even within white society the family were given a certain deference as industrious and churchgoing leaders of their race. Nor was this political speaker likely one of the patrician politicians whom Handy had emulated, such as Governor O'Neal; this now-aging generation of post-Reconstruction public men had tended to be comparatively benign toward people of color, or at least willing to fund education for blacks, so long as the primacy of the Democratic Party and the social customs of racial separation were maintained. Rather, Handy was experiencing for the first time the rising generation of younger white southern politicians who were Populist and explicitly racist in their appeal, and who would in his young adulthood labor to write the so-called Jim Crow laws of legal discrimination into their states' constitutions and statutes.

These overheard racial insults deeply stung the boy. He ran back home to Handy's Hill in tears and then retreated alone to the nearby woods. "There, point by point, I had undertaken to answer the man of ill will," he remembered with passion even as an adult. "Slowly, deliberately, I had torn his arguments to bits." Marshalling all his skills of elocution and logical argument carefully learned from other white examples like Governor O'Neal, the boy answered his absent tormentor "at the top of my voice." Standing solitary in this Alabama landscape, he listened as "my words of defiance echoed and echoed" among the pine trees and oaks. For perhaps the first time as an adolescent, Handy was experiencing the "confusion and doubt" that Du Bois claimed was the burden of the black artist. Despite his demonstrated musical and intellectual gifts, the boy remained a member, in Du Bois's estimation, "of a race which his larger audience despised." And despite his hearing a "harmony and beauty that set the ruder souls of his people a-dancing and a-singing," the young Handy had not yet formed the artistry of the blues in his mind; as yet "he could not articulate the message of another people." He eventually returned home to his family's cabin, where he later remembered that he at least slept more easily that night as a result of his shouted defiance.

His mother in the following days tried to console her son by her use of a biblical homily. One of her favorite passages was Genesis 16–21, in which a slave woman, Hagar the Egyptian, bore a son to the patriarch Abraham but was cast out into the wilderness with her child as a result of the jealousy of Abraham's wife, Sarah. As Handy's mother now lovingly explained to her son, all people of color were, in her description, "Aunt Hagar's children." Although promised by God in their exile to become members, in the deity's words, of "a great nation," Aunt Hagar's dark-skinned descendants, in Elizabeth Handy's retelling, were fated to lives of sorrow and rejection by the ruling white majority.

The story of Aunt Hagar's children did in fact make a profound impression upon Handy and would later provide the title to one of his best compositions, the cheerfully exuberant score of "Aunt Hagar's Children Blues." As both an adolescent and an adult, much of his later life and artistic ambitions can be interpreted as his attempt to recast his mother's story of biblical sorrows into a more joyful musical retelling. And, fortunately for Handy's twentieth-century blues compositions, not all of Aunt Hagar's children found in Florence in the 1880s were such sobersides as described to him by his mother.

In 1885, when the younger Handy was twelve, he was hired with his father's approval at three dollars a week as a water boy at the Muscle Shoals construction site of navigational Lock Number Seven, the first of the New South improvements along the Tennessee River. There, whenever possible, the boy escaped from his duties "to hear the laborers sing." These nineteenth-century work songs by the black construction gangs included, as Handy later repeated to a folk collector of the 1920s, such wonderfully profane folk ditties as

> Ashes to ashes, an' a-dus' to dus',
> Ef de whisky don't git you, den de cocaine mus'.
>
> .   .   .   .
>
> Let me be yo' rag-doll till yo' tidy come,
> If he can hear me raggin', he got to rag it some,
>   my honey,
> How long has I got to wait?
> Oh, can I git you now, or must I hesitate?

The "tidy" (possibly "titty") lover was the regular or "official" lover of the black woman so seductively addressed. This was powerful stuff to be heard by a twelve-year-old son of a minister, and it was a future inspiration—*Can I git you now, or must I hesitate?*—for his popular song of the year 1915, "The Hesitating Blues": *Hello Central, what's the matter with the line? / I want to talk to that High Brown of mine / Tell me, how long will I have to wait?*

Even at twelve years of age, Handy was not so foolish as to repeat within his father's hearing the ditties of the Muscle Shoals workmen he had found so fascinating in words and melody. Charles Handy had often made it clear to his son and his congregation that he considered such songs among the "devil's playthings." But by the time he entered high school, Handy had discreetly sought out the companionship of the town's most unrepentant performer of worldly tunes. This was the hard-drinking James "Jim" Turner, an itinerant African American fiddle player who was then approximately in his late twenties and who sometimes could be found playing for tips on Court Street or Tennessee Street in Florence. "The drunker Jim Turner was, the better he played," Handy remem-

bered. The carefree-living Turner and the earnestly self-improving
Y. A. Wallace were Handy's two lasting musical influences during
his Florence boyhood and the two most distinct embodiments of
Aunt Hagar's children. By age sixteen, in 1889, the young W. C.
Handy had come to know some of this fiddle player's songs.

Although obscure historically, Jim Turner was in his day one of
the most celebrated folk fiddlers of the Tennessee River Valley. In
addition to his performances on street corners and traveling road
shows as something of an uneducated fiddle virtuoso, Turner was
also sought out by whites in the states of Tennessee and Alabama as
a novelty act for private parties. Handy later recalled how Turner
delighted dance audiences in Florence and elsewhere by making
"jackass brays, rooster crows, all kinds of barnyard imitations on his
violin." (This became an early jazz and blues tradition, and such
instrumental, barnyard cacophony was later deliberately performed
by other musicians on early recordings.) Turner also played his
music in the barrooms of Memphis, the closest major city of any
consequence, and his stories of the city's famed Beale Avenue, with
its blacks-only saloons and bordellos—which in their opulence and
opportunities for vice equaled any establishments reserved for
whites only—fascinated the minister's son. Handy's friendship with
Turner was as close as this future composer ever got to the folk, or
so-called naïve, performers of the African American blues. As an
educated publisher and composer of the blues, Handy later had little professional use for nonscore-reading, itinerant African American performers who were his contemporaries from the rural South,
such as Charley Patton or Robert Johnson. Handy would consider
his published blues a "higher" art. However, he would always make
a personal exception for the talented and alcoholic Turner, provid-
ing him with employment throughout the 1910s, perhaps in remembrance not only of their early friendship in Florence but also of
Handy's first having heard from this fiddler the music that later
became Handy's polished and nationally popular art.

By 1888, Jim Turner had taught Handy at least one version of the
words and notes to the widely circulated folk song "Joe Turner."
This black folk tune, its title a corruption of the historical name "Joe
Turney," was the nineteenth-century "prototype of all blues," in the

opinion of Abbe Niles, a distinguished scholar of that music. The historical Joe Turney was the white "long-chain man" who was notorious among blacks living in post–Civil War Tennessee for arresting and transporting African American males in shackles from Memphis to the state penitentiary in Nashville. *They tell me Joe Turner's done been here and gone* was the lament expressed in this song by the wives and lovers who returned to their empty homes to find their men arrested and gone for years. This dolorous folk song later became the inspiration for Handy's rearranged and copyrighted national hit of 1915, "Joe Turner Blues." It is significant that Handy, as the future joy-seeking adult child of Aunt Hagar, would change *his* Joe Turner from a cruel white jailer to an affectionately teasing black lover, and the original folk song's lament of irretrievable loss becomes, in Handy's published lyrics, the carefree Joe Turner's boast to his woman about the good-natured wanderings of his carnal love: *You'll never miss the water till the well runs dry / You'll never miss Joe Turner till he says "Good Bye."*

Shortly around the time of his befriending Turner and learning from him this archetypal blues song, Handy also acquired the instrument by which he would later become known as a blues performer. This was the cornet. Like the electric guitar of the 1950s and 1960s, it was the instrument of choice for young musicians in the 1880s, owing to its preeminence in brass bands. Shorter than the standard military trumpet, the cornet is considered to produce more mellow sounds through its three valves and tubing than the more clarion-sounding trumpet. When a traveling circus had become stranded in Florence for lack of money, the adolescent's eyes were caught by the brass sheen of a cornet owned by one of the musicians. Handy quickly made a deal with the desperate circus player, purchasing the horn for one dollar and seventy-five cents, payable in installments.

He kept both this purchase and his subsequent practice on the instrument concealed from his father and Professor Wallace. At school, Handy outwardly attended to his lessons while on his desk he unobtrusively practiced his finger-work for the cornet's valves. Alone, he developed his skill of triple-tonguing on the mouthpiece, the technique expected of any accomplished horn player by which three distinct notes are played in one short exhalation. Handy's determination to master his instrument was motivated by his ambition to take a prominent place in the local American brass band.

Brass bands, not dance or symphonic orchestras, were at the time of Handy's adolescence this nation's most popular form of musical performance, for both white and black musicians and listeners. An estimated ten thousand bands were playing locally by the end of the 1880s, in performances by either professionals or amateurs. Before the advent of home radios or phonographs, a local band, predominantly playing brass instruments, gave the only opportunity for many small-town Americans to hear music outside their households or churches. Fraternal organizations, workingmen's associations, or private entrepreneurs were the organizers, and the bands' performances were significant civic events, playing at political rallies, store openings, or evening serenades in parks. Even the small town of Florence boasted two brass bands in the 1880s, one for its black musicians and another for its white citizens. As his skills progressed, Handy began practicing with the band members at the town's African American barbershop, once again without his father's knowledge.

The popularity of brass bands and the military-style marches they often played was due in large part to one of America's most prolific composers and charismatic band directors of the 1880s and 1890s: John Philip Sousa, who had been appointed director of the U.S. Marine Corps Band in 1880. Himself the child of Portuguese and Bavarian immigrants in Washington, D.C., Sousa as an adult made the military march and the quick-step patriotic song inescapably part of nineteenth-century American popular music. His band of forty smartly uniformed Marine musicians—Sousa made use of woodwinds as well as brass—toured for concerts and parades outside the nation's capital whenever possible, and to appreciative audiences and newspapers they became known simply as the National Band. The songs they played were exclusively marches, often composed by the band director himself. Between 1877 and 1889, Sousa composed and published thirty-eight marches, including his instantly popular "Semper Fidelis" (1888). The music was usually written in thirty-two-bar strains, although Sousa showed considerable skill and an even greater showmanship within the restriction of quick march time. Dividing his marches into thematic sections, all intended, in his words, "to make [even] a man with a wooden leg step out," Sousa included attention-grabbing solos by cornet and trumpet, and always made certain to end his compositions with an emphatic flourish—the "ice cream" after the "roast beef," he liked to say.

Such was the appetite for marches that black and white brass bands alike were welcomed as public entertainment. Adapting these popular marches for performance by smaller bands was consistently seen by Handy from his youth onward as an opportunity to succeed with Du Bois's "larger audience," playing a music that they did not despise or ignore. Indeed, brass bands would provide his most constant employment into the first decade of the twentieth century. Inside the Florence barbershop, Handy practiced assiduously on his cornet, even when he became, in his phrase, "lip weary" when playing such conventional Sousa marches as "Right-Left" (1883) or "President Garfield's Inaugural March" (1881).

Handy's forbidden musical activities came to his father's knowledge during his son's fifteenth year, in 1888. The occasion was not the minister's witnessing any public performance by the barbershop band, but as a consequence of his son's friendship with the even more disreputable Jim Turner. Engaged to perform with his fiddle at a local land sale and lacking a player to back his performance, Turner persuaded Handy to skip a day's school and join him. In his memoir, Handy does not specify the songs they played, but it is probable that Turner chose tunes then much favored by both black and white Alabama fiddlers such as "The Bucking Mule" and "The Old Hen Cackled and the Rooster Crowed," which would have given him the opportunity to show off his celebrated animal mimicry with his string work. Another folk song that Turner very likely would have played was then a great favorite of fiddle players of both races and immensely popular among white listeners in the 1880s. This was "Run, Nigger, Run or the Patrol Will Get You." Enjoyed by Alabama whites as a comic tune, it had originated as a black folk fiddle melody in the antebellum lifetime of William Wise Handy, when it was played with a quite different intention. A covert encouragement to absent runaway slaves, it was fiddled by blacks remaining on the plantation as they supposedly joined in their masters' excitement at the pursuit.

Handy's pay for this performance was eight dollars, as opposed to the three dollars a week he had earned as a water boy at the Muscle Shoals quarry. "I imagined that my father would have a change of heart" about secular music, Handy later wrote, and that night he impulsively sought out his father, explained how he had earned the money, and then put all his day's wages into his father's hands. The Reverend Handy was having none of it, however, and he refused the tainted cash. "Son," Handy remembered his father telling him, "I'd rather see you in a hearse. I'd rather follow you to the graveyard than to hear that you had become a musician." The next day, Handy's schoolmaster continued the remonstrance. "Your father was right," Professor Wallace told him. "What can music do but bring you to the gutter?" The schoolmaster then expressed his anger at Handy's unauthorized absence the day before and "finished the job by applying the hickory," in the blues composer's rueful recollection.

Turner thereafter left Florence and returned to the road working as a saloon fiddle player and as a musician with blackface minstrelsy companies traveling in the Northeast and West. Handy resumed his studies at the Florence school, although in a remarkable defiance of his father, he insisted on playing public engagements with the brass band. Any further quarrels between them over his musical activity were unrecorded in the composer's memoir.

Handy graduated from the district high school in 1891, and, unenthusiastically, acceded to his father's wishes by serving as a teacher's assistant in the black schools in Lauderdale County. The conflict between father and son over the morality of playing secular music remained unresolved, however, and the family home on Handy's Hill had become more physically crowded with the birth of Handy's brother, named Charles for his father, in 1889. (The younger Charles Handy always idealized his older brother and in many ways considered him a surrogate father.) Their mother, Elizabeth Handy, perhaps in an attempt both to reduce the emotional tension within the small log cabin between father and older son and in her hopes for her firstborn's ambitions, encouraged her older son "to venture into the world." Handy later recalled that his mother's support "may have been that she found her time fully taken up by my baby brother. But it was likely that she had simply seen a brighter future for me in the world beyond the horizon." One of his father's AME ministerial friends subsequently arranged a teaching position for the young Handy in the larger Alabama city of Birmingham, about a hundred and thirty miles farther south. In September 1892 he departed from the Florence train depot, permanently leaving his childhood home on Handy's Hill.

His heart was plainly not in teaching. Handy resigned the arranged job before classes began when he learned that he could more than double his monthly salary by working as a foundry laborer at the Howard-Harrison Iron Company in nearby Bessemer. The better pay was a means to continuing his musical vocation. "I organized and taught my first brass band" among the black residents of Bessemer in his off-hours, he later recounted. But despite his local success at promoting popular music, what Handy called his "wanderlust" and his desire for a larger audience soon resurfaced. For all his later professed love of Alabama, and his subsequent adult visits there from New York City as a professional musician, Handy in his youth tried to get out of his home state at the earliest opportunity. One day, for instance, he impulsively threw down his foundry tools, intending to walk out of work when his foreman called the black workmen "you niggers." (In Handy's account, they later reconciled, and he resumed work when the two discovered a mutual liking for brass band tunes.) Handy in any case was not long for Bessemer, and, once again, the nineteen-year-old was hearing the appeal of Sousa's march music, this time to be played personally by the bandleader at a distant world's fair. In the two years since President Benjamin Harrison had signed the 1890 bill authorizing the national quadricentennial celebration of Christopher Columbus's first landing in America, promotion of the World's Columbian Exposition scheduled for 1892 in Chicago had spread nationwide, even into Alabama. Sousa, who had resigned from the Marine Corps, was now touring with his own band to great success and was advertised as the star among the performers and bandleaders to appear at the exposition.

Handy was determined to go to this world's fair. One day in the late fall of 1892, he overheard a group of young black men singing in a Birmingham saloon, introduced himself, and persuaded them to travel with him more than six hundred miles to the fair. After his optimistic assurances that they could earn money by singing along the way, they met at night at the Louisville & Nashville rail yard in Birmingham, intending to jump a freight train traveling in the general direction of Chicago. (Handy does not mention in his memoir whether he informed his parents in advance of this decision. If so, his mother likely would have approved, albeit with misgivings; his father almost certainly would not have.) A week later, in a series of almost comical episodes, and after several jumped freight railway cars and talking themselves aboard for a short trip on a Tennessee River excursion boat, they were still in the state of Alabama, less than eighty miles from Florence. Handy persevered, however, and the five young men eventually made their way northward. They arrived in Chicago, "exhausted and pretty well on our uppers," he recalled, and headed toward that city's Jackson Park, in search of the world's exposition.

What they found was not the celebrated beaux-arts "White City" of the fair's later finished buildings but a muddy construction site on the windy shores of a chilly lake. Although for promotional reasons the locale of the Columbian Exposition had been officially dedicated on October 21, 1892, by Chicago's mayor as "a great day for America," the actual *opening* of the fair had been postponed until twelve months hence. Handy and his four companions had been unaware of the fair's delay. The panic, or economic depression, of 1893–96 had already begun to reduce local financing for the costs of the fair's construction, and negotiations between fair officials and the Carpenters and Builders Union of Chicago over such issues as a minimum wage and an eight-hour workday were becoming delicate in a city where the Haymarket violence between laborers and police was well within living memory. It would be October 1893, a year after the aspiring youths had left Chicago, before President Cleveland stood underneath patriotic bunting on the steps of the exposition's administrative building and pressed a gilded telegraph key that signified the official opening of the world exposition to the public.

Handy had been homeless and frequently jobless throughout the winter of 1892–93. The would-be singers had been unable to find any work, musical or otherwise, in Chicago. He and his four traveling companions were considered simply among the "great throng of professional idlers, adventurers, and semi-criminals" contemporarily described by the city fathers as having been attracted to Chicago by the promise of the fair. Handy, however, was ever optimistic and insisted that better times were down the road. The five, riding as what Handy called "blind baggage"—unseen jumpers upon passing freight cars—traveled as a group to the city of St. Louis to try their fortunes there. But what neither Handy nor his friends knew was that they were traveling across the country at the onset of the greatest national panic, or economic depression, in the United States since the Civil War. Unemployment across the nation between 1893 and 1896 reached historic highs, and in 1893 the number of displaced workers in St. Louis was estimated variously as between 18,000 and 75,000. The only civic relief available there to the unemployed was provided from a diminishing fund of $8,000, raised at a concert sponsored by the St. Louis police. Finding themselves still jobless, the group broke up after reaching St. Louis. The other four members presumably hopped the rails for a return to their homes in Alabama, but Handy chose to remain alone, confident that his musical talent would succeed.

He was rewarded with poverty and homelessness, and he found not a day's work in St. Louis as a professional musician. Handy did obtain what seems to have been some financial relief when he was hired, probably as an unskilled laborer, at the Elliott Frog and Switch Works company on the Illinois side of the Mississippi River in the city of East St. Louis. To obtain an advance in salary for necessary food, lodging, and laundered clothes, he left his watch in pledge to his employer. But when he had worked out his debt after two weeks' wages, the company refused to return the timepiece. Handy went to the police to no avail. Six decades later, he could still strongly recall his full resentment felt in 1893 at his reception by the East St. Louis constabulary, who in Handy's recollection were politically connected to his employer:

> I went to the police for redress, and they threatened to
> take me in for vagrancy if I pressed the charge. If you

don't think that in those days there was corruption in East St. Louis, you have but to do a little research.

In his greatest despair, Handy then walked hopelessly across the mile-long Eads Bridge over the Mississippi, back to the Missouri side of the river to join the anonymous day laborers at the St. Louis docks. By this time, Handy had heard and remembered the then-current black folk melody "East St. Louis": *Walked all the way from East Saint Louis / And I didn't have but one lousy dime.* At this moment he possessed even less, having only five cents in his pocket. But on his trip across Eads Bridge, there was to be one final humiliation. Frantically beginning to scratch at his shirt, Handy realized that his clothes were infested with lice. The child who had once been dressed in his mother's lovingly embroidered vest could not bear as a homeless young adult to keep his infested shirt close to his skin. "I tore off my lousy shirt and threw it into the Mississippi River," Handy later passionately recalled to a friend. Another pedestrian passing on the bridge, his skin color unrecorded by Handy, saw this act and assumed that this disturbed-appearing young man was taking off his shirt prior to deliberately jumping to his death in the river. He impulsively offered Handy a safe shelter of sorts on the Missouri side. Thus, according to his later recollection of the early winter of 1893, "I spent my first night in St. Louis at the race track in a horse's stall."

During his winter in St. Louis, Handy eventually was reduced to sleeping in the open air upon the cobblestone levees of the city's Mississippi River docks. The weather was particularly severe, even by Midwestern standards. In the bleak mornings he might find temporary pickup work as a stevedore unloading riverboats. Hundreds of other unemployed laborers, black and white, shared these outdoor living conditions, where personal safety and lack of toilet facilities can be imagined. He later romanticized his season as a vagabond, remembering in a prosperous old age how he first had heard on the docks of St. Louis the folk songs of his fellow anonymous laborers, such as "Lookin' for the Bully of the Town," and how his hungry, dangerous nights on stone bedding had inspired his later poetic beginning to the "St. Louis Blues"—*I hate to see that evening sun go down.* But in historical fact, the young William

Christopher Handy, despite his mother's hopes, his father's warn-
ings, and his own hard-won musical education in Alabama, was in
1893 just another faceless black vagrant among the unemployed
ranks of workers. (The following year, the labor leader Jacob Coxey
would lead hundreds of jobless Midwestern laborers to Washington, D.C., where they would join with hundreds more of the unemployed under Populist banners as a self-declared "army," demanding
federal spending to create jobs. They were met by policemen with
clubs.) Handy, cold and hungry, certainly had sufficient time to
reflect remorsefully upon Professor Wallace's earlier warning to
him, when he had expressed a desire to be a professional musician,
"What can music do but bring you to the gutter?"

Handy decided to leave St. Louis by the spring or early summer of
1893, perhaps considering a return home to Alabama and his father's
inevitable rebuke. Riding the freight cars as a hobo, he got off a train
in Evansville, Indiana, hungry and penniless. Although Handy does
not mention the fact in his later memoir, this community was significant in his family's history. A little over forty years earlier, the
Ohio River town had been the place where the abolitionist Seth
Concklin had been arrested along with the two fugitive slaves who
had been aided in their escape from an Alabama plantation by
William Wise Handy.

    W. C. Handy had better luck in Evansville. After a few weeks
working as an unskilled road grader, he talked his way into a paying position with a local brass band, the Hampton Cornet Band.
(Rubber-rimmed mouthpieces for cornets had come into patented
usage in 1876, and though Handy was unable to keep an instrument
about him during his penniless travels, he could at least carry a
mouthpiece in his pocket, ready to show his talent to anyone who
would lend him a horn.) For the first time, he was at last making
his living as a member of a professional brass band. For the next
three years, from 1893 to 1896, Handy played his cornet in light classical music and martial marches, including such favorite Sousa compositions as "King Cotton" (1895), "The High School Cadets" (1890),
"The White Plume" (1884), and "The Stars and Stripes Forever"

(1896). When a white Kentucky politician who was a former protégé of Sousa's heard Handy play, he encouraged him to perform across the Ohio River with the brass band of Henderson, Kentucky, organized there by local band master David P. Crutcher. Handy soon was playing both sides of the river.

Often the members of these Indiana and Kentucky marching bands were dressed in smart uniforms of gilt-trimmed short jackets, striped trousers, and military-style hats. The latter certainly pleased Handy. One of the well-known photographs of his youth shows him proudly standing in the uniform of the Hampton Cornet Band in 1893—less than twelve months from throwing away his lice-infested shirt in St. Louis—dressed in a brass-buttoned coat, matching trousers, a clean high white collar, and flat-topped hat with the band's brass insignia. The purchase of this uniform would have set Handy back about ten dollars, probably deducted from his pay. He prominently holds a J. W. Pepper silver-plated cornet in front of him. In the marches, he had a place of musical preeminence in the band. Even in brass bands featuring other instruments, the cornetists usually stepped in formation closely behind the bandleader, immediately after the wind instruments, their horns played in E-flat to be heard above the following drums and larger brass instruments. Handy with his skilled triple-tonguing would have been a noticeable marcher.

Score reading was a necessity for such musically and physically synchronized performances, and Handy's subsequent insistence upon a strict observance of the printed score and his later distrust of jazz improvisation was set in his mind during this period.

Also fixed into his personal habit at this time was his lifelong practice of abbreviating his name to W. C. Handy. To his mother, he was always "William"; to a few close friends, he was "Bill"; but from the beginning of his professional career, and in later playbills and printed scores copyrighted under his name, he was known as W. C. Handy. Perhaps this choice was an attempt at psychologically distancing himself from the name of his disapproving minister father; or perhaps it was his ambitious preference upon being known formally in public as a serious and respectable performer of music; or in this era of hot-lead type for printed material, it may simply have been at the insistence of the early Linotype operators, who always avoided casting into type what they considered unnecessary letters.

Ever ambitious, the musician now known as W. C. Handy also took an additional job playing in the serenade bands aboard the *F. W. Nesbitt,* an excursion steamer that offered pleasure cruises for whites southward from Cairo, Illinois, along the upper Mississippi River. The musicians there adjusted the tempo of Sousa's marches to allow for genteel two-step dancing by the passengers. The newly self-sufficient performer now kept in contact by letter with his family in Alabama and began sending them small presents as emblems of his musical success. By 1895, to supplement his pay with the Indiana and Kentucky bands, Handy also took a janitor's job at the Liederkranz Hall of German immigrants in Henderson, and there he came to the attention of the director of the hall's singing society, who kindly gave Handy further instruction in vocal arrangements. In Handy's optimistic words, "I obtained a postgraduate course in vocal music—and got paid for it."

Most important, he found a wife on the Kentucky side of the Ohio River. She was Elizabeth Price, a young black woman from a respected local family in Henderson. They had met at an Emancipation Day ceremony there, where apparently her attention had been caught by this young, ambitious musician in his smart uniform. Handy had by this time matured into a stocky, genteel-appearing man with closely cropped hair who spoke in a softly persistent, educated southern accent. Their courtship, in anticipation of her later life with the peripatetic Handy, was to be largely conducted by correspondence, as he traveled and played his music on the road and the river. On July 19, 1898, the couple married in a moonlight ceremony in Henderson, where brass bandsmen of Handy's acquaintance played accompaniment. He was then twenty-four years of age.

He was not a husband often at home. Earlier, to his lasting guilt, he had missed his mother's funeral in Alabama in August 1895, when a family letter notifying him of her death had been delayed in reaching him while he was performing aboard the *Nesbitt.* He had returned to Florence only in time to meet the mourners returning from the AME church, where so many of the black community had attended the funeral that the church's floor collapsed under their weight. The esteem with which the Handy family was regarded by the white community was also noted, by local standards, in the obituary of Elizabeth Brewer Handy. Her passing was headlined "A Good Old Colored Woman Dead," in the largely white-read newspaper, the *Florence Herald*.

Absence from important events, such as his mother's funeral, would be characteristic of Handy, who frequently would be away on engagements during the births, and on one occasion the death, of his children. By the time of his marriage in 1898, Handy was fully engaged as a professional musician in a vocation even more footloose.

He earlier had received a letter from a former member of the Henderson brass band now traveling as a minstrel, who had urged Handy to consider performing in a minstrelsy troupe as an opportunity to be heard nationally—with the added advantage of "cakes," as the three meals a day provided at no charge by the minstrelsy companies were then called by the black performers. Handy had decided in 1896 to join such a troupe. Now often away from home, he was learning a new form of highly popular, largely white-composed music, although, unlike the patriotic marches of Sousa, minstrelsy songs were considered racially insulting and socially lower-class by many in both the black and white races. "It goes without saying that minstrels were a disreputable lot in the eyes of a large section of upper-crust Negroes," Handy later circumspectly recalled, "including the family and friends of Elizabeth Price." Nevertheless, this gifted performer would "fight it out" over the next seven years, until 1903, as an increasingly celebrated cornet and trumpet performer in the traveling blackface minstrel show.

CHAPTER THREE

———

Jumping Jim Crow

HANDY AS A TRAVELING MINSTREL
MUSICIAN, 1896–1900

PROSPERITY'S FAVORITES
MAHARA'S COLORED MINSTRELS
40—People—40

WANTED
COLORED TALENT
of all kinds Musicians for Band
and Orchestra;
also Good Amateurs

ADDRESS JACK MAHARA, CARE
WINTERBURN PRINTING COMPANY
160 SOUTH CLARK STREET
CHICAGO ILL.

—Advertisement for new employees
by the Mahara brothers' minstrel
company

The 'Blues' are ambiguous." So a successful W. C. Handy would write in a 1919 article to the African American–owned newspaper the *Chicago Defender*, describing his new music as an admixture of remembered joy and pain. Handy at the time of this article would be more than a decade and a half removed from the young, gaudily dressed cornet player who had toured nationally in what he later recalled was "the genuine article, a real Negro minstrel show." But despite Handy's growing popularity in 1919 as a composer of blues music, his experiences of minstrelsy between 1896 and 1903 would leave their permanent marks on him. The musical stage routines of blackface entertainment were a precursor to the blues in their ambiguous emotions of pain and joy, which Handy experienced during his five seasons as a minstrel cornet player.

When contemporary Americans think of black minstrelsy, if they think of it at all, they recall it as a nineteenth-century stage grotesquerie in which white actors, known as "Ethiopian delineators," with their faces blackened with carbon from burnt wine corks, performed exaggerated dance steps and turns, and sang what they purported to be authentic African American folk songs. Foremost among early nineteenth-century whites who composed or performed for this antebellum minstrelsy were Stephen Foster, George Washington Dixon—who created the stage character of Zip Coon, an urbanized black dandy—and Thomas D. "Daddy" Rice, who first had popularized the routine that later was elaborated into the mid-nineteenth-century minstrel show. Rice, in blackface makeup, would energetically shuffle onstage dressed in colorful rags during the intermissions in "legitimate" theater of the 1830s, and then sing to the enthusiastic white audiences while making grotesque and frequently erotically suggestive contortions with his body: *I jumps jis' so / And ev'y time I turn about, I jump Jim Crow.*

There is "a curious lurch in the rhythm, that makes it stick in your mind whether you want it there or not," a twentieth-century scholar of popular music, John Strausbaugh, wrote of the singing and dancing by this white actor, whom Strausbaugh considers to have become the nineteenth century's version of Elvis Presley. In fact, Daddy Rice's black-inflected verses and outré dancing were, like Presley's, an early international pop phenomenon. Rice eventually performed in the 1830s to sold-out London crowds at the Surrey Theatre. In America, other stage entrepreneurs such as E. P. Christy added new songs, comic stage patter, instrumental solos, and group dances, all performed in blackface, and by the 1850s, the uniquely American minstrel show was an established popular entertainment.

Rice claimed to have copied the halting but antic dance steps of "Jump Jim Crow" from an African American he had observed who was dancing and working, in his various accounts, either at a stable in Louisville, Kentucky (in which case the black dancer probably would have been a slave), or across the Ohio River on the streets of Cincinnati (in which case the black dancer would have been legally a freedman). Yet what was billed as the "Ethiopian Mobility" of Rice's leg-and-hip-twisting dance moves was probably the only authentically African American influence upon his performance. Black folk music was neither adapted nor outright appropriated until almost the end of minstrelsy. The 1832 score of "Jim Crow: A Comic Song Sung by Mr. Rice," copyrighted in Baltimore, most resembles "an Irish folk song and English stage song," in the opinions of musical scholars. So too do the later tunes of antebellum minstrelsy, such as "My Long Blue Tail" and "Coal Black Rose." Despite the stagy African American dialect of the show's song lyrics and comedy routines, minstrelsy tunes until almost the end of the nineteenth century exhibited none of the techniques that European visitors to the antebellum South had noticed as unique to the folk songs of the African American slaves—an improvised variation in rhythmic accent and a keening-like use of minor notes. (An exception were the minstrelsy scores written by Rice's friend the gifted Stephen Foster, most noticeably in the off-the-beat accents of his "Gwine to Run All Night, or, De Camptown Races.") Daddy Rice's famous dance did have a lasting effect, however, upon later historical discussions about the lives of African Americans; by the 1890s, "Jim Crow" had permanently entered American usage as the description for this nation's laws enforcing racial segregation.

For a present-day reader, it is tempting to regard blackface minstrelsy and the Jim Crow routines that developed out of the caricatures of Daddy Rice as an aberration, or a confirmation, of America's deepest racism, and to regard its stage representations of urban black buffoons or contented plantation darkies as no longer acceptable to enlightened whites by the end of the Civil War. But such a moral judgment is not so absolute: blackface minstrelsy was an ambiguous mix in its emotions and motivations. The majority of Americans through the first half of the nineteenth century probably saw Daddy Rice's dance of jumping Jim Crow onstage just as proudly as a later generation in the twentieth century would offer African American blues and jazz to the rest of the world as among the best accomplishments of U.S. popular culture. It is no accident that minstrelsy first began to be popular in the 1830s, the Age of Jackson, when the United States was desirous of a national identity distinct from that of Great Britain.

But the question remains, why the choice of an African American to represent American popular culture on the nineteenth-century stage, rather than a white theatrical "Uncle Sam" or a New England Yankee? Perhaps it is because the burnt-cork makeup of minstrelsy can also be a convenient mask for licentiousness or confrontation, otherwise unacceptable. This unsettling national truth was consequently addressed by two twentieth-century American authors, with mordant humor by Flannery O'Connor in her short story "The Artificial Nigger," and in 1954 by James Baldwin, who wrote of what he called the "sleeping terror of some condition which we refuse to imagine."

> In a way, if the Negro were not here, we might be forced to deal within our selves with all those vices, all those conundrums, and all those mysteries with which we have invested the Negro race. Uncle Tom is, for example, if he is called Uncle, a kind of saint. He is there, he endures, he will forgive us, and this is a key to that image. But if he is not Uncle, if he is merely Tom [or a subversive, enticing minstrel who is uninhibitedly jumping Jim Crow], he is a danger to everybody.

"The whole minstrel episode is schizoid," the music historian Rudi Blesh subsequently wrote in 1971 in a tone of intellectual exasperation. "The comic portraits of the Negro that were drawn in burnt cork were at once sympathetic and belittling." Blesh, who in other publications belittled Handy's contributions to the blues, then perhaps unwittingly confirms the significance of Handy's career in minstrelsy to the composer's later accomplishments. He wrote,

> Though much of it was mere travesty, it was a sort of tribute to the charms and power of the real thing. From the 1840's [sic] on, it prepared the way for the acceptance of

Negro music, though it defined in advance much of the
nature and extent of the acceptance, very much as the
obnoxious poll tax at the end of the last century began to
define the political boundaries of poor Southern citizens
of both races.

When Handy enlisted with the Mahara troupe in the summer of
1896, blackface minstrelsy, like the poll tax, by no means was an
anachronism in the United States. He was joining a going business.
Traveling minstrel shows sustained a post–Civil War popularity
from the 1870s to the early twentieth century, and urban theaters
specializing in minstrel entertainment flourished in the late nineteenth century in New York City, Philadelphia, San Francisco, and
the Midwestern states. Even the future "March King," John Philip
Sousa, made his early musical livelihood by composing such non-
march tunes as "'Deed I Has to Laugh," for the Philadelphia company of the Cornecross and Dixie Minstrels in the 1870s. Some
minstrel shows advertised themselves as all whiteface, but many
others continued the tradition of blackface makeup. Burnt cork at
twenty-five cents to fifty cents per can was a necessary overhead
expense for early minstrel companies.

In an innovation well received by some African American audiences, by the time Handy went on the road, minstrel shows also
were beginning to be performed by actual people of color. The
Mahara troupe out of Chicago, which Handy had joined, was such a
company. Referred to in newspaper advertisements generically as
"Georgia" minstrels, or "colored minstrels," these African American
troupes were usually under a white manager and promoter, in
Handy's case the Irish family consisting of William Mahara and his
two brothers. The shows attracted largely white audiences, and
these managers frequently had to turn away black customers
because minstrelsy theaters reserved such small seating areas, usually in the topmost balcony, exclusively for African Americans. For
many African Americans, the colored minstrel show was their only
opportunity to see people of their own race perform professionally.
Intriguingly, colored minstrels themselves occasionally blackened
up for the stage, either in mockery or in competition with the white

minstrels. Thus by the time Handy left for his first tour, American minstrelsy consisted of white men onstage who performed as white men; white men onstage in burnt cork makeup who imitated black men; black men who blackened their own faces and then performed onstage in imitation of blackened-faced white men; and black men in unadorned faces—"the genuine article," in Handy's description—who performed as they were.

Handy departed for this strange theatrical world from Chicago by rail with the rest of the Mahara troupe for their opening appearance about seventy-five miles away in Belvidere, Illinois, on September 6, 1896. He played cornet in the marching band and both cornet and violin in the minstrelsy show's orchestra. During his first tour that season of 1896–97, aboard the Maharas' private train known as the Maharaja, Handy followed the circuit that colored minstrelsy had adapted from the traveling circuses, playing small towns during the late summer or early autumn harvest seasons, then closing with shows in larger cities such as Los Angeles, Denver, or Cincinnati. He also came to know well some of the more flamboyant members of the company, with whom he shared meals, sleeping quarters, and dressing rooms aboard the small train. One with whom he renewed his acquaintance was the itinerant violinist Jim Turner, who had so fascinated him in Florence with stories of life on Beale Avenue, and who was now traveling again as a minstrel with the Mahara company. Another was George Moxley, a charismatic and very light-skinned man who for years was the company's stage manager, solo tenor singer, and Mister Interlocutor, who introduced each night's performance and bantered onstage with the other performers. Another minstrelsy veteran in the Mahara troupe was Wilbur C. Sweatman, who was later obliged to make his living on the vaudeville stage with the novelty act of simultaneously playing three clarinets and who was to be a future friend to Handy in his blues career.

There were also the professional cross-dressers. Another "ace in our company," in Handy's description, was Johnny Stone, who under the stage name of Leroy Bland was one of the most skilled of the Mahara company's female impersonators, collectively known in the minstrel business together with the actual female performers as "soubrettes." (Although female members were among the companies' musicians and singers, female impersonation seems to have been a specialty act popular with colored, whiteface, or blackface minstrel shows.) Assorted acrobats, comedians, dialect humorists, and the occasional "whistling specialists" and "serpentine" dancers, along with Handy and other marching band and seated orchestra musicians, completed the Mahara company.

After advance publicity, arranged by Jack Mahara, consisting of posters locally pasted up and free tickets given to friendly journalists, the troupe would arrive in town aboard the Maharaja. After changing into their parade uniforms inside the Pullman car, Handy and the other black musicians would fall into line at the railroad yard for a grand parade at noon to the town square. Their uniforms, as Handy could still recall in his late middle age, were showily magnificent, and he had been fortunate in the timing of his arrival with the company. In the summer of 1896, the Maharas had outfitted all their minstrels with new attire for the parades, described by a contemporary newspaper as consisting of "silk vests and velvet knee pants. The six end men wear full satin suits, and the orchestra is dressed in satin suits with lace sleeves."

The parade was led into town by William Mahara, in an elegantly trimmed carriage accompanied by his Saint Bernard dog, Sport. Mahara sometimes arranged for four mounted buglers, usually also white men, to ride alongside him. Handy and the others played and marched far behind. Following the carriage, there first came the "walking gents," the star performers and acrobats, who cut capers for the crowd as they strutted and marched. Behind the walking gents, and intermixed with the occasional trick bicyclist, clowning trombonist, or comedic piccolo player, came the rows of uniformed minstrel musicians, including Handy.

Handy soon stood out by virtue of his talent. He received an early press notice on August 22, 1897, when a local newspaper described the Mahara troupe's arrival in Joliet, Illinois: "The parade included two bands, one large band of twenty pieces under the leadership of W. C. Handy, and a pickaninny band of fourteen pieces under Joseph Brink." Handy formally assumed the title and the pay of band master for the Mahara company on December 11, 1897.

On the night of each show, he would take his position on the stage behind the curtain among the thirteen other orchestra players, who were seated upon an elevated platform rather than in the orchestra pit as was the usual arrangement with legitimate theater or opera. Directly in front of this small orchestra were assembled two semicircles of standing performers, the most favored in the first semicircle closest to the audience, and the assorted acrobats and comedians standing behind them. George Moxley would receive his backstage order from a Mahara brother to "get them told," in stage parlance. The curtain would then rise on the minstrel company's singers and dancers. A painted backdrop visible to the audience behind the orchestra would portray an idealized plantation setting, or, in what was certainly an ironic remembrance to Handy, a scene of cotton bales and a river levee recalling to him his time in St. Louis.

Mister Interlocutor in his opening act would then welcome the audience and cheerily command the entire company, "Gentlemen, be seated." This was the cue for Handy and other musicians in the orchestra to take to their chairs in position behind the featured entertainers and strike up the overture of the show. What followed was a three-part stage routine common to all minstrel shows by the late nineteenth century. The printed program for the Mahara troupe's show at the Los Angeles Theater in California on January 31, 1898, gives a record of what Handy contributed, triple-tonguing on his cornet to the quick notes, to the orchestra's performance in the first part. At the top of the act, he accompanied the female imper-sonator Leroy Bland, possibly dressed in theatrical drag for comic effect, who opened the show with the number "Honey, Does You Love Your Man?" This song was followed by the more genteel "When Maria Johnson Marries Me" and then the sure crowd-pleaser "Young America."

Throughout this first part of the show, members of the orches-tra, Handy included, also provided background music or comic sound effects as Mister Interlocutor, now standing at the stage's center, introduced the performers. Acting as a straight man, Mis-ter Interlocutor also engaged in scripted banter with the two comedians positioned at stage right and left. These two main "end-men" were known as Mr. Tambo and Mr. Bones, and the two signaled their punch lines to the audience by shaking a tambourine or rattling a pair of castanets or, sometimes, horse rib bones. In an instance of the basically socially subversive nature of American minstrelsy, the two end-men traditionally always got the better of Mr. Interlocutor, who in the white companies usually had the only unblackened face onstage, and who in the Mahara company was played by the light-skinned Moxley. The following is representative of what was presented onstage in front of Handy and the other musicians as they played their accompaniment or sound effects:

MISTER INTERLOCUTOR: Do you know that the sun gives us life?

TAMBO: That's nothing. I know a judge who give us the same thing! . . . *(All laugh)* Does anybody live up in the sun?

MISTER INTERLOCUTOR: I don't think so. Because when you look at it through a telescope everything looks bare.

TAMBO: Then, maybe only women live there.

MISTER INTERLOCUTOR: No, no, all you can see in the sun is gas and hot air.

TAMBO: Oh, I see. They have policemen up there, too.

After this staged repartee and music of about sixty minutes' duration, Handy and the other orchestra members then provided numerous quick-paced musical segues for the second, equally long portion of the show, known as the olio. This was a rapid succession of dancers, comedians, "banjo comique," contortionists, "a genuine Mexican band" (presumably light-skinned African American troupe members), supposedly humorous stories told in purportedly Negro dialect, and whatever other novelty act the Mahara brothers hoped might amuse the crowd, including the antics of one Samuel Williams, who performed "a clever human frog act." At the Los Angeles show, the olio also included vocal numbers by the Blackberry Brothers and the Blackberry Sisters, and a "refined" comedian—actually the musical director Billy Young, who made a quick change of costuming. Handy, as he increased his skill with cornet and trumpet, was also moved up to become one of the featured olio acts. During the olio, the female impersonators costumed appropriately in frocks and artificially exaggerated bosoms would frequently sing "Mammy" songs or comically pursue one of the other male performers.

The final and third stage routine, or afterpiece, was an unrelated short musical sketch. At the Los Angeles booking, it was "a Farce-Comedy entitled 'The Rival Brothers.'" At some point in the evening's entertainment, Moxley would also announce to the delighted audience that the minstrelsy troupe would perform their most elaborate walk-around, the much-anticipated "peregrination for the pastry." This was the choreographed dance known as the cakewalk. Handy and the other musicians would then strike up a simple two- or three-chorded dance march in a one-two, one-two beat with a strong bass rhythm, perhaps also played with comical instrumental effects. This marching walk-around was perhaps the sole black folk tradition in minstrelsy and was based on the antebellum entertainment of a high-stepping, elbows-akimbo, buttocks-raised dance promenade in song. Here the racial "insult and imitation," which some scholars have maintained perennially characterizes America's cultural exchanges between the races, and American popular music in particular, subversively rose to the favored spot on the late-nineteenth-century minstrelsy bill.

Antebellum slaves are believed to have developed the cakewalk as a deliberate parody of what had seemed to them the pretentious and overly inhibited social dancing of their masters, as in the quadrille. But the white plantation owners, unaware of the joke, had enjoyed watching what appeared to them to be the natural exuberance of happy slaves, and at times had rewarded the best dancers with a cake. Minstrelsy in the 1880s and 1890s revived the cakewalk tradition, to immense popularity with their white audiences. So popular was the cakewalk, in fact, that when performed with more restrained stepping and posture and accompanied by a Sousa-like march, the dance in the late 1890s became a fad with young middle-class couples. Thus the original vulgar insult by antebellum blacks to the dancing by their masters became, through the venue of black minstrelsy, the late-Victorian pastime of genteel white Americans.

The cakewalking songs by the time of Handy's arrival to the minstrelsy stage also frequently employed lyrics of national political satire. In the late minstrelsy version, star performers in the promenade took the singing leads and would be answered in chorus by the other members of the company. U.S. presidents William McKinley and Theodore Roosevelt and presidential candidate Eugene V. Debs were all occasionally subjects of satire. An instance of this topical walk-around is the popular minstrel afterpiece number of the late nineteenth century, sung to Stephen Foster's composition of 1850, "Camptown Races," now with lyrics entitled "That Ain't No Lie":

> Went downtown for to cast my vote,
> Thought I'd swap it for a two-dollar note,
> Man says, "I'll give you five, sure as fate,
> If you'll vote the Democratic ticket straight"—
> I took the five, then another man
> Give me ten to vote the Republican,
> But to fool them both I couldn't resist,
> An' I voted for a no-account Socialist.

The producers and stage managers of the minstrel shows certainly remained fond of the songs of Stephen Foster, but blackened-faced or not, the performers singing the lyrics in the above cakewalk are a long distance from shouting "Doo-dah!"

At a sign from Moxley, following about two and a half hours' entertainment, Handy and his fellow orchestra musicians would then signal to the audience the end of the show. The curtain would slowly descend, and the acting troupe and musicians would softly sing or hum their farewell accompaniment, usually a nostalgic favorite like "Farewell Ladies," from the repertoire of the Christy's Minstrels show of the 1850s:

> Whenever again we make a call
> We'll do our best to please you all
> One thing is sure, we'll neber tire
> Unless, oh, some us should suspire!
> Fare you well, ladies. Fare you well.

The Mahara brothers then safely collected the door's receipts, the Maharaja car would depart the rail yard with the exhausted minstrels, and the theatrical company, Handy included, would be on their way for another engagement at yet another town on the circuit.

Handy was away from his wife in Henderson, Kentucky, during these five- or six-month tours on the road for much longer than when he had played the Ohio River towns in a marching brass band. Elizabeth Price Handy remained in residence in Kentucky with her parents during his first and following tours of 1896–99, with the couple usually reuniting during the winter off-season. His absences were perhaps an early source of marital discord between the couple, or at least between Handy and his in-laws. They had made clear to him their opinion that his new vocation as a traveling colored minstrel was more "disreputable" than his marching in a local brass band. Yet this itinerant life was also unavoidable for any ambitious and professional musician of color such as Handy. As George Moxley, after his retirement as Mister Interlocutor, reminded readers of the *Freeman* in 1907, for African American musicians who came of age in the 1880s and 1890s "there was no avenue for the colored entertainer but Uncle Tom's Cabin, the minstrels, and the [black gospel] jubilee companies." Unlike the other two types of nationally traveling musical shows, in colored minstrelsy the money was good. The Mahara brothers made certain that "the ghost walked," in the parlance of African American minstrels: that is, the white manager appeared at regular weekly intervals with the agreed-upon salaries for the company's members. (Minstrel company owners frequently dressed in showy white suits and traditionally paid their black employees by walking through the company and handing out small envelopes of cash. Hence, the image of the walking ghost from an African American perspective.) Handy eventually was making two hundred dollars a month with the Mahara troupe. Besides sending home a generous portion of his salary to his wife every week, he bought for himself, in his description, several "smart outfits, one being a suit, hat, watch fob, umbrella strap and spats, all cut from the same bolt of rich brown cloth." He also added to his wardrobe "a couple of diamonds."

"My association with them had made of me a professional musician," Handy later wrote of his five seasons playing with the Maharas' company. "It had thrown me into contact with a wistful but aspiring generation of dusky singers and musicians." In fact, for his generation and a future generation of both black and white Americans, a new art of performance was emerging from the ritualized routines of these minstrel shows. The future vaudeville theater of the 1910s and 1920s was taking shape from the fast-paced variety acts and comic bits of the nineteenth-century olio; and in the choreographed walk-around there was plausibly seen, by the remarkable Harlem Renaissance intellectual James Weldon Johnson, the recognizable beginnings of that distinctly American performance, the Broadway musical. Both in his stage performances of the 1920s and 1930s as well as in his later memoir, Handy defended colored minstrelsy "for the break it was" for black entertainers such as himself to have introduced authentically African American musical forms like the cakewalk to the national stage.

But however sophisticated and racially adaptive the minstrel show had become during Handy's years, there were also performed musical numbers "at once sympathetic and belittling," in Blesh's words. These songs have given American minstrelsy its historically bad name and explain why a number of educated nineteenth-century blacks such as the Price family—or W. E. B. Du Bois, who loathed the minstrel stage—disapproved of Handy's new vocation. At the Mahara troupe's performance in Los Angeles, for instance, the sentimental and patriotic numbers that Handy played had been preceded by his accompanying Rube Brown singing "Every Nigger Has a Lady but Me." In 1896, the same year that Handy joined the Maharas' company, the African American vaudevillian Ernest Hogan also copyrighted the words and music of the widely popular tune "All Coons Look Alike to Me." It subsequently became a necessary part of practically all minstrelsy companies' repertoire. Just as the name "Jim Crow" had entered American usage by the 1890s as a term for legal racial segregation, so had the "Zip Coon" of George Washington Dixon's earlier minstrelsy performances created an audience in the late nineteenth century for what were called "coon songs."

Coon songs performed in colored minstrelsy were of low repute with African Americans such as Du Bois and the Prices not for how they were played but for what they said. The music Handy and other minstrel musicians played for these songs was usually a simple-chorded ballad in common time, with a slight speeding up on the chorus. The lyrics were what defined this genre. Sung in an exaggerated, stagy African American dialect, the words inevitably portrayed people of color either as childishly simple or hopelessly larcenous; black males in particular were frequently portrayed as comically inept thieves or dice-rolling gamblers, perennially in trouble with "Mister Johnson," a slangy African American term for a white policeman. The lyrics of the coon song written and copyrighted in 1896 by the white pianist Ben Harney are representative:

> *A big black coon was lookin' fer chickens*
> *When a great big bulldog got to raisin' de dickens,*
> *De coon got higher, de chicken got nigher,*
> *Just den Johnson opened up fire.*
>
>   .   .   .   .
>
> *And now he's playin' seben eleben*
> *Way up yonder in de nigger heaben*
> *Oh! Mister Johnson, made him good.*

As a late-nineteenth-century innovation by the white and colored minstrel companies, coon songs became great crowd-pleasers for their predominantly white audiences. "Folks began whistling Ernest Hogan's songs on street corners and barber shops," Handy later recalled of these years in the 1890s. The same year Hogan copyrighted "All Coons Look Alike to Me," the composer Paul Dresser (who spelled his family name differently from his brother, Theodore Dreiser, author of the novels *Sister Carrie* and *An American Tragedy*) scored a national hit with his tune "I'se Your Nigger If You Wants Me, Liza Jane." Additionally, George M. Cohan, composer of "You're a Grand Old Flag" and "The Yankee Doodle Boy," also wrote "a number of songs in the coon vein." Coon songs continued their popularity in sheet music sales and public performances throughout Handy's seasons in minstrelsy, with such national hits as "Mammy's Little Pumpkin Colored Coons" in 1897; indeed, with the later performances of these songs by Handy's acquaintance the talented

Bert Williams, coon songs retained their popularity into the halcyon twentieth-century years of vaudeville and the Ziegfeld Follies. Perhaps this genre reached its fulfillment in the popular and almost pathologically obsessed song titled "Coon! Coon! Coon!" whose lyrics were written by Gene Jefferson in 1901.

Ernest Hogan, Bert Williams, and Handy were all persons of color. In their compositions or performances of coon songs for pay, they may have found justification in that they were simply giving to white people the illusions that they wanted and that would be provided to them by other performers if these colored minstrels did not do so. After all, it was the white audiences who were parted from their money, and it was the performers of color who left the stage doors each night in possession of very nonillusory dollars. In defense of Handy, Hogan, and others, it can also be argued that the coon songs, at least those composed or sung by African Americans, were subtle indictments of prejudice on the part of the white majority or its white pluralities, as in the hit by the African American composer Irving Jones, "St. Patrick's Day Is a Bad Day for Coons." Plausibly, "All Coons Look Alike to Me" and even "Coon! Coon! Coon!" are capable of a socially critical interpretation when sung in pathos by a performer of color.

And, for at least some black listeners, the pleasure of seeing African Americans such as Handy celebrated on the minstrelsy stage was greater than hearing the insults of the lyrics that these performers were required to sing or accompany. The ambiguity for Handy personally and for his career as he played accompaniment to what would later be regarded as racist songs was well presented by this praiseful review of the Mahara troupe, printed without adverse comment or distancing irony, by the Indianapolis *Freeman* on June 18, 1898:

> But the bright stars of the evening were undoubtedly Mr. and Mrs. Dan Avery. The unique rendition of several of the latest coon songs of Mrs. Avery and the droll and original comedy of "Happy Dan" elicited thunderous applause and compelled the clever team to take five encores. At the close of the present season the Mahara

show goes under canvas. Prof. W. C. Handy is the band-
master and undoubtedly has one of the best bands in the
country.

Handy in his memoir of 1941 refrained from specifically denounc-
ing the coon songs with which he had shared the minstrelsy stage in
the 1890s. He consequently has been criticized by twentieth-century
critics such as Rudi Blesh for having made an early and comfortable
living by "Uncle Tom"–ing in a racist business run by white owners
who deliberately caricatured blacks. Yet historically he frequently
had "to fight it out"—as he remembered his inheritance of character
from his slave grandfather, William Wise Handy—in order to survive physically on the minstrelsy road. His memories in *Father of the
Blues* of his flush salary and his growing skills as a professional musician are squarely placed beside nightmarish instances of racial violence. His memoir puts the lie to later accusations that Handy had
an easy ride as a comparatively privileged performer of color. In
fact, in recalling his life as a traveling colored minstrel within the
pages of *Father of the Blues,* he refers to what he vividly terms the
"nightmare" of minstrelsy.

The most vivid nightmare that Handy remembered occurred in
his fourth tour, in the 1899–1900 season, when the Mahara company
made its first circuit in ten years through the South and Texas, a state
that culturally and politically remained part of the former Confederacy. William Mahara at the time made many public boasts of pro-
viding his black minstrelsy employees with a private railroad coach
that included the services of a retained cook, a porter, and a waiter.
Such arrangements were prudently necessary for African American
minstrels while traveling through the South and the West in 1896,
when *Plessy v. Ferguson* was the law of the land. But despite the minstrel troupe's segregated travel, the brightly painted Mahara train
was fired upon, apparently for sport, by white locals with rifles as it
passed at night through the town of Orange, Texas. Handy, along
with the rest of the minstrels, stretched flat along the aisle of the
darkened train to avoid the bullets.

On a different occasion in Texas, Handy had a rifle waved in his
face, also apparently for sport, as he led the minstrels down a main

street in parade; during this same parade, minstrels were also las-soed, and rocks were thrown at the drums of the band and down into the brass instruments. Further along the southern tour, in Murfreesboro, Tennessee, Handy had to conceal himself in a secret compartment in their railroad car, which the minstrels called the "bear wallow," after a county sheriff and a posse came aboard the Maharaja, all of them talking lynching. They were looking for Handy after he had roughly rebuked a white man in the rail yard who had threatened a member of the minstrel troupe.

The risk of lynching for traveling colored minstrelsy companies was not limited to tours in the southern or southwestern states. Handy was also keenly aware of the fate of one of the former trom-bonists in the Mahara minstrels, Louis Wright, whom Handy recalled in his memoir as a "slim, sensitive boy." Wright, who had left the Mahara company for the rival Georgia Minstrels, was killed by a mob in Illinois in 1902 after cursing a group of white street toughs who threw snowballs at him. "He was lynched, his tongue cut out, and his body shipped to his mother in Chicago in a pine box," Handy wrote with a still-vivid memory in 1941.

Yet the worst nightmare of all occurred for Handy in late 1899, again on a tour in Texas. Handy's wife had temporarily joined him when the troupe stopped at Houston. Now advertising itself as Mahara's Minstrel Carnival, the troupe included "ten performing Shetland ponies," the trick bicycle rider Snapper Garrison, a female "slide trombone soloist" named Nettie Goff, and "Prof. W. C. Handy's grand military band of twenty-six pieces." Although she had come ostensibly for a short visit, Elizabeth Handy then decided to travel with him and the others aboard the crowded Maharaja to their engagements in the state capital of Austin and then to the east-ern Texas cotton town of Tyler. Perhaps she wanted to keep an eye on her husband while, handsome in his custom-tailored brown suit and his bright diamonds, he traveled in close quarters with female performers such as Goff. Handy later maintained that her accompa-nying him aboard the rail car was at his insistence, and that is cer-tainly one explanation of her decision. In any case, at least some nuptial privacy would be possible for the Handy couple as they com-pleted this last leg of the late 1899 season, since Handy optimistically assured his wife they could find room and board with respectable African American families in Austin and Tyler.

But what had been intended as a marital interlude became an endurance of smallpox infection and the threat of lynching as the Mahara railroad car rolled that autumn into the market town of Tyler. A trumpeter in the minstrel company whom Handy names in his memoir simply as Cricket Smith had fallen ill earlier in Austin and been diagnosed by a local physician there as suffering from a "slight skin infection." This was the talented horn player William Smith, familiarly known throughout his life as "Cricket" or sometimes "Crickett." Smith must have appeared worryingly ill, for upon the troupe's arrival in Tyler, he was excused by the Maharas from the opening day parade and told to see a physician there. Handy later recalled the stunning moment when the Tyler physician dramatically ran to the town square and interrupted the minstrel company's parade, waving his arms and shouting to the band and to the crowd, "Stop it! Stop this damn music!"

Handy in his memoir then repeated the doctor's frenzied announcement: "Ladies and gentlemen, these niggers have got the smallpox. If they don't get out of town—and that right quick—we'll lynch them all."

With what Handy called an instance of "native wit" among the minstrel troupe, the snare drummer of their marching band immediately struck up a double-quick beat to signal all the other African American performers, including Handy, at once to retreat to their railroad car. It was pulled to a siding a little distance outside the town for a temporary escape. "County officers came a short time later," Handy wrote, "to inform us that the appearance of one more case of smallpox among us would be the signal for them to burn the car and carry out the doctor's lynching threat with regard to the rest of us, men and women."

Elizabeth Handy now faced the possibility of having a burning brand tossed into the railroad car where she slept or lynching ropes stretched across a tree's branches for her and her husband as a consequence of her having decided to travel with Handy across Texas. Nor was the situation any less threatening for all the other black members of the quarantined minstrel troupe. "No provision had been made for the luckless Cricket," Handy wrote, "and no food, water, or sanitary arrangements were made for the rest of us." Fortunately for the immediate needs of his troupe, William Mahara, as a result of his prior experiences in transporting African American entertainers across the southern and western states, usually maintained a few days' supplies of water, food, and even firearms and ammunition aboard the Maharaja.

For what occurred later, there is only Handy's account, published in his memoir some four decades afterward, and he is not always strictly accurate or chronologically correct in his retellings. The local records and newspapers of Tyler for early 1900 make no mention either of a smallpox scare or of the quarantine of a colored minstrel troupe at the outskirts of town. It may be that the temporary quarantine of a group of out-of-town African Americans was not locally considered news at the time, or that any discussion of a possible threat of smallpox was withheld by the city fathers in order to avoid damaging local commerce during the important autumn cotton harvest and cotton brokering season. And perhaps out of a similar commercial fear of retarding the careers of African American performers, no mention is made in the *Freeman* of the Mahara troupe's smallpox predicament. The following events can be substantiated only by Handy's memoir, but they are narrated by him with a historical detail not usually found in *Father of the Blues*. His version of the Texas quarantine confirms that he considered his minstrelsy career at times to have been a psychological and physical "nightmare" to be endured and creatively escaped.

According to Handy, some relief came from a local white Tyler merchant who kindly supplied the troupe with better food than that which the county begrudgingly gave them during their quarantine after supplies aboard the Maharaja were exhausted. This merchant was, in Handy's memory, named John Brown. "Less militant than the hero of Harpers Ferry whose name he bore," Handy wrote,

> Mr. Brown was nevertheless a solid sender where we were concerned. After we had been quarantined a few days, he secured orders from the county to supply us with sow belly, beans, cornmeal, and molasses. In conformity with

his orders, he made out bills for this type of provision, but actually he was a sensitive man who understood we were not accustomed to this sort of food. While this may have been the diet the townsfolk had been in the habit of supplying their field hands, it was certainly not the grade of food that W. A. Mahara provided for his minstrels.

Thanks to storekeeper Brown, the African American minstrel troupe at least ate well.

Meanwhile, a total of fourteen minstrels had contracted smallpox while the company remained in quarantine, a fact urgently concealed from the white guards, since only one more case would be enough for the townspeople to carry out their threat of lynching. Handy began "to brush up on my shooting" with one of the three firearms he kept about him while on the road, and he attempted without success to teach his wife how to fire a small revolver. He also devised from wooden scraps in the rail yard what he called a "fortress of cross-ties" to protect her and himself. Clearly, desperate measures were required.

The nightmarish quarantine finally was ended by an act of theatrical trickery on Handy's part. "I got the band together," he wrote, "and played a concert behind our barricade. The townspeople, as usual, swarmed around like flies drawn to a molasses drop." As Handy and the company's other musicians continued to draw the attention of the guards, and a company acrobat joined in their diversion, the fourteen sick men by prearrangement were given a collection of money to travel out of Texas and seek medical care, and were dressed as "soubrettes" in women's clothing. The fourteen black men then individually and nonchalantly made their way out of the quarantined camp as "ladies," under the guise of relieving themselves in the nearby woods, and thus escaped. Handy was still playing his brass cornet for the diversion of the white crowd, and "out of the corner of my eye watched the would-be females make their way down the tracks." Handy does not mention whether among the tunes he played to divert the crowd was the national favorite, "All Coons Look Alike to Me."

The Mahara troupe shortly thereafter was allowed to safely leave

Texas. But some of the performers, Handy later recalled in his memoir, were so shaken by this incident they shortly thereafter permanently left minstrelsy. "Perhaps they found it hard to erase from their minds the nightmare of those minstrel days," he wrote. Handy, however, chose to remain a minstrel. Elizabeth Handy, having survived on the road during their Texas quarantine, was understandably upset when her husband later proposed that they continue to travel with the troupe throughout the early months of 1900; the Mahara company was booked for the late winter for appearances in Havana, Cuba. It was not usual for colored minstrels to overwinter in Cuba while performing there. The presence of McCabe & Young's Colored Operative Minstrels on January 16, 1892, for example, was reported by the New York show business newspaper the *Clipper* under the headline "Notes from McCabe's Minstrels—at Cuba." "The boys are highly amused at the odd ways that business is done in Cuba," it said.

Handy's wife was even more opposed to this trip when she learned that the Mahara brothers expected the minstrels to pay their own steamer fares and hotel expenses in Havana. Handy, however, was persuasive, or perhaps his spouse again did not wish to have her husband travel unaccompanied. In any case, she joined him as the troupe traveled in late January or early February 1900 from the Gulf of Mexico port of Tampa to Key West, Florida, and departed from there to Havana.

As Elizabeth and William Handy cruised into Havana harbor, they saw a ruined portion of the sunken U.S.S. *Maine* protruding above the water, a visible reminder of the Spanish-American War that had begun with the explosion of this battleship less than two years before. However, Elizabeth soon lost her misgivings about the dangers of foreign travel, at least in her husband's later account of their sojourn, and the couple found Cuba to be pleasant and its residents not as biased against persons of color, in their experience, as the majority of those in the United States. Listening to performances by Cuban musicians, Handy became fascinated by what he called the "Tangana rhythm," which he first heard on this trip. The haunting Latin rhythm stayed in his mind, and more than fourteen years later this remembered tango would delight listeners as one of the most memorable passages in his future masterpiece, the "St. Louis Blues."

The Cuban tour in the winter of 1900–01 was significant for Handy's future in another way. During this visit, Elizabeth Handy informed her husband that she was pregnant with their first child. Their daughter would be born in June of that year after the couple returned to Alabama and would be named Lucile. The couple's return to Florence later in 1900 likely was due in part to his wife's expressed desire for a more respectable and settled—and less dangerous—career for her husband after their child was born. Handy, however, was ever footloose. Although Elizabeth Handy would live at the home of one of Handy's relatives in Florence and give birth there, he would complete the spring and summer tours of 1900 frequently away from his wife while continuing to travel with the Mahara troupe.

When he temporarily retired from the road and returned to Florence to live with his wife and child from late 1900 to 1903, he would bring with him a new musical enthusiasm he had learned in minstrelsy that he again would soon want to take on tour. In the minstrel show's final contribution to American culture since the Jim Crow dance of Daddy Rice, the stage coon songs of the 1890s had introduced a new style of musical composition to national listeners. Within his published score of "All Coons Look Alike to Me," Ernest Hogan in 1896 had included an intriguingly syncopated passage that many in the following years found to be musically irresistible. "In the late 1890s, ragtime sung and performed by black musicians reached the mainstream popular stage," in the consensus of recent scholars, "but the real 'craze' commenced in 1897 with the inception of the 'ragtime coon song.'" Acknowledging that a "cunning amalgam of appreciation and mockery was a cornerstone of minstrelsy," the disturbing ambiguity of this popular entertainment "was perpetuated in ragtime coon songs." Handy was no exception in his appreciation for syncopated, or ragged, scores, despite their frequently distasteful lyrics. In his final seasons as a colored minstrel, he became fascinated by what he called this "odd new vogue" of ragtime.

CHAPTER FOUR

———

Aunt Hagar's Ragtime Son Comes Home to Alabama, 1900–1903

Old Deacon Splivins, his flock was givin' the way of livin' right,
Said he, no winging,
No ragtime singing here tonight.
Up jumped Aunt Hagar and shouted with all her might,
Why all this razzing about the jazzing?
My boys have just come home . . .
Hear Aunt Hagar's children harmonizing,
Hear that sweet melody.

—W. C. Handy, lyricist and
composer, "Aunt Hagar's
Children Blues," 1922

The Mahara Company toured the towns of northern Alabama and the Tennessee Valley shortly after its return from Cuba in early 1900. Handy in his memoir of this year includes an account of how his minister father, then living in Huntsville, Alabama, with his recently married second wife, made the momentous decision to attend the Mahara performance there on March 7, 1900, to see his son on the stage. W. C. Handy felt some personal trepidations about taking up his cornet before the show, knowing his father was in the audience; but the minstrelsy entertainment was otherwise avidly anticipated by many other Huntsville residents, black and white. The Mahara brothers had done their usual good job of promoting the show and befriending journalists.

"There will be a hot time in the old town tonight," the town's *Weekly Mercury* newspaper that afternoon had promised, enthusiastically praising the appearance at the Huntsville opera house that evening of the Mahara brothers and "their big colored minstrel show." The company by this time included, besides the unmentioned Handy, "Prof. Genther's trained troupe of dogs and ponies, without doubt the best aggregation of educated animals ever seen in this city"; Leroy Bland, the male "soubrette"; and also the celebrated Nettie Goff, "the only colored lady in the world playing the slide trombone." The "hot time" to which the *Weekly Gazette* referred was an allusion to the 1896 ragtime song by a black St. Louis saloon keeper, "A Hot Time in the Old Town Tonight," and the Mahara troupe, including their orchestra and its leader, gladly brought this new music to the Alabama audience. Handy certainly felt relief that at least his father had seen his musical son applauded at the performance's end. According to Handy, there followed backstage after the show an emotional reconciliation between the Reverend Charles B. Handy and his grown child, with the elder Handy telling him: "Sonny, I haven't been in a show [theater] since I professed religion. I enjoyed it. I am very proud of you and forgive you for becoming a musician."

This reunion may have occurred just as Handy sincerely described it; but the story may be an instance of Handy as an inveterate showman who was also given to an equally sincere embellishment. His version of the paternal blessing, published in his memoir in 1941, bears more than just a passing resemblance to that perennial fable of show business enacted in Handy's lifetime in the popular motion picture *The Jazz Singer* (1927). Therein the character of Jackie Rabinowitz, a blackface minstrelsy performer who is played by the white Al Jolson, reunites with his parents while on tour. His performance is so brilliant he is movingly forgiven and blessed by his dying, pious father.

Just before the Mahara moved out of nearby Florence to perform at other engagements, Handy in a late-night incident drew a pistol on a fellow minstrel. It apparently was the settling of an old grudge. Handy accused the man of having earlier insulted him and his violinist friend Jim Turner, and the man advanced on Handy as if to strike him. Handy scared the fellow away by firing several shots— harmlessly—into the air. Knowledge of this incident in Handy's life may have contributed to his subsequent reputation with Beale Avenue's scofflaw gamblers as a bandleader in Memphis not to be trifled with. Unmentioned by Handy in his memoir's account was the likelihood that the shooting affair, if they learned of it, would have been confirmation to his in-laws of the morally degrading consequences of their son-in-law's practicing "this or that monkey business" in colored minstrelsy.

After completing this tour of early 1900, Handy returned to his wife in Florence. Perhaps his decision was a result of her insistence that she and her husband lead a more settled life preceding the birth of their first child. If so, it is noteworthy that he chose to live among his relatives rather than near Elizabeth Price Handy's parents. They may still have been expressing to him their disapproval of his earlier vocation. Handy moved with his wife into a house belonging to his aunt, Mattie Jordan. Lucile Handy was born there on June 29, 1900.

The two-year residence in Alabama was the longest Handy lived and worked in one state since leaving for the world's fair in 1892. He came to know his father's second wife and children in Huntsville (throughout his career Handy was remarkably friendly and cordial to his step-siblings), and he reacquainted himself with his younger brother, Charles, who was then eleven. In his hometown much was unchanged since his last visit, for his mother's funeral: the courthouse square, with a newly erected Confederate monument; the earnest Professor Y. A. Wallace; and the white politicians in the lobby of the Exchange Hotel. Handy by his own account found Florence "just a trifle dull" after his national tours as an exuberant and flashy minstrel playing ragtime.

This judgment reflected more than just the cosmopolitanism of the hometown traveler who had seen Chicago and Los Angeles, or his ambition. He was once again living in a state where, as his late mother had consoled him, African Americans were "Aunt Hagar's children," the inheritors of the ruling majority's distrust and rejection, a race prudently advised to accommodate themselves to their lower station in life. In fact, Florence had become more racially restrictive than it had been during his childhood. Alabama was now under the control of a new generation of white politicians like those whose racist rhetoric had so shocked Handy as an adolescent when he heard it proclaimed on the courthouse square. The state was now in the process of codifying into its local and state statutes the Jim Crow social proscriptions that were earlier only informally enforced. Black and white children were legally forbidden even to play together. African American adult males by 1903 were to be excluded by law from voting in the primaries of the state's dominant Democratic Party, and, together with a rigorous enforcement of the poll tax for would-be voters of color, these laws effectively disenfranchised even the "black and tans" of the state's diminishing Republican Party, which included Handy, his father, and Professor Wallace in nearby Huntsville.

For the next two years, 1900 to 1902, Handy tried mightily to accommodate himself to these changed circumstances and to his mother's biblical homily. But the imagery of himself as a child of Aunt Hagar, preordained by the color of his skin to aspire no higher than to be an educator or a minister for his people, conflicted with his musical creativity. Twenty years later, in 1922, he celebrated creativity's victory in one of his best blues songs, "Aunt Hagar's Children Blues" (also titled "Aunt Hagar's Blues") in which the jubilant, blues-and-ragtime-loving grown child returns home and musically "liberates" a black congregation from the dreariness of socially approved music and behavior. His mother's consoling and melancholy words, and his own joyful refashioning of them, would evolve slowly from these years of Handy's adult return to Alabama. In Florence he was inescapably finding his calling. Shortly after resettling with his family there, Handy resumed his collaborations with Turner, who also had stepped off the Maharas' train to stay and play his fiddle in Florence for a while. Handy organized a small orchestra and began to play engagements with Turner in the northern Alabama area. Together these two former minstrels led the other musicians in playing at local dances the increasingly popular new music heard on the minstrelsy stage. They were not yet musically "jazzing" or "razzing" their songs, but they were certainly "ragging" them.

Ragtime in 1900–02 "was terrific," Handy later recalled. His earlier career as a minstrel in fact had coincided neatly with the advent of ragtime in minstrelsy and its subsequent national popularity. By

1895, the celebrated cakewalks had begun to be scored in ragtime melodies such as "Rastus on Parade," and Ernest Hogan's ragtime song of 1896, "All Coons Look Alike to Me," was widely performed on and off the theatrical stage. Whether the lyrics of these coon songs were found to be offensive or not, American composers such as Handy were intrigued by this popular music's unique offbeat rhythms, known as "ragging" or syncopation. The felicitous, foot-tapping appeal of syncopation can be appreciated by tapping a pencil on a desk in a regular, two-four beat of *one*-two, *one*-two. Now imagine a second pencil tapping the desk in accompaniment on the off beats, for a dual rhythm of one-*two,* one-*two.* The rhythm now retains the forward movement of a fast-time march but with the added effect of spontaneity. In ragtime, this syncopated beat can be performed on the piano by playing the bass accents with the left hand while accenting the offbeat notes with the right, or by adding a second instrument, such as the banjo or Handy's horn.

Obviously there has been syncopation since there has been music, and syncopated passages had been played or composed in European folk and classical music before the nineteenth and early twentieth centuries. Martial marches are easily syncopated, and some musicians consider "I Wish I Was in Dixie Land," composed by the white minstrel Daniel Emmett in 1859 and later adopted as a battle song by the Confederacy, as an early rag. But practically from the arrival of African American slaves in this country, syncopation had been noticed by white auditors as uniquely favored by black performers. The ragtime beat, in fact, may have originated in this country with the early African American recreation of "patting Juba," a music played on the body by regularly tapping one foot and simultaneously clapping and lightly slapping the thighs in a counterbeat. In Georgia the antebellum poet and musician Sidney Lanier recalled with admiration that

> I have heard a Southern plantation "hand" in "patting Juba" for a comrade to dance by, venture upon quite complex successions of rhythm, not hesitating to syncopate, to change the rhythmic accent for a moment, or to indulge in other highly-specialized variations of the current rhythmus.

Almost any score can be ragged. But syncopated songs, particularly when played on the native African instrument the banjo, or, later, the piano, still were traditionally identified by some national listeners as a distinctively African American musical novelty. In 1900, the ragtime style of piano playing was occasionally known as "jig piano." Racially identified, the heavily syncopated sixteen-bar measures of ragtime, even when played without patronizing lyrics, were often composed and marketed as just a new style of coon song, such as in the popular rags "Happy Little Nigs" (1898), "Whistling Rufus" (1899), and "Ragtime Rastus" (1900).

By the time of his arrival in Alabama, Handy and other composers and performers of color, such as Scott Joplin and Artie Matthews, were looking beyond what Joplin called the "bad words" of ragged coon songs to a more complex and less racist music. Joplin in particular was experimenting with ragtime pieces in a complex stanzaic architecture of three or four passages without lyrics, in which the syncopated line of one stanza introduces the first line of the next. The effect is an elegant playfulness, as in his often-revived song "The Entertainer" (1902). Joplin's earlier "Maple Leaf Rag" (1899), also a non–coon song, became very popular among whites as a danceable two-step and was a particular favorite of Handy's. Even that paterfamilias of American music, Sousa, was by 1900 including ragtime marches by a classically trained white band member in the group's performances.

Handy's orchestra played nonsyncopated waltzes, marches, and light classical music as well as ragtime. When the African American president of the State Agricultural and Mechanical College for Negroes, William Hooper Councill, heard Handy play a concert in the summer of 1900, he invited him to join the college's faculty in nearby Normal. Handy accepted. The college's budget did not allow for a professor of music, so he was hired for duties commencing in September 1900 at the rank of an instructor in English, with the understanding that he would teach the college students in band, orchestra, and singing classes. In addition, he was expected to be a proctor at nightly study sessions, to assist in Tuesday night prayer services, to teach lessons in the college Sunday school, to conduct or perform with the college choir, and to complete any other duties as specified by the college president, among which were for Handy to count the cows and keep an inventory of all other livestock in the college's barns. His salary was to be forty dollars, one-fifth of what he had earned per month playing for the Maharas. Handy was trying very hard to be the Aunt Hagar's son of his mother's advice—and not the frolicking and carefree show-business child of his imagination.

W. H. Councill was a formidable mentor and employer. Twenty-five years older than Handy, Councill was a bespectacled but power-fully built man who had spent his boyhood not attending school as a minister's son but, rather, surviving in the slave pens of Richmond, Virginia. Brought into Alabama along with his sickly mother by slave traders in 1857, Councill until his mother's death in bondage had "carried her row," that is, he had done his mother's work in the fields as well as his own, in order to prevent her from being physi-cally punished or sold to another owner. After the Civil War and the death of his mother, Councill had managed to educate himself at a school for blacks in northern Alabama established by Quakers in 1865, and by the end of the state's Reconstruction in 1872 he had emerged as a leading educator and political leader of the Democra-tic Party among northern Alabama's few enfranchised black citi-zens. Unlike the father and grandfather of W. C. Handy, and unlike Handy himself, all of whom were stalwart members of the state Republican Party of immediate post–Civil War Alabama, Councill had accommodated himself to his southern state's resurgent white Democrats. The state legislature established his small college in tacit exchange for northern Alabama's few Democratic black votes before the eventual disenfranchisement of people of color by the state government.

At the time he hired Handy, Councill was determined that the lit-tle land-grant college at Normal become "an island of formal edu-cation," in his words, in a sea of black illiteracy and uplift what he regarded as the rude folk music of untutored local African Ameri-cans. Six years earlier, in the summer of 1894, he had led a male quartet and two female elocutionists selected from among his col-lege's best students on what he styled a Tour of Conquest and

Melody to twenty-seven northern Alabama and Tennessee towns and cities. The performances likely were of hymns and classical numbers. After each free performance, Councill had asked for a show of hands from those in the predominantly black audience who were willing to pledge that they would educate their children and that they themselves would attend at least some school in the coming year. It was while traveling through the South on such an educational and promotional trip that Councill, after paying his fare, was evicted from a whites-only car on the Alabama Great Southern Railway Line. "He was handled roughly, but fought like an enraged lion, until overcome by the train crew," a professor at the college later recalled.

Such a man as Councill would have little sympathy for the musical routines of colored minstrelsy. Handy lasted less than two full academic years in Normal, leaving the college permanently in late 1902 to rejoin Mahara's Minstrels after he had affronted Councill by conducting a concert of ragtime music at a college assembly. In his memoir, Handy passes over this incident as having been due to an almost-comical disagreement over the musical merits, in his words, of "an odd new vogue called 'ragtime.'" But the differences between this ambitious instructor of music and the battle-hardened college president, both seeking respectability in a white world, were a continuing part of the debate over proper ambitions for African Americans, as illustrated by the public disagreements between Booker T. Washington and Du Bois. The new music of ragtime, so enjoyable to Handy and so repellent to Councill, was anything but a superficial and odd vogue of little importance to these two men.

Long before Handy's first composition of the blues, both popular and classical white composers who had listened to black-composed syncopation were, like Joplin, Handy, and Matthews, fascinated by ragtime's potential for more than coon songs. One classical composer, Charles Ives, who recalled as a youth in the early 1890s having gone to Poli's Theater in New Haven, Connecticut, and hearing "blackfaced comedians ragging their songs," incorporated this new music into his suite "Ragtime Dances" (1902–03). Tin Pan Alley composers, who were then predominantly German or Jewish, also adopted ragtime syncopation for popular noncoon songs, in part because of the ease with which earlier traditional-time tunes could be ragged. During the two years when Handy was forgoing minstrelsy and attempting to become an academic, at least forty-three new ragtime songs were published nationally. This was an average of just under two new ragtime songs published every month. Handy was certainly justified in his enthusiasm for ragtime, both for his own future compositions and as a crossover success with white audiences. He later adopted ragtime stanzaic structure into the score of his first nationally popular blues tune, the "Memphis Blues," and by the next decade ragtime ultimately reached the irreproachable success of commercial acceptance by urban and sophisticated white audiences: inclusion into the Broadway revue and musical. In 1918 the first professional musical collaboration between George and Ira Gershwin, for the revue *Ladies First*, included a showstopping composition that the Gershwin brothers entitled "The Real American Folk Song (Is a Rag)." That same decade the then-rising music critic Hiram Moderwell declared that "the one distinctive element which America has contributed to music is the so-called 'ragtime.' Ragtime therefore should be the basis, or at least one of the chief ingredients of our national music," which Moderwell presumes was the fulfillment of the "Dvořák Manifesto."

Councill in 1900 was unconvinced, and he was no ragtime man. The president's understanding of music and his educational philosophy were in the utilitarian tradition of his fellow Alabama educator Booker T. Washington. In addition to courses in electrical engineering and nursing, Councill's underfunded northern Alabama college, like Washington's Tuskegee Institute, offered its young men and women practical courses in shoemaking, mattress making, and cooking. He opposed the notion of a distinctive and independent African American musical aesthetic and an African American professional class composed of other than ministers and educators, as urged by Du Bois. Public performances of music by African Americans were to be restricted, in his opinion, to matters of racial uplift, as in the college's performance of spirituals, or of classical music, in order to demonstrate a playing ability and correctness of taste equal to that of whites, as in his hard-fought Tour of Conquest and Melody.

Indeed, Councill may have hired Handy in hopes of reforming him. At a college chapel meeting called by the president, the faculty discussed a recently published article condemning ragtime. Councill, who in Handy's later description was "a stickler for the classics" in regard to music, had delivered for good measure a lecture to his employees on the evils of ragtime, which Handy recalled as "sarcastic and derisive in the extreme." Following the lead of Councill, the faculty declared its opposition to ragtime, with one noticeable exception. Handy had risen and spoken in defense of the new music; the president then had directed a look at Handy that the latter described as appearing "disappointed and sad."

But if Councill had hopes of reforming this musical child of Aunt Hagar with a look of disapproval, he had misjudged his man. At a subsequent chapel assembly, Handy arranged for the college orchestra to play the musical number "My Ragtime Baby," composed by an African American in Detroit. The role of the musical trickster being irresistible to Handy, he had introduced the piece as a classical composition, supposedly entitled "Greetings to Toussaint L'Ouverture," revealing it as ragtime only after Councill enthusiastically had expressed to the audience his pleasure at having heard it played. The college president even had been observed tapping his foot in accompaniment to the song's syncopation.

Handy was rebuked for this chapel-hall trickery when it was revealed, and he exacerbated his situation by reminding the college administrators that he "was a two-hundred-dollar-a-month man in a forty-dollar job." His employer was not pleased. In defense of Councill's conservative musical tastes, one should note that ragtime in the first decade of the twentieth century was not fully separated from the syncopated coon song. Despite ragtime's increasing adoption by Tin Pan Alley and classicist composers for more genteel compositions, Scott Joplin as late as 1913 uncomfortably noted that

> I have often sat in theaters and listened to beautiful ragtime melodies set to almost vulgar words as a song, and I have wondered why some composers will continue to make the public hate ragtime melodies because the melodies are set to such bad words.

The ragtime style of performance in 1902 also retained its earlier association with the bad company of minstrelsy or vaudeville, or, worse, the saloon or the brothel. Thomas Turpin, the popularizer of "A Hot Time in the Old Town Tonight," played ragtime piano in both. To many upward-striving educators of color, ragtime in the early 1900s would have been as demeaning as the sight of Daddy Rice in blackface, much like the sound of some rap music is to presidents of historically black colleges today. Among the most frequently played ragtime songs for white audiences in 1902 was not the "Maple Leaf Rag" but the "Bully of the Town," with its following representative lyrics:

> *Some coon across my smeller swiped a watermelon rin'*
> *I drawed my steel that gentleman for to fin'*
> *. . . looking for that bully and he must be found.*

Handy knew the latter ragtime song very well, and he envied its commercial success, despite its vulgarity. He remembered having heard the original "Bully of the Town" as a folk tune popular among black stevedores along the Mississippi River levees of St. Louis when he vagabonded there in 1893. This folk tune's later transformation into a ragtime success had been accomplished by May Irwin, a white female vaudeville singer of Junoesque proportions who saw its possibilities as a crossover novelty song intended for white audiences, particularly when comically sung by a white woman of a certain physical presence looking to do battle with the town's African American male bully. This ragtime coon song anticipated Handy's own subsequent attempts to achieve a crossover success by rearranging syncopated black folk blues for a white audience, despite the folk songs' disreputable origin and sometimes salacious lyrics.

"I had watched the joy-spreaders rarin' to go," Handy subsequently wrote of May Irwin's version of the "Bully of the Town." "I wanted such success." This was a disturbing contradiction between a gifted black individual's ambition for success and the uplifting of his race that Councill was unwilling to accept. It was precisely to displace such low folk music or theatrical clowning among black people that Councill had traveled on his musical tours in northern Alabama and Tennessee—the same route that was so recently taken by the minstrels in the Mahara troupe—where Councill for his efforts had been beaten and removed from a Southern railway car.

After the concert incident, the ragtime-loving Handy was asked by Councill's college administration before the end of his second year of employment to find another position in which he could presumably obtain what he considered his true worth. Handy reacted by placing a notice in the Indianapolis *Freeman,* no later than the autumn of 1902, advertising his availability as a musician. Among the responses was an envelope stamped with a Chicago postmark and colorfully printed with an illustration of a watermelon slice with what appeared to be oversized black seeds. When Handy looked closer, however, he saw that the supposed black watermelon seeds on the envelopes were in fact miniature portraits of grinning African American performers in the Mahara minstrel troupe. Seemingly inescapably, the white ghost of his past stage history of colored minstrelsy was returning:

> *I jumps jis' so*
> *And ev'y time I turn about,*
> *I jump Jim Crow.*

Inside was a letter from F. A. "Frank" Mahara, the third of the Chicago show business brothers, inviting Handy to rejoin the family's minstrelsy company for the remainder of the touring season of 1902 and to continue touring into 1903. Handy signed on for his fifth tour. By the Christmas season of that year, the roster of the Mahara company touring the Midwest listed "W. C. Handy and his band and orchestra." Elizabeth Handy stayed in Florence, raising their daughter Lucile and also a second daughter who recently had been born, Katharine. This minstrel tour in 1902–03 was the last for Handy, and there were the familiar indignities and dangers during his final run aboard the Maharaja. Among his pleasures, Handy by this time was one of the best paid members of the troupe, as he was leading both the company's marching band and its seated orchestra, apparently having replaced William Malone in this latter position. Some time earlier, because of his increased minstrelsy earnings, Handy had been able to buy himself a new gold-plated C. G. Conn cornet. The manufacturer of that instrument was then widely regarded as the best in the U.S. market.

Additionally, Handy was able to resume his associations, after the intellectual provinciality of Normal, Alabama, with what he liked to call the "aspiring generation of dusky singers and musicians." Since his first year in minstrelsy, he particularly had sought out the skills of the former U.S. Army African American military band members who subsequently had joined the Maharas' company. These included his acquaintance George A. Swan, who had played cornet with the U.S. Colored Ninth Cavalry Band. While on this final minstrelsy tour, Swan arranged for Handy to play with his former company's black band at Fort Robinson, Nebraska. Through association with such former military performers, Handy gained a further knowledge of the quick-step marches such as Sousa's, which were then very popular with American civilian audiences.

This exposure to martial music apparently continued for a year or so to compete with Handy's interests in adapting ragtime or black folk music, such as "Bully of the Town," as a means of achieving national popularity. Handy began to attempt composing light marches and martial-like, nonsyncopated overtures in 1902 and 1903, and by his last season of minstrelsy he was announcing to his fellow black musicians his ambitions to became prominently known as an African American "March King." Indeed, he would carry these ambitions with him when he left colored minstrelsy for good.

Handy finally "closed with Mahara's," in the minstrelsy vernacular, in midseason on July 9, 1903. Before his departure, however, he made a triumphant return and final performance in February of that year with the Mahara troupe back to his hometown and his wife and children in Florence. The response of the local audience at the town's "opera house" was ebullient, even allowing for hometown boosterism. "As a violin and cornet virtuoso, Prof. Handy has few equals, and as a band master has been called the colored Sousa," one of the two white-owned newspapers in town, the Florence *Times,* praised. The paper further noted that "only the inducement of a fat salary had persuaded him" to leave black academia. The competing Florence *Herald* was even more praiseful in its review of the minstrelsy show, approving the "two hearty encores" that Handy had performed at the audience's demand following his cornet solos. Even the rear of the opera house "was crowded," the newspaper further described, with happy auditors expressing their delight at the musical show with "roars" of enthusiasm. Aunt Hagar's son finally had come home to public approval, as one of the "joy-spreaders rarin' to go." And after this hometown approval, Handy was indeed ready to go. Shortly thereafter he would permanently leave Alabama with his family to spread his joyful music in other states, finding musical work other than as a minstrel and returning to Florence only occasionally for family visits.

Handy had been lucky both in the timing of his joining minstrelsy in 1896 and in his leaving it seven years later in 1903. Ragtime had been the final innovation of the minstrel show, and despite the music's rising popularity with classical and popular composers, outdated Stephen Foster–inspired numbers such as James Bland's number "Oh! Dem Golden Slippers" (1879) remained the musical bread and butter of the minstrel companies. Thus even before the expansion of cinema and vaudeville theaters nationwide, blackfaced and colored minstrelsy in the United States had become a nostalgia act. Had he continued with minstrelsy past the 1903 touring season, W. C. Handy might have wound up as just another once-celebrated but now obscure minstrel performer of color, such as the dialect comedian Ike "Old Stretch" Simond—or at best a forgotten Tin Pan Alley composer of dated sentimental ballads, such as the once well-known Paul Dresser, or an unjustly forgotten ragtime man and arranger such as Arthur Matthews. The minstrelsy world had given to Handy by 1903 all it could as inspiration to a future blues composer. Handy's five seasons with the Mahara company had provided him with a knowledge of national music that probably exceeded that of any other American, black or white, at that time. Before him as he performed on the minstrel stage had passed, as if in a pageant for Handy's personal education, practically all the popular music listened to and enjoyed by all the people of the United States in the late nineteenth and early twentieth centuries: the sentimental and narrative ballads in the Stephen Foster tradition, African American hymnody, martial marches for brass instruments, banjo and fiddle improvisations, politically satiric airs, European light classical selections, "Habañera" rhythms, and ragtime.

William Christopher Handy had heard it all, and he could play most of it. All that was lacking to complete his musical education in order to make him a great *"American* composer"—in his own later emphatic words, and in fulfillment of Dvŏrák's prophecy—was his exposure to the African American folk blues melodies then being played and sung in the American South. This final musical education would come when, after his last season with minstrelsy, Handy would take a job as a band director in 1903 in the western Mississippi market town of Clarksdale. There, Aunt Hagar's musical child would fully emerge. Near the rural intersection of railroad lines that the local blacks called "where the Southern cross' the Yellow Dog," Handy would hear the folk songs he later would blend with ragtime and his own distinct notation to make them among the first of America's published blues music. Ahead for this future composer was the Mississippi Delta and the origin of his blues.

———

CHAPTER FIVE

Where the Southern Crosses the Yellow Dog

HANDY AND THE MISSISSIPPI DELTA, 1903–1905

> *Clarksdale's in the South,*
> *And lays heavy on my mind.*
>
> —"Clarksdale Moan," blues song
> composed by Eddie James
> House Jr., "Son House"
> (1902–1988), born in the Yellow
> Dog district, two miles from
> Clarksdale, Mississippi

When the Mahara troupe stopped in Michigan in 1903, Handy had been tempted by a job offer there to become band director for a local organization of white musicians. But his attention had already been caught by an offer to direct a band organized by the Knights of Pythias, an African American fraternal society, in Clarksdale, Mississippi. Handy chose Mississippi. It was a decision pregnant with meaning for the future of American popular music, and Handy thoughtfully revisited his choice of musical vocation four decades later in his memoir.

"The Michigan thing was miles ahead," he wrote, "more money, more prestige, better opportunities for the future, better everything I thought. Yet, for no good reason I could express, I turned my face southward and down the road that led inevitably to the blues." He may have chosen the Mississippi job to remain reasonably close to his father in Huntsville, or from a desire to associate with the mercantile and professional class usually attracted to Pythias membership. His new employer, fully named the Knights of Pythias, North America, South America, Europe, Asia, and Africa, was a rapidly growing international fraternal society founded by a black Mississippian in 1880 for men of color. It eventually enrolled roughly 300,000 members, then about 6 percent of all African American males in the United States. Colloquially, the society was known as the Colored Knights of Pythias. This fraternal society also marched and performed in the brass bands organized by its lodges.

It is also possible that Handy as a minstrel may have established friendships in Clarksdale during his performances there with the Mahara company prior to his later move. But for whatever unrecorded reason, by the end of 1903, Handy had moved with his wife and two daughters to Clarksdale, one of the comparatively larger towns in the area known as the Delta. Handy was living permanently in the South for the first time since his childhood, now as a performing musician and a married man. And, it must be understood, he was now living as a black man not in the comparatively Progressive South as experienced in Florence, Alabama, with its small farms, distrust of a plantation oligarchy, and some history of Republican sentiment, but instead in the much "deeper" South of the Mississippi Delta.

Shaped like the giant leaf of a cottonwood tree and pointed downward with the Mississippi River as its central vein, the Delta is an area of approximately 8,700 square miles that in 1903 was almost an inland island cut off from the rest of the state by the great river to the west and the curling Yazoo River to the east and south. This idea of insularity, particularly in Handy's day, was apt: roads from towns like Clarksdale to places within and outside the Delta were poor even by Mississippi standards (the first gravel road was not laid down in any of the fourteen Delta counties until 1915), and hundreds of square miles of the lowland Delta were still forested with hardwood timber uncut since the Mississippi Territory had been organized in 1798 during the first presidential administration of John Adams. William Faulkner, who set some of his greatest fiction, such as "The

Bear," in this Mississippi wilderness at the turn of the twentieth century, recalled it as being both "rich and foul," an

> impenetrable jungle of water-standing cane and cypress,
> gum and holly and oak and ash . . . along the rivers Talla-
> hatchie and Sunflower which joined and became the
> Yazoo, the River of Death to the Choctaws—the thick,
> slow black unsunned streams almost without current,
> which once each year ceased to flow at all and then
> reversed, spreading, drowning the rich land and subsiding
> again, leaving it still richer.

This description of the Delta's waters as both drowning and
enriching the land—and its inhabitants—is accurate. Nearly every
spring the Mississippi and its tributaries overran their banks and
flooded this inland island; but when the floodwater receded, it also
left behind in its silt the best topsoil from the more than 1.25 million
square miles of the Mississippi River's drainage basin in the upper
United States and Canada. Thus, almost as a providential gift of
grace, some of the most desired soil on earth had been deposited
onto this remote quadrant of the state of Mississippi. The deposits
had accumulated over thousands of years. When commercial
planters first began substantially clearing the Delta lands in the last
quarter of the nineteenth century, they were astonished to find that
in drilling for their plantation wells, the drill bits frequently went
down through soft alluvial soil for seventy feet or more before
reaching bedrock. And where that soil was cleared of its green and
low-hanging canopy, it was wonderfully fertile for growing cotton
or sugarcane.

By the second decade of the twentieth century, more than four
million acres of forest had been cleared in the Delta by lumber and
railroad companies, and the resulting cultivated land consistently
produced the highest cotton-bale-per-acre yield in the world. This
area was thus in the middle of an extraordinary economic boom
when Handy arrived with his family in 1903. With the characteristic
overoptimism of the irrepressible showman, Handy described to
others his new place of residence as a "Green Eden." It did appear

so. The problem of the Delta's miserable publicly financed roads was being solved by the steel rails of newly financed private railroad lines, chief among them the Yazoo & Mississippi Valley Railroad (Y&MV), which began laying track in 1882 northward from Yazoo City into the Delta. This railroad and others serviced many of the vast post–Civil War plantations newly established in the Delta by white entrepreneurs, such as the Dockery Farm, a 10,000-acre cotton plantation and sawmill established in 1895; there the Y&MV line eventually constructed a station building and employed a full-time ticket agent. Dockery's itself employed 2,000 black workers. Handy thus was the rare exception in 1903 among the 400,000 African Americans then living in the Delta counties in that he was a skilled performer who lived in a town, was paid in cash, and was not an agricultural worker living as a tenant on a plantation. However Edenic the Delta land appeared to Handy when he arrived, this black majority was fated to live in a state of near-bondage to white landlords, owing to the system of sharecropping and the "perpetual debt" to plantation commissary stores for such necessary items as tools and cotton seeds.

"This system," Du Bois wrote in 1907, "is not a system of free labor; it is simply a form of peonage. The black peon is held down by perpetual debt or petty criminal judgments; his rent rises with the price of cotton, his chances to buy land are either nonexistent or confined to infertile regions. Judge and jury are in honor bound to hold him down; if by accident or miracle he escapes and becomes a land-holder, his property, civil and political status are still at the mercy of the worst of the white voters, and his very life at the whim of the mob."

Du Bois's lethal "whim of the mob" was, in unvarnished terms, the threat of lynching to any African American at the turn of the twentieth century in the South—including Handy—who perchance fell afoul of the county sheriff or an enraged white landlord, or who objected too openly to his social or economic station in life. Eighty-seven people of color were lynched in the United States in 1903, the year Handy moved to Mississippi. (Louis Wright, the young man whom Handy had known in the Maharas' Minstrels, had been lynched and had his tongue cut out by a mob in Missouri the year earlier.) Among those eighty-seven were fifteen African Americans lynched in Handy's new state of residence. Of those, four were killed by white mobs in the isolated Delta counties. That same murderous year, James Kimble Vardaman was elected by the white citizens of Mississippi as the state's new governor. Vardaman, a white-suited, Stetson-hat-wearing young veteran of the Spanish-American War who happily had adopted the political nickname "the White Chief," publicly called for lynching as a means of maintaining social order. Thus, even for an ambitious, educated black man such as W. C. Handy, there was always present—like the coiling Yazoo River, the Choctaws' "River of Death," deceptively passive and unmoving at the foot of the Delta—the potential for lethal violence in this supposed Eden.

Clarksdale was a mercantile center for the surrounding area of Coahoma County and was located on the banks of the tannin-stained Sunflower River—one of Faulkner's slow, black, verdant-shaded streams. The town had reported a population of 1,773 black and white residents in the census of 1900. With the advantages of both a railway station and the rare crossing of two major roads, Clarksdale's commerce was rooted in its yearly supplying of the nearby plantations and farming communities such as Tutwiler, Alligator, Hushpuckena, and Indianola with cotton seeds, tools, fertilizer, and black laborers. Clarksdale's prosperity in the Delta's high-cotton years was directly responsible for its comparative progressivism (a black man was employed as a teller at a local bank, for example) and for its white citizens' patronage of a brass band from the African American lodge of the Knights of Pythias. Although the fraternal society's members themselves had provided for hiring Handy as band master, the white merchants had assumed the expenses of outfitting the band with fine uniforms, at a cost of ten dollars per fitting. Their motives were not purely philharmonic; the Pythias band was expected to give free weekly concerts on the town's main street, presumably on Saturdays, as an inducement for farmers to come to town and trade with Clarksdale merchants. The musicians were also available for entertainment at socials given by the local white lodge of the Masons and at political rallies for the state's all-white Democratic Party.

"The music played was nearly all marches and waltzes," recalled S. L. "Stack" Mangham, an African American who was the clarinetist for Handy's band in 1903. Mangham also specifically remembered at least one ragtime song, Scott Joplin's "Maple Leaf Rag," as a crowd-pleasing number played by the band during his years. He further recalled that when Handy first arrived in Clarksdale "his ambition was to write marches. He brought a march with him that he had written that was published as 'Hail to the Spirit of Freedom.' He said then that he was going to be the March King—another John Philip Sousa." Handy's experience with the army bands on his last minstrel tour was apparently still paramount in his mind. "I didn't pay much attention to the blues and that music until Handy came here," the clarinetist recalled. "He didn't either at first," he added.

Chance and locale, however, were determining that Handy become a blues king rather than the March King when he moved to Clarksdale. Organizing a commercial ten-piece orchestra from among the twenty members of the fraternal band to entertain at dances for white couples, Handy traveled extensively from Clarksdale in order to book engagements. (A traveling dance orchestra composed exclusively of black musicians would not have been an exceptional sight on a weekend or holiday in the Delta. African Americans, either as slaves or servants, traditionally had been the musicians at plantation dances for whites since the nineteenth century.) Local trains contributed to the music's success. The Yazoo & Mississippi Valley Railroad by now had completed its steel tracks from Yazoo City to Clarksdale on a line known locally as the "Yellow Dog." Handy's attempts to find bookings for his orchestra took him on this railroad through even smaller Mississippi towns southward in a four-county Delta area known as the Yellow Dog district, the rural and wilderness area between the tracks of this route westward to the Mississippi River.

These rail stops included the obscure Mississippi hamlets of Tutwiler (where a later historical plaque commemorates Handy's visits), Parchman (the site of the Mississippi State Penitentiary Farm, where a railroad spur delivering visitors to the black prisoners was the inspiration for the well-known folk blues song "The Midnight Special"), and Moorehead (where in local black parlance "the

Southern cross' the Dog," that is, where the tracks of the Y&MV crossed those of the Southern Railroad). Handy came to know thoroughly these stops along the Yellow Dog. Like other riders, he was never able to determine the provenance of this train's nickname. Some later historians speculate that the Southern Railway engineers dismissed their competitors whose tracks they crossed at Moorhead as operators of a mere "yellow dog" railroad. The line from Clarksdale to Yazoo City was also known as the "Yazoo Delta Line," and Handy thought that perhaps the initial letters of the first two words poetically had suggested the nickname "Yellow Dog" to local African Americans. Writers for the Works Progress Administration researching the area in the late 1930s more prosaically suggested that a yellow-colored canine that once lived in Rome, Mississippi, population 250 in 1938, was known to have excitedly chased the Yazoo railroad cars for years.

The railroad brought Handy his first exposure to the Mississippi folk blues. One night in late 1903 or early 1904 (the year is not exact in Handy's memoir), half asleep while waiting inside the station in Tutwiler for a delayed train back to Clarksdale, he was startled by hearing a strange music:

> A lean, loose-jointed Negro had commenced plunking a guitar beside me while I slept. His clothes were rags; his feet peeked out of his shoes. His face had on it some of the sadness of the ages. As he played, he pressed a knife on the strings of the guitar in a manner popularized by Hawaiian guitarists who used steel bars. The effect was unforgettable. His song, too, struck me instantly.
>
> *Goin' where the Southern cross' the Dog.* The singer repeated the line three times, accompanying himself on the guitar with the weirdest music I had ever heard.

W. C. Handy at last heard the folk blues potentially as art, fully awakening him as a future composer. Having been intrigued since a schoolboy in Florence by the plangent work songs of black plowmen he had heard singing outside his classroom and the chants of the black laborers constructing the Muscle Shoals dam and locks, he

now heard in the repeated lines of this unnamed guitarist's song—
"the effect was unforgettable"—a creative structure for the three-
line chorus of many of his later polished blues. Unlike the sixteen
measures of ragtime, this music when later written down by Handy
would contain no more than twelve measures for its short folk
lyrics, with a space at the end of the final measure for an improvised
lyric or musical note. What kept this repetition from becoming
monotonous, and made it sound to the musically educated Handy
as "the weirdest music I had ever heard," was the flatted, or minor,
note deliberately played out of scale by this guitarist with the dull
edge of his knife pressed against the strings. By the conventional
European musical scale, Handy would have anticipated—and himself played—a major note. But the emotional satisfaction of this
so-called wrong note was striking. He remembered how white audiences listening to his band's ragtime or dance marches had not
seemed fully to appreciate his black musicians' score-reading skills
when compared to those of white bands, despite "how perfect ours
was." He had complained thus to his aunt in Alabama. "Honey," he
recalled her advising him, "white folks like to hear colored folks
make some mistakes." Decades after this night and the success of
his published blues that evolved out of it, the advice of his aunt
Mattie remained treasured in Handy's memory. "In this one remark
can be hidden the source or secret of jazz," he wrote in 1941.

The "mistake" of the unanticipated minor or flat note, along
with repetition and syncopation, had been noticed in black folk
music long before Handy heard it. "They are a musical people," an
educated white northerner had observed of rural southern blacks
during the Civil War. "All their songs are in a minor key." (This was
an exaggeration but gives an indication of how black folk music
sounded to white auditors accustomed to the European scale.) A
more musically sophisticated listener, Sidney Lanier, wrote in 1876
with even greater artistic sympathy of the "ecstasy and glory" of
black folk music, wherein "the semitone that *should* come according
to the civilized *modus*" [original italics] is replaced by a "tone that
would shake any man's soul." Before the advent of phonograph
records, it was impossible to exactly reproduce the keening-like
lyrics, the improvised shifts from major to minor, and the strange

vibrato effects of worrying the strings of a guitar with a knife blade or a broken bottleneck. Here ragtime had possessed the early commercial advantage, because syncopation can be readily scored. But what Handy realized that night was that, as a result of his musical education and sense of pitch, he could *approximate* that sound of the folk music onto the printed score. The result was what in the following decade would be called Handy's "World Famous Blue Note." What was yet to be determined for this ambitious bandleader by 1904 was how his white audiences would react to his introduction of this African American style.

Any remaining doubts of Handy's that "a simple slow-drag and repeat could be rhythm itself," or that the "weirdest music" he had ever heard could be commercially resold to a white audience, vanished the night Handy and his orchestra gave a performance for a white audience down at the Yellow Dog in Cleveland, the closest town of any consequence to the Dockery plantation. While Handy and his musicians took an intermission to smoke cigarettes, a rustic-looking black string band consisting of players of a battered bass, mandolin, and guitar, led "by a long-legged chocolate boy," in Handy's description, took the stage and began to play the new music later known as the blues. It was, as Handy had described the sound of the song he heard at the Tutwiler station, "one of those over-and-over strains" that "seem[s] to have no very clear beginning and certainly no ending at all" and therefore was open to improvisation in both its playing and its shouted lyrics. It was the "kind of stuff that has long been associated with cane rows and levee camps," Handy wrote, certainly not the sophisticated ragtime, quick-step marches, genteel dance music, or even ragged coon songs that Handy had made his living playing since 1896. He wondered how the white audience in this hamlet of Cleveland would react.

Highly profitably to the musicians, Handy soon learned. "A rain of silver dollars began to fall around the outlandish, stomping feet" of the three countrified musicians, he later wrote in his memoir. "My idea of what constitutes music was changed by the sight of that silver money cascading around the splay[ed] feet of a Mississippi string band." Thus was born, if not the Father of the Blues, at least the Father of the Commercialization of the Blues. "I returned to

Clarksdale and began immediately to work on this type of music,"
Handy wrote. "Within a day or two I had orchestrated a number of
local tunes, among them 'The Last Shot Got Him,' 'Your Clock
Ain't Right,' and the distinctly Negroid 'Make Me a Pallet on Your
Floor.' My hunch was promptly justified, for the popularity of our
orchestra increased by leaps and bounds." Although still regarded by
most white audiences as only an entertaining musical novelty, these
well-paying blues performances gave encouragement to Handy's
ambitions far beyond what he previously had achieved playing
Sousa marches or ragtime. "That night a composer was born, an
American composer," Handy later wrote emphatically of his witnessing the reaction of the white audience to the rural string band.
"Those country black boys at Cleveland had taught me something
that could not possibly have been learned from books, something
that would, however, cause books to be written."

With his added repertoire of this new music, syncopated but not
quite ragtime, urgent but not crude, Handy's orchestra became *the*
group to book at Clarksdale parties, in the mansions of Yazoo City,
and at any point in between, wherever the Yellow Dog railroad
could carry the musicians and their instruments. These earliest
compositions with equal accuracy might be called bluesy rags as
much as published blues in terms of their overall structure. Handy
was still much influenced by ragtime and sentimental melodies. But
what he accomplished creatively by his thirtieth year justifies his
later boast that he became "an *American* composer." In a brilliantly
creative and apparently ad lib choice, Handy was able to closely represent the sound of the folk blues onto scores with his use of the
"blue note"—technically, an unexpected minor third, fifth, or seventh within an otherwise major strain, a very unusual dissonance in
the popular music of his day—to approximate these worrying and
keening sounds. The presence of this blue note defines to some listeners the uniquely American music of the blues itself, or at least of
the published urban blues. "The more of such notes, the meaner the
blues," one scholar of the blue note in the 1920s insisted.

Consider, for example, Handy's scoring during this early blues
period of what he called the "distinctly Negroid" folk tune "Make
Me a Pallet on Your Floor." This song had been published in 1911 in
an academic journal by the white sociologist Howard W. Odum.

Characterizing it as the complaint of a rejected lover "who pines around the house," Odum heard it performed by a traveling African American guitarist in Lafayette County, one county removed from Coahoma County and Handy's residence in Clarksdale. Regardless of how remarkable he found this folk song, however, Odum was limited by his technology to writing down only the various lyrics of the tune, which he called an example of the "secular songs of the southern Negro." It was reserved for W. C. Handy to reproduce for listeners the tonal melancholy once heard in an unknown Mississippi guitarist's singing and playing of this blues song. Handy later rewrote the "Make Me a Pallet" melody into his own copyrighted "Atlanta Blues," in which flatted thirds are played, in one version of the lyrics, to accompany the following two italicized syllables as they are sung: "I'll grab me an arm*ful* of train before you know / So make me one pallet on your *floor.*" These minor notes change the imperative "make me" into a blues-filled plea, with a return to the tonic on the last word of the lyrics giving the song a finality. There is also a haunting half rhyme at the ends of the last two lines. Handy got it just right.

Although his field work is valuable, Howard Odum himself had no ear for the blues. As the style gained popularity in the second decade of the twentieth century, he denounced the music in an academic publication as "openly descriptive of the grossest immorality and susceptible of unspeakable thought." Ironically, many a blues musician and listener would agree with the latter assertion, that the blues communicate what is otherwise not capable of verbal articulation or musical scoring, as in the "Clarksdale Moan."

Handy's popular blues-playing orchestra often performed at public rallies for the Clarksdale district's perennially elected congressman, John Sharp Williams (served 1892–1908), and, more discreetly, for white patrons at the black-staffed red-light neighborhood of brothels then known as the New World, located across the Y&MV tracks. "Between playing for dances in magnificent plantation mansions from one end of the Delta country to another," Handy later recalled, "striking up the band for an occasional political candidate and conducting jam sessions in the New World," he was profitably performing what he confidently called "the stuff people wanted."

Notably, the people listening or dancing were predominantly

white. Stack Mangham recalled that he and the other members cus-
tomarily received a flat five dollars per man for playing at white
dances, then a considerable fee, but had to settle for a lesser "script"
at black dances, usually a subscription of whatever African Americans could pay at the door. This was presumably much less than five
dollars a man. Despite the remembrance of Mangham that Handy's
orchestra played for "both white and colored," another Delta musician of color, who was a ragtime guitarist and personally knew both
Handy and Charley Patton, qualified that assertion by saying that
African American listeners and dancers were never Handy's first customers of choice. "Handy never played for no colored," William
Moore later told an interviewer. "The colored folks didn't hire him
'cause they didn't have the money," he further explained: "Onliest
way the colored folks would get a chance to dance to Handy's
music, he play for the white folks until about one o'clock [in the
morning], then he play for the colored from one until train time."

Handy's early success in the Delta at scoring and copyrighting
such folk blues and then profitably marketing these songs to white
audiences later led to the appearance of what one blues scholar aptly
calls the composer's "Mississippi problem." Handy's fame "rests on a
kind of cultural appropriation," in this assessment of the problem,
and in the belief that he never suffered the Deep South racism of the
"sort that marked the lives of the 'real' bluesmen whose music he
appropriated." Handy himself certainly did not help the popular dis-
abusal of his "Mississippi problem" by his noticeable patronizing
within his memoir of these same "real," African American bluesmen, who are inevitably pictured in Handy's words as his social or
educational inferiors. As he later wrote:

> A picture of Clarksdale during the years I spent there
> would be incomplete without the blind singers and foot-
> loose bards that were forever coming and going. Usually
> the fellows were destitute. Some came sauntering down
> the railroad tracks, others dropped from freight cars,
> while still others caught rides on the big road and entered
> town on top of cotton bales. A favorite hangout with
> them was the railroad station. There, surrounded by

crowds of country folks, they would pour out their hearts in song while the audience ate fish and bread, chewed sugarcane, dipped snuff while waiting for trains to carry them down the line.

There is also Handy's considered description, for instance, of the railway station black guitarist with "outlandish, stomping feet" that "peeked out of his shoes" and whose "clothes were rags." While this may have been an accurate description of such early turn-of-the-century Mississippi bluesmen as Henry Sloan, who lived in nearby Indianola and who taught a young Charley Patton how to play blues guitar (Sloan is believed by some to have been the bottleneck guitarist Handy heard at the Tutwiler station), it encourages an inaccurate notion of Handy's having been socially indulged by the white planter class and immune from the Jim Crow discrimination of his time. If, in B. B. King's celebrated later remark, for an African American to play or compose the blues is "like being black twice," then Handy is accused of having been black only once, and a privileged once at that.

Handy and his nine other smartly dressed musicians playing for Mississippi audiences of white planters and merchants and their families are sometimes seen by blues historians as having attempted to "ape Mr. Eddie," in the black vernacular of the time—that is, to act in slavish imitation of the white man. (In fact, Handy published a blues song in 1922 with this title, almost certainly intended ironically.) It is true that Handy had no desire to be a poor, itinerant Mississippi bluesman. Neither did the frequently poor, itinerant bluesmen who later played around the Clarksdale area and who were nationally celebrated only after their deaths, such as Tommy McClennan, Robert Johnson, or Charley Patton, the last certainly having preferred playing blues for paying audiences to working as an agricultural tenant at the Dockery Farm. Handy's success in his lifetime as a musician and a blues composer should not be held against him, at least not simply because he desired prosperity for himself and his family and because he lived long enough to obtain what he wanted. And in his earlier years of the "nightmare of minstrelsy," Handy received or witnessed in Mississippi his share of racist threats and violence. Nor did his position as a black musician necessarily make him privileged or immune from his state's institutionalized racism or its accompanying violence. Performing once with his orchestra for a white dance in Batesville, he was struck in the eye, apparently for sport, by a white man, and Handy fought back. In the composer's words, "a battle royal" broke out, and the Batesville constables refused to intervene. Handy and his orchestra fled on foot for their lives, some of the musicians being able to run to a train station in the next town and escape, Handy hiding all night in the fields. In his account, he was found the next morning by a white farmer who, after Handy identified himself as a member of the black order of Masons (Handy was an enthusiastic joiner of fraternal societies), provided him with breakfast. This fellow Mason then protected him against the townspeople with a shotgun until Handy could safely board a train out of town.

Courageous also and not sufficiently appreciated was Handy's conducting of what he called "a kind of bootleg business," selling copies of African American newspapers such as the *Freeman* to Clarksdale's blacks and the area's black farmers. Particularly on come-to-town Saturdays, blacks knew they could stroll by the Issaquena house of Handy, give the resident "the high sign," in Handy's term, and then surreptitiously buy from him a copy of the national newspapers intended for the uplift of African Americans. "This may sound like a tame enough enterprise to those whose memories are short," Handy wrote in 1941 with a passionate restraint, "but oldsters of those parts will not have to be told that I was venturing into risky business. Negro newspapers were not plentiful in those days, and their circulation in cities like Clarksdale was looked upon with strong disfavor by certain of the local powers." Indeed, if Handy's part-time vocation had ever come to the attention of the Clarksdale constables or a Vardaman-supporting county sheriff, it would have gone far better for him if he had been found bootlegging corn whiskey rather than copies of the *Freeman*.

Even his membership in and employment by the Colored Knights of Pythias was a dangerous choice of affiliation at that time in Mississippi. The Pythians were bitterly denounced for their use of the Damon-and-Pythias myth of Western Europe and for their adoption of the name of the all-white lodges of the Knights of Pythias, an older fraternal organization that explicitly forbade membership or initiation into its secret rites for any male of color. Early in the twentieth century, the white Pythians, along with other whites-only fraternal societies such as the Elks, protested to state court and police authorities over the use of their organizations' names by the black fraternal societies. Jim Crow still jumped, vigorously, even in fraternal lodges dedicated to universal brotherhood. To professional men such as Handy—and to his future business partner and member of a "black" Elk lodge, Harry H. Pace—the controversy was less over the right to a fraternal society's generic name than to the right of African Americans legally to organize themselves—for example, to call themselves Democrats or Methodists. In 1904, Mississippi whites legally stopped the use of the "Elk" name by black fraternal societies in their state, and the white Pythians throughout the South began legal action against the Colored Knights of Pythias. Handy had been extraordinarily lucky that the Batesville Masonic farmer had been willing to acknowledge that fraternity's secret sign of brotherhood from a black Mason.

As a prosperous entrepreneur, Handy must be considered among the number whom W. E. B. Du Bois in *The Negro Problem*, coauthored with Booker T. Washington and published in 1903, famously termed "the talented tenth." Explicitly rejecting Washington's advocacy of gradualism and vocational training as most beneficial for the political and cultural advancement of the nation's people of color, Du Bois had called for the support by all African Americans for a "talented tenth," an elite of intellectually sophisticated people of color who would solve "the problem of developing the Best of this race that they may guide the Mass away from the contamination and death of the Worst, in their own and other races."

Du Bois likely would have considered blues, if he had heard them by the first decade of the twentieth century, to be at least a "contamination" of black culture. (In *The Souls of Black Folk*, also published in 1903, Du Bois makes no mention of African American popular secular music other than minstrelsy tunes, which he abhorred.) There is no conclusive evidence that Handy had read Du Bois's essay on the talented tenth when it appeared in September 1903, other than discussions of it in the *Freeman*. But the superior educational and social training that separated Handy from his Clarksdale black neighbors, his own sometimes patronizing descriptions of uneducated folk musicians, and his voluntary undertaking of risky political activism make clear that he considered himself to be one of those whom Du Bois had distinguished as the talented tenth.

The great divergence of opinion between Handy and Du Bois was that Handy considered blues music a high art, once it was properly scored by a member of the select tenth such as Handy himself, and that it then could be proudly presented to the largely white nation as a notable accomplishment of what Du Bois called "the Best of this race." And as Handy surely would have argued, the blues—"pathetic, tender, passionate, melancholy," in the words of Antonín Dvořák, describing African American melodies—were the outlines of what Dvořák had predicted to be "a great and noble school of music" for America, and, for Handy, his credential to be a great and noble American composer.

But to those white Mississippians of Governor Vardaman's political persuasion, Handy was not perceived as a talented American composer—indeed, not even fully a human being—but simply as a suspiciously well educated and ambitious member of that dark-skinned inferior race whom the governor habitually described on the speaking stump as "brutes," "coons," or "niggers," who could be socially controlled only by the threat of lynching. In the first year of Vardaman's governorship in 1904, seventeen black men and one black woman were lynched by mobs in Mississippi. This woman, along with her husband and three other men described afterward simply as "unknown," was murdered on the single horrific night of February 7, 1904. The five murders were committed in Doddsville, in Sunflower County, just down the Yellow Dog tracks from Clarksdale. The violence was encroaching even closer to Handy's residence. Also among the number lynched that terrible year were two men in the nearby hamlet of Cleveland, where Handy had heard the rural blues string band. Here was Du Bois's "whim of the mob," which he decried as the brutal means by which the white Delta society and economy were kept unchanging. Historically and figuratively, the "Clarksdale moan" was not yet the title of a celebrated blues song or the remembered expression of a night of carnal pleasure; rather, by 1904–05, it could be the dying ululation of a lynched and tortured black person.

Ever since his discovery of the folk blues, the area around Clarksdale and the Yellow Dog district had been where Handy had "made more money" playing rearrangements of this new type of music than he had ever earned as a minstrel or bandleader. His family responsibilities had increased alongside his income with the birth of his first son, William Jr., in 1904. Yet even a successful man of color could ignore the reality of lynching only at his peril and that of his family. In a grotesque perversion of Handy's musical artistry, he and his band once were forcibly kidnapped late at night after playing a local engagement. They were made to stand ready with their instruments in order to play his recently scored blues tune "The Last Shot Got Him," while a white farmer viciously beat a white storekeeper in the street prior to the farmer's announced plan to then shoot the man to death. "Keep perked up, you boys," Handy recalled the homicidal farmer telling him and his band. "Then when I raise my hand and give you the high sign, you strike up 'The Last Shot Got Him.' Understand? When I kill him I want to hear you playing like sixty." Despite the farmer's attempted scoring for murder, the storekeeper after his beating managed to crawl off and escape with his life; and then, after commanding Handy's band to play more songs for his and his friends' amusement, the farmer finally released the band members.

But the band's night of terror was not over yet. On their hasty way out of town, Handy and his musicians met one of the farmer's white friends who had enjoyed their music. "He had a rope around a Negro's neck," Handy later wrote. "In the next few hours three Negroes were murdered. They had to kill somebody," he added scornfully.

There were reasons of economics and ambition, as well as racism, for Handy now wanting to leave this now-demotic Eden. His traveling blues orchestra was practically limited in its engagements in the Delta by the route of the Yellow Dog, or the equally poetically named, even more circuitous branch of the Y&MV, locally called the Pea Vine. (The Pea Vine, which was considered an "all-Negro train," ran in a roundabout way from Cleveland to the Dockery Farm.) Furthermore, the revenues Handy earned from his traveling orchestra's bookings, unlike those of the urban bands that were retained at urban cabarets or bordellos, were strictly seasonal, dependent upon the Democratic Party's candidates holding political rallies at town squares in the summer or the plantation elite's celebrating holidays or successful cotton harvests in the autumn or early winter. Handy likely was ambitious to try his talents in a larger city, perhaps motivated in part by the potential profits and pleasures he had witnessed playing music for white patrons in the Clarksdale district of the New World.

It has long been a rueful home truth repeated among Mississippians of all skin colors that for ambitious residents, the state has two big cities: Memphis, Tennessee, and New Orleans, Louisiana. In plainer words, that state's residents traditionally had to leave Mississippi in order to succeed. In his decision to move his family and his performance business from Clarksdale, a decision he made perhaps as early as the winter of 1905, Handy acted no differently from thousands of others before him, black or white.

Clarksdale itself was located on the routes of out-of-state emigration. The town, in Handy's day as now, is sited to the south of the intersection of two roads that are now designated Highway 61 and Highway 49. (This supposedly is the Mississippi crossroads, one of several proposed in blues lore, where the guitarist Robert Johnson a generation later was said to have met with the devil at midnight and to have traded his soul in exchange for blues mastery.) For those headed east or west out of Mississippi, Highway 49 is the chosen route. But if one elects to go north on Highway 61, the road leads directly to Memphis, or, if one travels southward, the highway ends at New Orleans. The latter city in the first decade of the century was the larger of the two, with a population of 287,104 residents in 1900, in comparison with Memphis's 102,320.

Memphis, the northernmost of the two cities, is located on the east bank of the Mississippi River about eighty miles north of Clarksdale. By late 1905 or early 1906, Handy's family relocated there and likely was boarding at the house of Matthew Thornton, an African American porter and general laborer who worked along the

city's Beale Avenue and who, active in the city's black fraternal organizations and Republican Party, had organized a Colored Knights of
Pythias orchestra there.

Earlier, Handy had arranged with Thornton to instruct the
Pythian band twice a week in Memphis while he was still living in
Mississippi and, in Handy's words, still "doing the Dog and Pea Vine
out of Clarksdale" for local bookings. There was therefore some
musical work guaranteed him in Memphis. But in casting his lot
to settle in the western Tennessee city as a musical manager, performer, and composer, he was, perhaps unknowingly, also opening
himself to regional influences of the developing blues uniquely different from what was then being played by Jelly Roll Morton and
other African American musicians four hundred miles farther south
down the Mississippi River at New Orleans. The city of Memphis is,
in fact, closer geographically to St. Louis than to New Orleans, and
the influence of Midwestern ragtime performers, as well as riverboat musicians working on excursion boats along the Ohio River
Valley, had—despite Morton's later protestations—played a large
part in the national development of the blues. Handy, unlike other
pioneers of the blues such as Morton or Louis Armstrong, probably
played in his formative blues years no closer to New Orleans than
Yazoo City, approximately two hundred miles from that Louisiana
city. The Yellow Dog district, and Mississippi generally, like his earlier career in minstrelsy, had given all they were capable of giving
musically to Handy by the first decade of the twentieth century. He
had come to Clarksdale professionally disinclined toward the black
folk tunes he had heard in his travels as a minstrel, college instructor,
and vagabond, and he had instead determined to become known
nationally, if not as a ragtime performer, then as a March King, a
sort of African American counterpart to John Philip Sousa. After
two years of extensive travel to the predominantly black small
towns of the Delta along the tracks of the Yellow Dog and the Pea
Vine, he was now leaving with his head full of the possibilities of a
very different music. As a determinedly *American* composer, Handy
was intent to fashion the black folk songs he had heard in Mississippi
into both a commodity and an art that he planned to sell as a
national music for whites and blacks—a music expressing the erotic

joy that was imitated by Daddy Rice, the syncopation that was celebrated by ragtime, and the pathos and dignity that recently had been
degraded by coon songs.

Four years before his death in 1958, Handy recalled to an interviewer that in about 1905 he proudly had watched his new son,
William, take his first adventurous steps within Matthew Thornton's house in Memphis. At this time, few professional musicians
outside the South had heard the term "blues." The word long had
been used as a colloquial synonym for melancholia, appearing in its
modern musical meaning in only a few song titles by composers
from New Orleans and Charleston, South Carolina. But the intelli-
gent and ambitious Handy, now in his early thirties, was beginning
to take his first artistic and commercial steps to becoming the Father
of the Blues. The location was to be the rough-and-tumble city of
Memphis, Tennessee.

———

CHAPTER SIX

Mr. Crump Don't 'Low

THE BIRTH OF THE COMMERCIAL
BLUES, 1905–1909

My aim would be to combine ragtime syncopation with a real
melody in the spiritual tradition.

> —W. C. Handy, on his first
> composition of blues songs for a
> national market, in Memphis,
> Tennessee

The Mississippi Delta has been described as beginning southward from the lobby of the Peabody Hotel in Memphis. But with as much accuracy it can be described as terminating there. Memphis, the new city of residence for Handy and his growing family, long had considered its commercial and cultural interests to face as much westward and eastward as southward. Located at the extreme southwestern line of the border state of Tennessee, and originally built upon four natural, low elevations overlooking the Mississippi River, the Chickasaw Bluffs, the city in its history contains as many incidents of the old southwestern frontier as it does of the antebellum plantation. Shortly after its founding in 1819, for example, Memphis was visited by the celebrated backwoodsman David Crockett, who hosted a midnight whiskey-drinking party long remembered by Native Americans as one of the greatest debauches by a white man ever to occur on the Chickasaw Bluffs. This frontier settlement, "a tough and uninviting place," in the words of one southern historian, rapidly became the center for legitimate business as well as vice offered to travelers south of St. Louis and north of New Orleans. By the time of the Handy family's arrival, the city had established its preeminence as an east-west venue of commerce and culture along the southwesterly flowing Tennessee River valley. Rail connections to Chicago and New York City were good, and four times more passenger railroad lines headed east-west out of Memphis than north-south.

Among them at the time of Handy's residence were the major lines of the Missouri Pacific Railway and the Nashville, Chattanooga & St. Louis Railway, making easy transit for ragtime musicians traveling to Tennessee from St. Louis and Kansas City, Missouri, both of which were then national centers for ragtime composers and players. In particular, Kansas City players were beginning to experiment with songs composed with blueslike twelve measures, rather than the sixteen measures common to ragtime; these songs made their way down the Ohio River Valley from Cincinnati and other Midwestern cities, then eastward along the Tennessee River, not up the Mississippi River. Excursion riverboats from cities in the Midwest also brought to Memphis their commercial musicians, frequently African American, who played in a different style than was heard in the bordellos or on the streets of New Orleans farther down the Mississippi River.

In its wide-open vices as well as its music, Memphis in the early decades of the twentieth century continued to compete with New Orleans. In Handy's day, as well as later, the prostitutes of Memphis were well known by their reputation throughout the Mississippi Delta for carrying a "ration sack" or, variously, a "nation sack" of coins hanging between their legs, which the women would jingle to entice prospective customers as they walked along the Memphis levees. A generation later, the Delta blues musician Robert Johnson made mention in 1936 of his lover's "nation sack," in one of Johnson's few recorded songs, "Come on in My Kitchen."

In both its legal and illegal commerce, Memphis upon Handy's arrival also had its Jim Crow codes, with the seating in streetcars legally segregated since 1903 and with separate brothels for white and black patrons, or with black men being admitted only very late, after "three o'clock in the morning." The color line also remained in force along many of the railroad tracks in the Midwest and West connecting to this Tennessee city. However, Memphis also was comparatively a refuge from small towns in the South and Midwest for ambitious and educated people of color such as W. C. Handy. Just a few miles down the great, indifferent river, for example, unthinkable in the state of Mississippi, was the franchise by which black males would be allowed to vote. But within a few wards of Memphis, blacks were allowed the franchise, and black males there even were allowed by the city to serve as policemen within the "colored" precincts. Handy's band employer and briefly his landlord in Memphis, Matthew Thornton, occasionally was employed as a city policeman.

These carefully dispensed civil and political rights were granted by a white civic government within one of the blackest of cities of the South. Memphis was home to 52,440 African Americans by the end of the first decade of the twentieth century. It was thereby a majority black city in its total population and in absolute contained more black people—greater in number than in Atlanta, Birmingham, Nashville, or Richmond—than any other southern city except New Orleans. There also lived in Memphis a substantial African American middle or professional class, much larger in their numbers than any Handy had seen in the cities of his minstrelsy travels, and certainly not in Florence or Clarksdale.

Robert Reed Church Sr. was the acknowledged leader of the black Memphis bourgeois community, and his and Handy's paths soon crossed. Church, a real estate investor who had been born a slave from the union of a white steamboat captain and a black seamstress, was reputed to be the South's first African American millionaire. When Memphis in the late nineteenth century had declined to finance any public recreational facilities for its citizens of color, Church at an expense of $50,000 out of his own pocket in 1899 had ordered constructed at one end of the predominantly African American street of Beale Avenue a six-acre landscaped site for the enjoyment of Memphis's black residents. It included a two-story theater, bandstand, and refreshment counters. Theodore Roosevelt had been the honored guest at Church's Park and Auditorium in 1902, speaking to an audience of more than ten thousand people, mainly black. Within a few years of his arrival, Handy would be hired as a bandleader by Church to play his new music on the park grounds on Beale.

"You'll see men who rank in the first of the nation / Who come to Beale for in-spi-ra-tion." Handy thus wrote this lyric, optimistically and expansively, to one of his most popular scores, "Beale Street," in the decade subsequent to his arrival in Memphis. There is no doubt that Handy from the moment of his arrival considered the city among "the first of the nation." Memphis, although still keeping many of its rough frontier violent habits—it was for several years reputedly the murder capital of the United States—had grown up into a regional metropolis. As a sign of its civic progressivism, white males in the city sported lapel buttons—made of celluloid like the century's later Edison recording cylinders—advertising the fact that their city's population had exceeded 100,000. By 1905, electric trolley cars were running on the paved streets (with Jim Crow seating at the rear), a skyscraper building or two had been raised overlooking the muddy flats of the Mississippi River, and, perhaps most impressive to Handy, well-dressed and professionally attired men of color were seen confidently walking down the city sidewalks along Beale Avenue.

Handy himself was soon among the confident Beale Avenue walkers, despite a humble start in the city. After leaving their temporary shelter at Matthew Thornton's house, the Handy family bought a small frame dwelling at 246 Ayers, in the questionable neighborhood known locally as Greasy Plank. The house lacked indoor plumbing, and the neighborhood, one of the poorer "colored" areas of Memphis, was crisscrossed by water-filled gullies considered to be both malarial and septic; it was located literally in a backwater to the east of the commercial district among the bogs of the Mississippi. In terms of their domestic comforts, the living standards of the Handy family had declined significantly from their Clarksdale residence, even considering their former location across the railroad tracks from the bordellos of the New World.

But his new employer, the local lodge of the Colored Knights of Pythias, rented impressive headquarters at 435 Beale, the location of a black church, and the Pythian membership included many of the city's leading black merchants and professionals. (The avenue itself was not officially renamed Beale Street until many years later, after the national sales of Handy's popular composition celebrating the street.) At the time of Handy's arrival, this mile-long urban street that ran past Church's Park on the east and ended at the Mississippi River's docks and levees on the west was officially named on the city maps as Beale Avenue, but, culturally and racially, this avenue was accurately known even then as "the Main Street of Negro America."

As a boy in northern Alabama, Handy had visited Beale Avenue, and he also had heard from the peripatetic fiddle player Jim Turner stories of its celebrated gambling dens, saloons, and brothels available to males of color, just as had thousands of other rural African Americans growing up in northern Mississippi, Alabama, Arkansas, and Tennessee. But by no means was Beale Avenue exclusively Memphis's scofflaw or red-light district for people of color. At its heyday, which coincided with Handy's arrival, Beale was also the central thoroughfare of commerce and residence for Memphis's law-abiding, middle-class African American citizens and the invisible demarcation of that city's Jim Crow commercial line. A few blocks from the river, Beale crosses the north-south axis of Main Street, an intersection that by the early twentieth century marked the invisible boundary of white downtown Memphis. Northward up Main Street from Beale Avenue, African Americans could enter shops only at the entrances marked "Colored" and be served only after the white customers. But along Beale Avenue to the south and east of the street, African American insurance agents, lawyers, bankers, dentists, undertakers, barbers, and other entrepreneurs had their businesses freely open to the neighborhood's traffic, and Jewish and Italian merchants, primarily in the clothing and entertainment businesses, respectively, actively sought black customers to come in from the sidewalks and sample their wares. And at Beale's eastern end, around Church's Park, were respectable residential neighborhoods. Most of the saloons and gambling dens catering to a "colored" clientele, later to be celebrated by Handy in "Beale Street Blues," were located in a two-block stretch between the intersections of Beale Avenue with Hernando and Fourth

streets. The bordellos for which the city was amorally celebrated—
"You'll see pretty Browns in beautiful gowns," Handy later would write
in his lyrics—were mostly found in a line of small frame houses
along Mulberry, a street that dead-ended into Beale and that also
was located a few blocks south of Main Street and the Peabody
Hotel's lobby.

But from 1905 to 1909, W. C. Handy was not yet the celebrated
blues lyricist of Beale Avenue and its vices; he was not even considered the best African American musician or orchestra leader to be
found along that avenue. Handy initially would have been recognized by old-timers on Beale Avenue simply as one of Turner's
musical protégés, and perhaps not even as a blues innovator in his
own right. "Long before Handy's day," reminisced George Lee, an
insurance salesman along Beale and a political lieutenant in Robert
Church's organization of the Republican Party, "Charlie Bynum
organized the Bynum and Jim Turner Band. Bynum was the first
[band]leader on Beale Street to play the blues, but, not realizing
their potential commercial value, he never thought of trying to set
them to music [score them]." Lee also recalled two local musicians,
Will Stewart and Powers Thornton, the latter remembered by Lee
for playing "the sweetest violin along the avenue."

Handy's personal talent for collecting the blues and "realizing
their potential commercial value" would rise above Memphis to a
national stage within a few years, but from 1905 to 1909 he was simply another horn player and bandleader, though skilled certainly in
arrangement and composition. He was also now in his midthirties
with a wife and three children under the age of ten. His own mor-
tality, and increased family responsibilities, had been presented to
him by the death of his father in 1908. Thereafter the composer's
younger brother, Charles E. Handy, with whom he was remarkably
close, moved to Memphis and for several years stayed with Handy.

To improve his livelihood, Handy as he had done in Clarksdale
organized a smaller musical group from the Knights of Pythias brass
band he was instructing. However, by his own admission, this
"dance orchestra stepped out on Beale Street only fourth best"
among the other Memphis orchestras. (In this era when brass bands
still dominated public performances of most popular music, an

"orchestra" was used to denote a group of musicians playing a number of strings and softer wind instruments. A "band" as colloquial shorthand for any ensemble of popular-music performers was just coming into popular usage.) Handy's orchestra initially received fewer bookings than the Bynum and Turner group or the dance orchestras organized by the more established black musicians in Memphis, such as R. K. Eckford. Other than his regular pay for the Pythias instruction, Handy in his first years in Memphis made most of his money with the larger Pythias band by playing at funerals, happily being referred frequently to the Memphis bereaved by T. H. Hayes, a local African American undertaker and a fellow black Pythian.

Handy, however, was just as capable a spotter of musical talent in Memphis as he had been of the folk blues songs in rural Mississippi, and for his dance orchestra he was able to recruit—or, less charitably, to steal from other leaders—the fiddler Jim Turner, Will Means, and George Williams, the latter two respectively a bass player and a trombonist and guitarist, from the Bynum and Turner group; he also recruited a cello player and a flutist, both from Reuben Brooks's Vicksburg orchestra; and he outright hired the Wyer brothers, Paul and Edward, who were between engagements, as additional violinists and clarinet players. (Their father, also named Edward, was known to Handy as a former army bandsman, and he had entertained colored minstrels from Richards and Pringle's Georgia Minstrels at Wyer's home in Pensacola, Florida.) James Osbourne, a pickup musician who played the tenor saxophone, an instrument then still considered something of a novelty, completed the group. Handy himself played cornet and trumpet.

Musicians would come and go in Handy's many local musical groups. There is later evidence that he may have been a difficult employer, but by that same year he had assembled many of the musicians who permanently constituted his bands. This collection of talent was not yet known as a blues group (indeed, with a cello, a flute, and three violins it would not be recognized as one today), but as its ambitious leader later recalled, with this assembly "the boom was on where the Handy dance orchestra was concerned." His arrangements of folk blues still continued to be called for in the

Delta, primarily as novelty numbers, and his Memphis group traveled out of the Tennessee city into northern Mississippi to play the parties at "great houses down on the roads that crossed the Dog," in Handy's expansive words; but his group also "played the river," as the fiddling Jim Turner would have put it, with more conventional music. These engagements were to play dance music aboard Ohio River Valley and Mississippi River excursion riverboats, such as the *Majestic,* which worked out of Cincinnati down to Memphis and which offered "colored" cruises for African Americans. There was also the *Idlewild,* operated by the West Memphis Packet Company and considered one of the finest pleasure boats on the Mississippi, and the *Pattona,* the resident excursion boat of Memphis and a frequent employer of Handy and his orchestra for short round-trips from the city docks, usually conducted at night.

Waltzes, schottisches, and one-steps and two-steps (both danceable ragtimes) were what was called for. Improvisation was not required or wanted by the management in this style of floating ballroom music (it would have confused the dancers), unlike in the performances of musicians in New Orleans. There the musicians were beginning to experiment with a horn player or others playing a melodic "first line" while other members of the group on clarinet, trombone, or piano played improvised solos. This polyphonic improvisation in the "Dixieland" style of playing would have sounded arbitrary and cacophonous to a strictly "reading band," religiously keeping to their scores, such as Handy's group. An indication of the importance to Handy of his bands' adherence to printed scores was the manner in which he hired Ed Wyer's brother, Paul, whom Handy encountered one night on a Memphis levee when he had stepped off a riverboat after an engagement. Wyer, seeking work as a violinist or a clarinet player, assured Handy that he could play "anything." Then, taking a moment to consider and perhaps remembering what he knew of Handy from his father and brother, he immediately qualified himself: "Anything that's written," he added. *I'm no uneducated bordello musician from New Orleans or some Delta crossroads musical novelty,* Wyer seems to have been telling him. Handy hired him on the spot.

Performing by arrangement on resident excursion riverboats such as the 150-foot-long *Pattona* (which first had arrived in the city of Memphis in 1909 with President William H. Taft aboard as an honored guest) was a significant source of income for Handy. An account book kept in his handwriting and recording his band's engagements and payments for the years 1914–16 frequently notes requests for his *Pattona* performances. The money was hard earned. His account book records payments of amounts varying from a little over seven dollars to fifty dollars for the excursion performances, which on Sundays could last the entire day and night. Handy would be a familiar sight hurrying down Beale with his cornet on these mornings, to the city's cobblestone docks where the boats were waiting by ropes tied to heavy iron rings. On some Sundays he would have to be aboard the riverboat *Charles Morgan* by eight o'clock in the morning and then return to land and board the *Pattona* for the two-thirty and seven-thirty p.m. departures and shows, returning to his home after eleven. Handy later humorously recalled that he would say his best Sunday prayers while crossing the intersection of Main and Union streets, hoping to make the boat in time.

Handy's skill began to gain him an outstanding local reputation as a riverboat musician and orchestra leader. One former white society debutante of Memphis told a historian in 1958 that one could not consider having "been on a river excursion unless Handy's band played for the boat." Such praise probably tells much more about Handy as a genial "colored" entertainer at the bandstand rather than his musical innovation played at that time aboard the riverboats. He loved the great rivers of his youth—the Tennessee, the Ohio, and the Mississippi. When he was asked, at age eighty-one, whether he would enjoy a riverboat trip out of Memphis, he laughed and answered, "Why not? As far as it's going." Other black bands from Memphis, such as R. K. Eckford's, sometimes had been aboard for performances on these excursions, and during smoke breaks with the other black musicians, if not in their set performances for the white audiences, "that music," Handy said—meaning variations on such black folk tunes as the "Joe Turner" melody—"spread all over the country." Handy in this 1954 interview then recalled with pleasure the small-town Mississippi River boat landings of 1909–1916 with their evocative, enigmatic names: Friars' Point, Sherard, Rena Lara. "I used to play for dances down there . . . Oh, yeah."

The year of the *Pattona's* first arrival in Memphis in 1909 was also the year when Handy as a national composer at last made the blues—or at least his written version of "that music." The occasion was the Memphis mayoral election. One candidate was another former resident of Mississippi who had sought his fortunes in Memphis. Edward H. Crump was making his first run at that city office from which he eventually would dominate the entire state of Tennessee for decades as the revered, and feared, Boss Crump. The race was predicted to be a tight one. The city's *Commercial Appeal* newspaper reported that over $20,000 in bets had been wagered on the election's outcome. About six thousand votes were needed to win a majority for the mayoral office, a number considerably less than the politically prescient Crump knew his supporters could deliver from their white wards. But about two thousand African Americans were eligible to vote in this city, many of them concentrated along Beale Avenue, which ran through the city's Fifth, Sixth, and Seventh wards. Crump was determined to turn out these voters and have them mark their ballots for him, and, by receiving their plurality, to gain the mayor's office.

Music at this time was the means by which large numbers of people could be reminded of the candidate's name and induced to gather at a designated place. Once a crowd was assembled or led to a site by an orchestra, particularly along Beale Avenue, there would be little difficulty for the Crump organization in obtaining votes for its candidate: popular saloons for blacks along the avenue, such as Hammitt Ashford's, were employed as voter registration sites. There, any delinquent poll taxes were paid for the new voter, very likely with several drinks of liquor also having been proffered and paid for, and a receipt for the paid tax—along with a ballot pre-marked for Edward Crump—was then handed back to the voter. Crump's political operative Jim Mulcahy determined to hire an African American orchestra to promote his candidate among Memphis's potential black voters. "We were hired to beat the drum and blow the horn for Mr. Crump," Handy later recalled, "and we did—in our own way."

Handy's orchestra, however, was not the only African American musical group paid by white campaign managers to "beat the drum" for their mayoral candidates in the election of 1909. Charlie

Bynum's group, Bynum's Superb Orchestra (the name was changed from Bynum and Turner, after Handy had hired away Turner) and yet another competing Memphis ensemble, the Eckford and Higgins Imperial Orchestra, were hired by Crump's two rivals to draw black crowds. However, nothing had prepared the competitors or the listening public of Memphis, black or white, for the musical number that Handy composed for his orchestra to play at the opening of the Crump campaign.

By his later account, Handy began writing his new composition leaning against the cigar counter inside Pee Wee's Saloon at 317 Beale Avenue, although he later completed the scoring at his new house at 246 Ayers. He gave only a slight consideration to the martial marches that had so fascinated him in his early Mississippi years. He may have arranged this new composition with its unique blue notes because his orchestra was being paid to draw a specifically African American crowd, and Handy believed, like Dvořák, that certain music was expressive of certain national or racial identities (as in Handy's earlier characterization of the "distinctively Negroid" melody of "Make Me a Pallet on Your Floor"). Or perhaps during this creative time inside a Beale Avenue saloon, Handy initially arranged the notes on paper as he did simply to show off the musical novelty for which his group was known. In any case, he chose to open Edward Crump's mayoral campaign with what he described as "a weird melody in much the same mood as the one that had been strummed on the guitar at Tutwiler."

Handy called his new song "Mr. Crump." Both in its original 1909 version and its later rearrangement in 1913 retitled as "The Memphis Blues," it has become recognized as among the first of the written blues. George Lee, the Beale Avenue habitué who heard the first public performance of "Mr. Crump," also immediately recognized the folk blues influence of Handy's novel composition. Lee later described it as musically expressing "the same backward, over-and-over wailing that characterized the sorrow songs of those people farthest down." Lee may have intended "people farthest down" to refer to those people of color living farther southward on the Mississippi River, or living in the lower economic classes, or both. But the people of Memphis—both white and black and of all economic classes—reacted joyfully to Handy's new jaunty, melancholy tune when he and his band first played it from atop a mule-drawn band-wagon on the city's courthouse square in 1909.

"The crowd in the streets literally went wild over it," Lee wrote. "They shouted until they were hoarse, demanding to hear it again and again. They whistled and danced with the rhythmic sway of the music, as the words floated out upon the air:

> *Mr. Crump don't 'low no easy riders here*
> *Mr. Crump don't 'low no easy riders here.*

Seated with Handy upon chairs inside the wagon were the Wyer brothers, along with Jim Turner on violin, George Higgins on guitar and vocals, Archie Walls on bass, Robert Young on clarinet, James Osbourne on saxophone, and George Williams on trombone. Handy, of course, played cornet.

As a popular American cultural phenomenon, probably nothing similar to this Memphis crowd's reaction to "Mr. Crump" had been witnessed since the nation's audiences delighted in Daddy Rice's dancing and singing "Jump Jim Crow." But this time, in Memphis, the African American–influenced music was being performed not by comedic white men in burnt cork makeup, but by respectable men of color whose musical leader had serious artistic and voca-tional ambitions. No one, not even the white or black enthusiasts of ragtime, had ever heard anything quite like Handy's song. This was, after all, the year when among the most popular commercial songs was "The Whiffenpoof Song," a sentimental ballad of misbehaving Yale University undergraduates.

This public performance of "Mr. Crump" is considered the birth of the published blues. Yet, for a blues composition, "Mr. Crump" had a remarkably cheerful sound. Handy's tune might just as accu-rately be described as being a very bluesy rag. He composed his song in a ragtime AABBTCCCC stanzaic architecture. The "A" and "C" strains were written in the twelve bars of folk blues, with what Handy specified as flat thirds and sevenths, or blue notes, enclosing a sixteen-bar middle of ragtime with its bouncy syncopation and slight suggestions of martial music. The listener is therefore made to feel slightly blue, only to be uplifted by the bouncy repeats of ragtime, or what George Lee called the song's "backward, over-and-over" melodies, sounding both energetic and melancholy. (To experience some of the blues novelty first heard in Handy's ragtime-influenced "Mr. Crump," the reader perhaps should listen to Scott Joplin's jaunty "The Entertainer" immediately followed by Handy's more elegiac and melodically complex ragtime mixed with blues.) There are in Handy's composition two solos, each two measures long, to be played legato, or in one breath or motion. One of the solos is written in the treble clef (violin, clarinet, or saxophone) and the other in the bass clef (trombone or tuba). Handy likely had written these passages with the specific talents in mind of George Williams on trombone or the Wyer brothers on violin. After this slight melancholy of the solos, the song returns in its structure to the repeated, upbeat syncopation.

But not before violinist Paul Wyer made blues history. A friend and patron of Handy, the New York lawyer Abbe Niles later described the Memphis scene:

> [W]ith the first performances by a capable Negro orchestra of "Mr. Crump" something new and unheard-of took place; at a certain point in the third and final air, one musician [Paul Wyer] went wild. He deviated from the score and put in some licks on his own account; he licentiously patted his feet. Up to then this, like every other dance orchestra, had played as best it could what was set before it in black and white. . . . The leader had learned something from this; from then on his musicians had carte-blanche in the breaks of his blues.

Paul Wyer had just played the first notable blues break, an individual's improvisation at the end of a final bar before the group's resumption of the melody in the following bars. Handy, always a "reading" musician, may or may not have planned what Niles's later account calls such a spontaneous deviation from the score. In later performances, such as the recordings made in 1917 in New York City by "Handy's Orchestra of Memphis" (not including either of the

Wyer brothers), the musicians under Handy's direction follow the scores almost to the point of stiffness. After all, he had hired Paul Wyer off that Memphis levee because of the latter's assurances that he was a reading musician who could faithfully follow what was set before him. But this daring, improvisational leap by Wyer lends further credence to this performance in 1909 of Handy's composition as having established the historical birth of the commercial blues. And as for the bandleader himself, Handy was certainly enough of a canny showman to notice the shouting, hand waving, and dancing at the Tennessee courthouse following Wyer's blues break.

For the general listener, the historical significance of this remarkable blues break perhaps has been best defined by the ragtime and early blues scholar David Joyner:

> The "break" at the end of each phrase of a blues chorus is used in published blues as the point for the piano or orchestra to play a responsive embellishment. This is where the folk blues performers would have put their "Oh (Lordy!)" or added a similar response to their vocal. The break became the essence of instrumental jazz.

As Joyner implies, the blues break certainly had been performed by folk performers prior to the first public playing of "Mr. Crump." But the musicians led by Handy were among the first professional and trained musicians unexpectedly to deviate from the expected melody, and Handy literally was on the bandwagon when it happened.

The crowd's enthusiastic reaction may also have been because "Mr. Crump," both in its performance and composition, was much greater than the sum of its parts. "Snatches" of the blues, as Handy liked to call them, had certainly been heard before in Memphis. Just as itinerant black blues guitarists had gathered on Saturdays at the rail station in Clarksdale, so had Delta guitarists played their versions of the blues along the Beale Avenue sidewalks on the weekends. Ragtime and martial marches also were certainly nothing new to Memphis music lovers by 1909; nor were twelve-bar strains played to or with ragtime a novelty to audiences in the city. Ragtime composers in Memphis prior to the performance of Handy's composition had experimented, perhaps influenced by the Kansas City ragtime men, with writing twelve-bar strains in their published works. Most intriguingly, there was the "Bull Dog Rag," composed with a twelve-measure strain by a female white music teacher then living in Memphis, Geraldine Dobyns, and published in the city in 1908, one year before the first public performance of "Mr. Crump." What Handy did with all these influences—with more than a little help from Wyer—was to make these sounds into something new: not in the sense of originally creating them, but in the sense of his refashioning them, *making* them into a nationally popular and marketable music.

"The melody of 'Mr. Crump' was mine throughout," Handy later wrote, perhaps somewhat defensively, in his 1941 memoir. But as he then immediately and frankly added:

> On the other hand, the twelve-bar, three-line form of the first and last strains, with its three-chord basic harmonic structure (tonic, subdominant, dominant seventh) was that already used by Negro roustabouts, honky-tonk piano players, wanderers and others of their unprivileged but undaunted class from Missouri to the Gulf, and had become a common medium through which any such individual might express his personal feelings in a sort of musical soliloquy. My part in their history was to introduce this, the "blues," to the general public as the medium for my own feelings and my own musical ideas.

Or, as he later expressed his artistic intentions: "My aim would be to combine ragtime syncopation with a real melody in the spiritual tradition."

In his song's lyrics, Handy also demonstrated his individual talent for introducing colloquialisms (albeit with standardized spelling), as in the celebratory descriptions of the city's "easy riders" and "barrel-housing." In 1909, no other American song lyricist or fiction author—including Jack London in his novel published that year, *Martin Eden;* Theodore Dreiser in his earlier novel of genteel prostitution, *Sister Carrie;* or Gertrude Stein in her novel *Three Lives,* published in 1909 with an African American female as one of the main characters—so effortlessly and so confidently employed the language that real people, white or black, used in the United States at that time. For the sound of true, twentieth-century literary Modernism, compare this passage from *Three Lives*—"Rose laughed when she was happy but she had not the wide, abandoned laughter that makes the warm broad glow of negro sunshine. Rose was never joyous with the earth-born, boundless joy of negroes" (original spelling and punctuation)—with Handy's humorous and to-the-point dismissive remark in his lyric "Mr. Crump can go and catch himself some air."

Mr. Crump was told to go elsewhere and "catch himself some air" because Handy, always something of a musical trickster, apparently had found it irresistible to gently mock the candidate whose name he had been paid to celebrate in music. Edward Crump was running for mayor on a moral platform, pledging to "reform" the city's illegal saloons, gambling dens, and brothels, or what were considered by many others simply to be the features of "a good-time town like Memphis." (Reform was to become a much-loved concept of Crump and the members of his subsequent political machine; indeed, so beloved was reform by this urban politician that four decades later Boss Crump or his picked candidates were described by V. O. Key in his *Southern Politics in State and Nation* as still running for public office in Tennessee on a promise of future reform.) The commercial vices of Beale Avenue were never permanently threatened by any Crump mayoral administration. Handy's lyrics gently mocked in syncopated rhythm their candidate's pledge to drive out the raffish inhabitants of Memphis:

> *Mr. Crump don't 'low no easy riders here,*
> *Mr. Crump don't 'low no easy riders here,*
> *We don't care what Mr. Crump don't 'low,*
> *We gonna barrel-house anyhow,*
> *Mr. Crump can go and catch himself some air!*

"That was Handy's sly joking," a local historian later explained:

The words said in Beale Street lingo that folks didn't believe Mr. Crump, the fiery young redhead, could or would reform a good-time town like Memphis; folks would go on barrel housin' and guzzling liquor, just the same. The words also had funny double meanings: to Beale, *easy riders* meant pimps; to Main Street, political grafters and protected vice lords.

Part of the audience's delight—the whistling, dancing, and shouts of joy that George Lee described—may have been, particularly among the African American listeners from Beale Avenue, at the audacity of this composer of color musically telling a prominent white man to "go and catch himself some air." In fact, there is something of the exuberance of the afterpiece of the minstrelsy show both in the score and the lyrics of "Mr. Crump," and it is easy to imagine the entire cast of an African American minstrel troupe, cakewalking and high-stepping to Handy's tune, momentarily celebrating the reversal of authority and the emotional release of their music by singing, *"We don't care what Mr. Crump don't 'low!"* Crump himself apparently never knew, at least until a year or so later, the lyrics of the song bearing his name. "Folks went wild about it," Handy later wrote of this first blues success. Handy then added with a nice choice of words: "No doubt Crump would have gone wild, too, in quite a different way, had he been permitted to hear the words. But he didn't go with the band, so he never heard the song that many like to think whisked him into office on a reform ticket."

(That year was also politically memorable for Handy in another matter. Given his later success as blues composer, it is sometimes overlooked that for the first six years of the century he made his living as the leader of Pythias bands. At every weekly meeting that year of the Memphis fraternal lodge, Handy, along with all other members of the Colored Knight of Pythias throughout the United States, was asked to donate a dime to help pay legal expenses for this African American fraternity to defend itself in court against suits denying the right of its members to call themselves "Pythians." The white Pythians of Tennessee in 1909 had joined with white lodges in other southern states in pursuing these suits. These combined suits eventually reached the U.S. Supreme Court. In 1912, the last full year of the Taft presidency, this black fraternal organization won definitively its legal trials. Handy and his fellow members were allowed at last legally to organize and to call themselves the Knights of Pythias North America, South America, Europe, Asia, Africa, and Australia.)

The immediate and wild success of "Mr. Crump" meant that Handy's dance orchestra now "stepped out on Beale Street" as first among the popular music groups of Memphis. When President Taft arrived in town in 1909, it was to this bluesy tune of "Mr. Crump" that the chief executive was greeted, played of course by Handy's orchestra. This was the first of Handy's much wished-for "crossover" appearances or national successes with white audiences. The following year, after construction was completed in 1910 on the eleven-story Falls Building to provide offices for cotton merchants, Handy and his orchestra were retained to play at nights in the cabaret atop the building's uppermost story, the Alaskan Roof Garden, which he later remembered as being the "leading uptown dance spot of white Memphis." And if Handy had not yet gained the acceptance he desired from the leading black bourgeois and black capitalists of Memphis, he and his music were at least making inroads upon the younger generation. A photograph from that period identified as "Handy's Memphis Blues Band" is inscribed by Handy to "my esteemed friend," R. R. Church Jr., the adult son of the Beale Street millionaire Robert Church Sr., and shows Handy and seven other musicians dressed in formal evening clothes. Handy appears prosperously sleek, his cornet expectantly half-raised. Ed Wyer, the violinist, is shyly smiling. James Osbourne, cradling his saxophone lengthwise across his lap, appears pensive.

The demand locally and regionally around Memphis among white audiences for Handy's new music was such that he eventually hired more than sixty musicians both full- and part-time to front as many as twelve different Memphis orchestras—or sometimes to play in what would by the 1930s be known as a blues combo, consisting of just a piano, drums, and possibly a guitar. Thus his success after 1909 directly led to the large number of local musicians around Memphis, many of them quickly hired music students from the city's black high school, who later claimed to historians to have "played with Handy's band," although not necessarily accompanying Handy himself on his trumpet or cornet.

"When we played, no matter where, the people could not refrain from dancing," Handy subsequently reminisced to a reporter from the New York City *Age* newspaper in 1916 about his first performances in 1909 of "Mr. Crump" in Memphis. "They danced in parks, halls, stores, on sidewalks, streetcars—anywhere." He further described to the *Age* how the public's pleasure at hearing the song became the "town talk."

Praise nationally for Handy's music eventually was just as positive in print from both black and white writers. Among white audiences, Hiram Moderwell had established himself by 1915 as one of the nation's most regarded commentators on both theatrical and popularly performed music, and that year he praised to the readership of the recently established periodical *The New Republic,* the music of ragtime as the "one, true American music." Objecting that for too long ragtime had been "officially beyond the pale," Moderwell distinguished Handy's composition by name—albeit considering it a "rag"—specifically noting the "tender pathos of 'The Memphis Blues.'" James Weldon Johnson also wrote with pride, in an article for the genteel readership of *The Literary Digest* entitled "The Negro's Contribution to American Art," of Handy's transmuted ragtime song possessing "not only great melodic beauty, but a polyphonic structure that is amazing."

Yet for all this future critical acclaim, Handy in a practical sense might just as well have gone and caught himself some air. For most of his songs' popularity in the early decades of the twentieth century, he gained not a penny in royalties. In what was unquestionably the worst business decision of his professional life, within three years of composing "Mr. Crump," Handy had lost control of his copyright claim to the score. Handy had indeed made one of the nation's first blues songs, but he would lose ownership of it by 1912 in exchange for a quick fifty dollars.

———

CHAPTER SEVEN

Handy's Memphis Copyright Blues, 1910–1913

That melancholy strain, that ever-haunting refrain
Is like a Darkies' sorrow song, . . . the Memphis Blues.

—"The Memphis Blues," new
words and arrangement by
George A. Norton, 1913

Handy came into my office in 1910, about a year after I was elected," Edward Crump reminisced in the late 1930s to a Memphis newspaper reporter. Handy must have approached this visit to the new mayor's office with some trepidation. Even in his initial year of political power, Crump was an intimidating presence. A very tall, truculent-looking man with fiery red hair contrasting with nearly translucent white skin, Crump dressed with a noticeable vanity in custom-made suits with blue silk shirts and showy cravats, which almost distracted a visitor's attention from the habitually grim set of his prominent jaw. The "Red Snapper" was how the mayor was known by his political associates, although never so called to his face. For his part, Handy had brought something exceptional, and, perhaps, familiarly insulting, to show the new mayor of Memphis. However risky to Handy personally, he felt he must obtain the mayor's permission in order to use what he handed over. "He had the words of the song written out on a big piece of brown wrapping paper," Crump told the reporter.

"The song" was, of course, Handy's "Mr. Crump," which the

bandleader had been playing throughout that year to patrons at the Alaskan Roof Garden and at other cabarets in the city. Crump had been seemingly unaware of this song bearing his family name as having been performed with such enthusiasm throughout all the wards of Memphis, where the city's new mayor was breezily told in song "to catch himself some air." Yet he that day had found time between serious matters to glance quickly at Handy's lyrics. "He asked me to read them and asked my permission to name the song 'Mr. Crump's Blues,'" the mayor later recalled.

It must have been encouraging to Handy that he had been at least allowed to meet with the mayor in his office that day in 1910. Whatever his failings, Boss Crump was no Governor James Vardaman, the die-hard White Chief during Handy's prior residence in Mississippi. Within limits, Edward Crump was willing to consider African Americans as his constituents, an instance that showed Jim Crow politics could on occasion make for strange bedfellows. Crump from the beginning of his mayoral reign in 1910 knew that his political dominance of Memphis and his future control of much of the state of Tennessee depended upon his ability to deliver the votes of his city as a bloc to his personally chosen candidates of the Democratic Party. Memphis, the most populous city within the state, could—if properly controlled by Crump—outnumber the voters of the rural counties or the returns of the precinct boxes from the smaller cities of Nashville or Knoxville. As blacks were registered in significant numbers within his Mississippi River city, they therefore were an important plurality for Crump in his planned political state machine. Crump's political machine, including its Memphis black votes, would in fact succeed in controlling elections in Tennessee until the end of the first Truman administration. In 1910, Crump well appreciated the benefits to himself, and to his future ambitions, of a limited franchise for blacks, and he was willing to reward it so long as it was controlled by him. The Red Snapper might have been pitiless toward those who dared oppose him (at least until the 1940s, white politicians from Nashville who opposed Crump avoided speaking in Memphis upon what may have been well-founded fears of murder by the Memphis underworld of undercover police officers), but among Crump's better qualities was an inclination to help those who had helped him, or at least not thwart them. For example, among the first actions he took upon assuming his mayoral office in 1910 was to fund, at long last, a municipal park for the city's African Americans.

Therefore, in regard to this black composer, Crump probably did not care what Handy had sung about him on the courthouse square or along Beale Avenue, or even at a white supper club, so long as Handy helped bring out the African American votes for him. The mayor looked up from reading the words on the brown wrapping paper. "I told him it would be all right," Crump later recalled saying to Handy.

Handy's visit had been a chosen risk in his campaign to market his new song. As he later told the New York *Age*, he had become "tired of writing so many manuscripts" by hand for its local admirers, and he was determined to sell the score locally and nationally in a printed version. In the early handwritten versions, the song perhaps had been known as "Mr. Crump's Blues," as the city's mayor later specifically remembered it. But by 1912, when Handy first sought a publisher, he decided to broaden its appeal nationally and in the state by awkwardly retitling his blues tune "Memphis Blues or (Mr. Crump)."

Handy optimistically spent some of the future revenues from this song by purchasing a slightly larger house for his family at 659 Janette Street, a comparatively more respectable street of Greasy Plank. A one-story "shotgun" style wooden frame house, with front and rear doors aligned in a straight shot for better cross-ventilation in Memphis's sweltering summers, it boasted the respectability of neatly painted trim; a front porch, perhaps ten feet in length, on which to receive visitors; and a large, curtained front window. This small house would become quite crowded, as a fourth child, Elizabeth, was born to the Handys there, joining the household with her brother, William, and sisters, Lucile and Katharine. A second son, Wyer, soon followed. A child who did not survive infancy, Florence, named for her father's Alabama hometown, had been born at the Ayers Street house. (Handy was away at the time of this child's death, playing an engagement in Mississippi.) Handy's younger brother, Charles, already had moved from Alabama to join the six others at this Memphis house, following the death of their father.

Handy's hopes of national financial success for "The Memphis Blues or (Mr. Crump)" in 1912 rested upon the individual sales of printed scores and not upon industrially manufactured recordings. The Edison Records Company that same year had introduced the Blue Amberol record cylinder, made of celluloid and capable of playing recorded music for about four minutes at a fidelity quite superior to the older technology using wax cylinders; but neither this new technology nor the even newer shellac-coated disks, or "records," were yet widespread. Neither were the machines required to play the cylinders or disks. Success in the music business in 1912 remained the purview of individuals who bought music scores.

These usually middle-class purchasers were prompted to purchase a score either by its prominent display in retail stores or by its performance onstage by popular artists. Theatrical adaptation of a song was therefore vitally important. Equally essential to a song's success was for the nationally distributed printed sheets to be scored for the piano for home performances. The year of Handy's original composition of "Mr. Crump" in 1909 had coincided with the peak of ownership of pianos by households in the United States. "A considerable number of homes in those days had a piano with a stack of sheet music," a gentleman from Memphis recalled in 1960 of his boyhood growing up within a genteel white neighborhood of that Tennessee city half a century earlier.

Accordingly, Handy tried to sell "The Memphis Blues or (Mr. Crump)" arranged for the piano to New York City music publishers with national distributions. He had no success. Apparently quickly scanning Handy's manuscript as a ragtime but failing to appreciate the effects of its twelve-bar measures, the publishers wrote Handy to try again and resubmit later, after he had completed the final four bars for the usual sixteen-bar strains. Rather than changing his composition, Handy on the advice of a Memphis sheet music salesman paid out of his pocket a total of $32.50 to the Otto Zimmerman & Son music printing firm of Newport, Kentucky, to print one thousand copies of his song as he had written it, and he tried himself to sell printed scores to music stores in Memphis. He had hopes thereby of attracting the attention of music salesmen on their southern sales calls and obtaining a national publishing contract for his song. The Memphis counter salesman promised Handy he would do his best to promote the song at the local department store where he worked.

Handy soon discovered that although the early blues in 1912 were "the stuff people wanted," as he had observed about the Mississippi folk blues played to white audiences, it did not necessarily follow that blues composers known locally to be African American were particularly marketable. He was shocked when a white merchant whom he had considered his friend, Oliver Kershner Houck, refused to stock any of the printed scores for "The Memphis Blues or (Mr. Crump)" at his music company on Front Street, north of Beale and the city's invisible Jim Crow line. The reason was not any fear by the merchant of offending the new mayor. Rather, in Handy's recollection, Houck told him that the merchant's "trade wouldn't stand for his selling my work," that is, scores by a composer well known in Memphis to be a man of color. When Handy gently pointed out to Houck that there were displayed at that moment in the store's front window popular musical scores by the popular minstrel and vaudeville team of Bert Williams and George Walker, as well as by other "colored" composers, Houck smiled. "I'll never forget that smile," Handy wrote. "Yes," this Memphis merchant pleasantly agreed in his final refusal. "I know that—but my customers don't." Handy left the store without a sale.

(The times, and the trade, changed. Houck's store within the next decade began to advertise its large inventory of "talking machine records" about the time that Handy would leave the Tennessee city for residence in New York City; and before the O. K. Houck Piano Company permanently closed its doors in Memphis in 1967, four decades after the death of its founder, the store's celebrated customers had included both B. B. King and Elvis Presley, the latter a lover of African American music who in 1955 bought his first upright piano at Houck's.)

Handy consequently made the worst business decision of his life. He sold his claim to the copyright to "The Memphis Blues or (Mr. Crump)" for fifty dollars. The buyer was Theron Catlin Bennett. A white music publisher with connections in New York City, Bennett (1879–1937) was a Missouri native and a popular ragtime composer, and, like Handy, had an ear for folk and street music. Indeed, Bennett's musical career might be considered almost a parody of Handy's later artistic accomplishments and ambitions. Bennett was the author not of the "St. Louis Blues" but of the "St. Louis Tickle," which he had composed in 1904. Bennett was also the composer of the then often-played bluesy rag "Pork and Beans" (1904), and, eventually, as published blues commercially supplanted ragtime music in 1916, the author of "Some Blues (For You All)." His purchase of "The Memphis Blues or (Mr. Crump)" in 1912 was not a philharmonic act, much less an altruistic attempt to aid a struggling fellow blues artist. Rather, Handy seems to have been the victim of a considered confidence game played by Bennett and a Memphis music salesman, L. Z. Phillips.

Phillips was the local sheet music salesman who had encouraged Handy to have his song printed at Handy's own expense. He rented space behind the music counter at Bry's Department Store, then perhaps Memphis's finest retail store, located at Main and Jefferson, and was also an acquaintance of Theron Bennett's. The latter, with his sales connections outside of Memphis, would promote sales of the score outside of Tennessee, Handy had been told by Phillips. One thousand copies enclosed in smart blue covers, paid for by Handy, thus had been subsequently delivered to Memphis. The scores had been printed with the title "The Memphis Blues (or Mr. Crump)" with white lettering against a blue background, and credited in type to "Handy Music Co., Memphis, Tenn.," with the additional line of "Theron C. Bennett as selling agent." Bennett had turned up in Memphis apparently by chance just as the proofs for the scores had arrived and generously had agreed to let his name be associated with these two amateurs' efforts.

"The Memphis Blues or (Mr. Crump)" went on sale at Bry's, advertised as Phillips had promised, on September 28, 1912. Handy, as previously recounted, had taken some of the scores to sell on his own, at such smaller businesses as the O. K. Houck Piano Company, leaving the bulk of the order for Phillips to move. But after Handy had returned, nearly sale-less, to check his inventory a week later, his bad fortune was compounded by what he was shown behind Bry's counter. Nearly a thousand copies remained, seemingly unsold. Bennett then declared himself willing to take this appar-

ently unsellable song off the hands of the composer and his friend
Phillips. The ragtime man offered Handy fifty dollars for all future
copyright rights (Handy had presumptive rights as publisher but had
not yet registered his copyright with the Library of Congress) and
for all future royalties to the "The Memphis Blues or (Mr. Crump)."
Handy accepted.

Only later in 1912, when Handy saw a new printing and retitling
of "The Memphis Blues" (now with the parenthetical reference to
"Mr. Crump" excised, and identified as a "southern rag"), did he
learn the full duplicity of Bennett and Phillips. The score was illustrated with, in Handy's words, a "white fiddler" on the cover. Handy
subsequently learned that Bennett, after his purchase of the copyright privileges, had ordered ten thousand new copies printed from
Zimmerman & Son in order to fulfill anticipated orders for the blues
song, which Bennett on the sly had been talking up to music store
owners in large cities outside of Memphis as a most "unusual tune."
And, as Handy also later learned, the thousand apparently unsold
copies he had been shown by Phillips at Bry's sales counter were the
second order for a printing, received in secret. The first order of a
thousand copies of Handy's song had sold out in Memphis within
three days. Bennett two decades later revealed that he had known,
and presumably had been in collusion with Phillips, about this
deception. Within a year after Handy had first seen the original blue
covers of his first printed song, the republished score of "The Memphis Blues," copyright registered and now legally owned by Bennett
and a New York publishing firm, had another press run of fifty thousand copies on September 20, 1913. Handy received not a penny in
royalties.

As a sad consolation, Phillips and Bennett's near-larcenous
action—"song sharking" as it was known by the turn of the
century—apparently was a professionally enacted "long con" that
might have fooled even a more worldly man than Handy. The song's
unusual twelve-bar structure had made credible to Handy, at least
when shown the "unsold" second thousand copies by Phillips, that
customers looking for entertaining music to play on their pianos at
home had avoided buying the unfamiliar and difficult scoring of
"The Memphis Blues or (Mr. Crump)." And as a cold comfort,

Handy and his orchestra at least received some free publicity when he was credited on the cover of the new printing of "The Memphis Blues" as its composer. When a New York City music publisher, which subsequently joined forces with Bennett to market this song, paid George A. Norton to write lyrics (Handy's revised version of the "Memphis Blues" having had none), Norton generously referenced Handy prominently in the new lyrics:

Folks, I've just been down, down to Memphis town,
That's where the people smile, smile at you all the while.
Hospitality, they were good to me.
I couldn't spend a dime, and had the grandest time.
I went out dancing with a Tennessee dear,
They had a fellow there named Handy with a band you should hear.
And while the dancers gently swayed, all the band folks played
Real harmony.
I never forget the tune that Handy called the Memphis Blues.
Oh them blues.
They had a fiddler there who always slicks his hair
And, folks, he sure does pull some bow.
And when the big bassoon seconds to the trombone's croon
It moans just like a sinner on Revival Day, on Revival Day.

That melancholy strain, that ever haunting refrain
Is like a Darkie's sorrow song.
Here comes the very part that wraps a spell around my heart.
It sets me wild to hear that loving tune again, the Memphis Blues.

These are the words to which "The Memphis Blues" was first sung in 1913 on a national tour promoted by Bennett and others. And, with a cruel theatrical irony, the performer featured on this tour was a vocalist who onstage merely pretended to be an African American. He was the blackface minstrel and theatrical contemporary of Al Jolson, George "Honey Boy" Evans. An immigrant from Wales who had gained fame as a whiteface minstrel singing the 1907 sentimental number "I'll Be True to My Honey Boy," Evans on this national minstrel tour in blackface now sang the lyrics, supplied by a white author, that purportedly expressed a "darkie's sorrow song." Almost certainly the lyrics irritated Handy on his first hearing them—the words lack the sure poetic and colloquial grasp of his lyricism at its best—and he later rather sourly speculated that Norton in his lyrics referred to an instrument of Handy's group as a bassoon, which the band did not use, because Norton probably never had heard a saxophone, which Handy's band did employ. But the lines do show that Norton had an ear cocked for the piquant, overheard expression. Particularly good is the memorable line *Folks, he sure does pull some bow.* Either of the Wyer brothers employed on violin, Ed or Paul, could not have asked in 1913 for a compliment of more brio.

"The Memphis Blues" subsequently has become known by Norton's lyrics, which are sung by Louis Armstrong in his urbane versions of Handy's compositions recorded in the 1950s. Despite whatever dissatisfactions one may speculate that Handy had with these words as white "cover" lyrics, they later would have a remarkably bluesy and authentically rural sound when sung by the African American vocalist Monette Moore in 1925 with the Texas Trio. To current-day blues listeners, many of whom exclusively identify the blues with a primitive, or at least simple, arrangement and with lyrics that are plangently sung, Moore's version is remarkably affecting, partially because she uses a "shouting blues" style and is accompanied on this recording for Ajax Records only by a ukulele, a banjo, and a harmonica. Her version, rather than Armstrong's orchestrated recording, gives modern listeners more of a feel for what prompted its first audiences to regard "The Memphis Blues," as Bennett had promised them, as an enjoyably "unusual tune."

Folks, I've just been down, down to Memphis town, / That's where the people smile, smile at you all the while. Handy probably heard this verse seemingly innumerable times throughout 1912–1913, but he was perhaps the only resident of Memphis who on hearing the blues song had no reason to smile. He could only watch, not participate in, the commercial triumph of "The Memphis Blues." The minstrel tour of his song for white audiences was followed by a Columbia Phonographic Company issue of "The Memphis Blues" with its Norton-composed lyrics sung in an affected black dialect by two white comedians, the "coon duo" of Arthur Collins and Byron G. Harlan. In an effort to reach exclusively African American markets, the song also was performed with great success by the black vaudevillians Arsceola and Birleanna Blanks. They were a dancing-and-singing sister act who played the TOBA circuit of Jim Crow vaudeville theaters and whose performances of the song to black audiences included appearances at Memphis theaters. The sisters also took the song on the road. The *Freeman* in 1914 reviewed the Blanks sisters' appearance on the vaudeville stage in Indianapolis, noting that the two "wore green and gold for the 'Amazon' number and then the quick change for 'The Memphis Blues' revealed the ladies in satin and lace." The year earlier, the *Freeman* hyperbolically had observed in Dallas, "the whole town whistling 'Them Memphis Blues.'"

After the blackface vaudeville success of Honey Boy Evans and his minstrels on tour singing "The Memphis Blues"—and the rapid selling of the press run of scores—the song achieved an even greater crossover success in the spring and late summer of 1914, when it was adopted as a signature tune by two professional and highly popular ballroom dancers, the white couple Vernon and Irene Castle. It was recorded as a dance tune in October of that year by the Victor company under the supervision of the Castles and performed by the Castles' all-black touring orchestra, Europe's Society Orchestra, in an arrangement by the orchestra leader, James Reese Europe. The Castles devised easy-to-learn dance steps to an arrangement of "The Memphis Blues" that consequently swept the nation's ballrooms as the wildly popular dance known as the foxtrot. (Playing in Europe's orchestra was Handy's former colored minstrel acquaintance Cricket Smith, who as a member of the Mahara troupe had occasioned the Tyler, Texas, lynching threat during Handy's minstrelsy tour with his wife.)

The Castles credited Europe with creating the music for their dance, but Europe—like Handy an Alabamian with classical music training, an orchestra leader who was beginning to sell significant numbers of the new phonograph discs for the Victor Talking Machine Company, and an arranger who at thirty-four years of age in 1918 might have given Handy a run for his money for the title of "Father of the Blues"—consistently told newspapers that the credit

for his dance composition and the foxtrot "really belongs to Handy."
Europe then intriguingly added, "You see, then, that both the tango
and the foxtrot are really negro [*sic*] dances." Europe's assertion in
1914 that the tango was becoming a distinctively African American
rhythm for dances was in step with Handy's long fascination with
the "Tangana" rhythms and his adoption of the tango rhythms in his
composition of 1913, "Jogo Blues" and, most famously, in his 1914
composition the "St. Louis Blues."

But as for the song of the moment, "The Memphis Blues" was
justly considered by later critics to have been the first "diffusion of
the blues into mainstream American culture." Handy, of course,
also profited at least indirectly from the national publicity of the
song's lyrics—*a fellow there named Handy with a band you should hear*—
and he continued to be the preeminent popular-music orchestra
leader throughout Memphis and northern Mississippi and Alabama.
But until twenty-eight years later when the copyright expired in 1940
and he was able to repurchase the rights, this word-of-mouth publicity was all Handy gained from his song's publication. And, in what
must have been a further coruscating irony to Handy, the Houck
Piano Company later displayed Bennett's new reissue of "The
Memphis Blues" prominently in its storefront window with a life-
sized photograph of Handy that was placed, as the composer later
remembered it, "standing beside a Victor talking machine with an
ear bent to hear the new Jim Europe recording of my song."

Considered legally, of course, whenever Handy referred to "The
Memphis Blues" in 1914 he could no longer speak of this blues com-
position being "my" song. But as the Beale Avenue easy riders
whose antics Handy celebrated in his 1909 original version of "Mr.
Crump" would have put it, he at least had been wise to the main
action, even if he had not succeeded in getting himself a piece of it.
When he had published his original "The Memphis Blues or (Mr.
Crump)," the tempo had been printed on the score as "Tempo à la
Blues," indicating that the blues were by then sufficiently familiar to
pianists so that most performers would know to play Handy's song
more slowly than ragtime's usual tempo. The blues were then
beginning to displace ragtime as the nation's most diverting popular
music, and Handy was well positioned to take advantage of this

change in the popular taste. This change had begun, at least on paper, more than a decade earlier, when an African American songwriter from Charleston, South Carolina, Christopher "Chris" Smith, published in 1901 his composition "I've Got de Blues" with the Lyceum Publishing Company of New York. This was probably the first published musical work with the word *blues* in its title used in the modern sense. For the remainder of the decade, few other American songs entitled with "blues" were published or registered for copyright, with the notable exception of Antonio Maggio's composition published in New Orleans in 1908, also titled, interestingly, "I Got the Blues." By the end of 1912, "The Memphis Blues" had become the fifth tune registered for copyright or published that year in the United States with a "blues" title. These five songs show the birth of published or urban blues as a modern and important genre. And, as with the advent of any birth, they soon changed all that came later in popular American music.

None of the five composers that year seemed then to have known one another, nor were they exclusively African American. Certainly, for the next few years, with the notable exception of "The Memphis Blues," this music would have predominantly African American audiences. But the simultaneous appearances in 1912 of these five songs—written or published in Memphis, Oklahoma City, Dallas, New York City, and St. Louis—indicate that Handy was placing his finger firmly upon the pulse of what was to become the rhythm of a popular *national* music, for blacks and whites alike.

Of these early blues songs and their composers—Chris Smith's probably reworked earlier song of 1901, now in 1912 titled "I've Got the Blues (But I'm Too Blamed Mean to Cry)"; Hart Wand's "Dallas Blues"; Leroy White's "Negro Blues"; Arthur Matthews's arrangement of the signature stage tune and lyrics written by the black vaudevillian Franklin "Baby" Seals, entitled the "Baby Seals Blues"; and "The Memphis Blues"—none were "country" blues, as the black folk blues were then known. And none had been performed earlier as they were now scored by rural musicians such as Charley Patton, either from the Mississippi Delta or elsewhere. (As will be seen later, Patton admired Handy's blues but felt unable to play them.)

The later exclusive understanding of the blues as a folk music originating in the Mississippi Delta and performed by formally untrained musicians such as Patton would belong to a later generation. The blues as they first were known nationally or regionally in the early twentieth century were composed by urban men such as Handy, and all five of these composers had worked successfully in other forms of commercial musical entertainment before writing their blues in 1912. Handy and Leroy White had been, respectively, a colored and a blackface minstrel; Chris Smith was a popular composer of such earlier nonblues songs as "Good Morning, Carrie"; Hart Wand was a professional violin player and the leader of a dance orchestra; Baby Seals was a greatly celebrated vaudeville performer on the black circuit; and "Artie" Matthews was a ragtime composer and, later, a music teacher at a Cincinnati conservatory. Yet all these composers together employed verbal and musical phrases used earlier by itinerant, nonurban blues singers, and their designations of their songs as "blues" rather than "rags" indicate that they were aware they were composing in a new genre.

In fact, Chris Smith (1879–1949) stole a march from Handy in 1912 when Smith also registered a copyright that year for his arrangement and words of "The Last Shot Got Him," a country blues that Handy had tried to claim as something of a signature tune for his band in the Mississippi Delta. Had he not chosen to continue in ragtime and to concentrate on adapting popular theatrical numbers, Smith, much like James Europe later in this first decade of the twentieth century, could have given Handy a serious run for his money for the historical title as a potential Father of the Blues.

Of these five early blues songs of 1912, only "The Memphis Blues" achieved a popularity beyond the regional. Upon this song's success firmly rests Handy's later preeminence as the "Father of the Blues." However, given his unquestioned reliance upon rearranging country blues, three questions must be addressed in evaluating Handy's "The Memphis Blues" as among the progenitor of America's blues music: What did Handy originate, what he did copy, and what did he rearrange?

Foremost in his use among these four other composers was Handy's very free adaptation of what are sometimes called "floating" blues phrases in twelve bars from the folk blues. Handy personally called them "snatches," and he had used these melodies and words in such earlier Mississippi compositions as his folk-adopted "Make Me a Pallet on Your Floor." Both the twelve-bar introduction and saucy lyrics of "Mr. Crump" recall snatches of the earlier black folk tune "Momma Don't Allow." And, as will be seen, black Memphis vaudeville performers also had heard, and adapted, the folk "Momma Don't Allow" at the same time Handy was claiming this melody as his own. This was not to be the first black folk blues adopted by Handy that black vaudeville artists claimed they had adapted before him.

But it was not simply African American composers or performers who took inspiration from the black folk blues. The truth was that both black and white composers and performers since the time of Daddy Rice had utilized black folk music for commercial performances. Handy simply claimed the snatches more frequently. Black folk tunes also had been adapted in 1912 not only by the African American composers such as Handy and Chris Smith but also by a former blackface minstrel, the white performer Leroy White, in composing the musical notes and words of his "Negro Blues." Recorded later on Columbia Records by the white comedian George H. O'Connor, who specialized in mimicking African American dialect, and retitled for release as the "Nigger Blues," White's folk-inspired lyrics ran: *Oh, the blues ain't nothing, / Oh, the blues ain't nothing / But a good man feelin' bad.* Both in its melody and words, this phrase had been floating around African American folk blues for years.

Additionally, Hart Wand's "Dallas Blues" also shares some floating black folk lyrics—*"I've got the blues but I'm too mean to, I said mean to, I mean cry."* (To his credit, Wand's copyright registration refers to the music as "anonymous," although the same certainly could also be accurately said of Wand's lyrics, which are simply a pastiche of black folk blues lyrics.) Chris Smith in turn had also used this folk lyric from Wand's "Dallas Blues" to be the title of Smith's own blues song published that same year, "I've Got the Blues (But I'm Too Blamed Mean to Cry)." The scholar of black folk blues Abbe Niles later called the variations of this African American folk verse—"got the blues but too mean to cry"—the "common property of the race." This common use of floating black verbal and musical phrases among these five should not obscure its novelty. The daring use of African American folk phrases by Handy, Smith, White, Wand, and Seals in what were intended as popular songs for mass audiences was certainly innovative in 1912. Among the most frequently performed songs that year were "The Sweetheart of Sigma Chi" and "When It's Apple Blossom Time in Normandy."

In using such black folk snatches, Handy—perhaps only equaled later by his fellow Alabamian Baby Seals—must be considered to have been the quickest to realize the artistic and performance possibilities of the call-and-response structure so idiosyncratic of black spirituals and folk blues lyrics and, later, the published blues lyrics. For instance, in Handy's version of what was described in the 1920s as "the prototype of all the blues," the folk song "Joe Turner," transcribed by Howard Odum in northern Mississippi at the turn of the century, there is a tripartite line arrangement that can normally be sung in two-four time, or common time, within four bars:

> They tell me Joe Turner's come and gone,
> Tell me Joe Turner's come and gone,
> Got my man—and—gone!

In his adaptation of this tripartite folk snatch structure of "Joe Turner's Blues" to his more sophisticated, published version of the song in 1915, Handy recognized that the first lyric line of a folk blues could be repeated in the second line, and then be written to be answered by the third line in an irreverent, rueful, or salacious manner. He had begun this gleeful use of the twelve-bar measure and lyrics as early as 1909 in his lyrics to "Mr. Crump":

> Mr. Crump don't 'low no easy riders here,
> Mr. Crump don't 'low no easy riders here,
> We don't care what Mr. Crump don't 'low!

This call-and-response was subsequently heard and exuberantly used in the published "Baby Seals Blues." (Seals, like the Blanks sisters a performer for the TOBA, died on the road in Anniston, Alabama, in 1915. As early as 1913, this articulate vaudeville performer was being promoted in black society as the "Famous Writer of 'Blues.'") Baby Seals's crowd-pleasing call-and-response in his signature tune during his brief lifetime was repeated licentiously in countless small Jim Crow vaudeville theaters throughout the South, including Memphis by 1912:

> Oh sing 'em, sing 'em,
> Sing them blues,
> 'Cause they cert'ly sound good to me!

As also can be seen from the above, the early published blues at times—but not always—had a melancholy theme, or told of an unfaithful or absent lover. But sometimes, as in the early blues of Handy or Baby Seals, this new genre of the blues, like early rock and roll decades later, celebrated the overthrow of social authority, as in "Mr. Crump," or the pleasures of carnality, as in *"They cert'ly sound good to me!"*

Handy, like Hart Wand in his "Dallas Blues," additionally established another distinct convention for composers and performers of the published blues that continued into the 1920s. This was their choice of balladlike storytelling and geographic wandering along specifically named sites. Here again Handy was the quickest among all these competitors to notice what popularly worked. Although Wand's song was little more than the bluesy lament of a hungover easy rider returning home told with "floating" blues lyrics—*"Baby, bring a cold towel for my head (my aching head) / Got the Dallas blues and your loving man / Is almost dead (almost dead)"*—Handy would later compose music and write lyrics at greater length of the narrative of a wandering easy rider set along the route of the Delta & Mississippi Valley railroad line in his celebrated song "Yellow Dog Blues." He also would wonderfully tell in a later song the specific events and sights of a typical day and night among African Americans in the geographically titled "Beale Street Blues."

And, finally, each of these five compositions of 1912 also shared, to one extent or the other, the "blue note." Handy probably first had reliably transcribed this sound of the folk blues into a written score, and by the second decade of the century he was personally identified with its innovation. A cover sheet of "The Memphis Blues" printed soon after Handy's sale of the copyright advertises the score as "George A. Norton's Song, Founded on W. C. Handy's World Wide 'Blue' Note Melody." Yet other composers, either in imitation or independently, used these unexpected minor and flatted notes. Some blues songs, such as the "Negro Blues," have few of them; others, such as "Dallas Blues," make greater use. This latter score also contains twelve-bar strains, and the performer is instructed to play it "Tempo dí Blues (Very slowly)." Hart Wand's underappreciated song thus actually sounds more "bluesy" and less like ragtime to modern listeners than does Handy's original score of "Mr. Crump." But after the national appearance of "The Memphis Blues," Handy more than any other of these early blues composers achieved preeminence by his skill at inserting blue notes, combining the call-and-response of the three lines of black folk music, and employing the tonal architectures of ragtime into a new, published blues. Handy now was just a year away from writing the most famous call-and-response to the most famous published blues song of the twentieth century, the "St. Louis Blues."

Thus were the commercial blues born in 1912–13, W. C. Handy of Memphis being their practical maker and their nominal father with at least four other black and white composers in attendance. "The Memphis Blues" can with accuracy be called the foremost if not exactly the first of the published blues, and it was Handy's composition that gave that popular genre its commercial future. This future eventually would include the success of the "St. Louis Blues," and for Handy would be both prosperous and troubled, part of the ambiguity that always defined his life as a person and as an artist.

With the success of "The Memphis Blues" and the emergence in 1913 of the urban blues as a popular musical art, Handy had "stood at the door of his big opportunity," as his Beale Avenue acquaintance George Lee later put it. But with his rash sale of his copyright to two song sharks, Handy had closed this door for himself, at least in regard to financial rewards for the particular song, for nearly the next three decades, until that song's copyright expired. Before then, he would have to re-create his success as best he could. Whatever his justified anger or bitterness, however, Handy did not dwell on these feelings, at least not noticeably.

As part of his chosen persona as an artist and businessman, W. C.

Handy always appeared as a sort of black "Mr. Micawber," the perennially optimistic and frequently penniless fictional character created by Charles Dickens, always confident that "something would turn up." Handy believed all reversals were merely temporary, or at least instructional. "A headache and heartache" was how Handy pithily chose to summarize his decades of lost royalties to "The Memphis Blues"—and he expressed that lament in print only after he finally was able to repurchase that song's copyright in 1940. But in 1913, whatever his unadvertised heartaches over his lost song, Handy already had determined to lose no time in replacing its popularity by writing new blues tunes. That year he began his extraordinary five-year period of musical creativity at Memphis, during which he would write the songs that would enter his name permanently into the canon of great blues composers—"Yellow Dog Rag," later "Yellow Dog Blues" (1914); "Beale Street," later "Beale Street Blues" (1917); and the "St. Louis Blues" (1914). As the original dates of composition and later retitles indicate, he was beginning to trust the use of the word *blues* in his titles.

"Mr. Handy is just at the meridian of life," a reporter for the *Freeman* wrote for its readers in the autumn of 1914, the year that the forty-one-year-old Handy composed the "St. Louis Blues" and one year after the first national marketing of "The Memphis Blues" under another man's ownership. This reporter found him "pleasant and unassuming in manner, an interesting conversationalist with that lack of self-assertiveness that is peculiar to the true genius"; and, interestingly, presumably as the result of a visit to the composer's house, now at 659 Janette Street, the reporter also noted that Handy "has one of the most complete musical libraries owned by a Negro anywhere." After the inevitable observation that Handy's unhappy sale of "The Memphis Blues" for fifty dollars has "brought many thousands of dollars to its purchaser," the *Freeman* reporter further continued his profile of Handy and his career in words that were remarkably prescient for the future evaluation of "The Memphis Blues," as well as remarkably accurate in regard to Handy's personal ambitions and the Dvořák prophecy. As the reporter wrote:

When Mr. Handy wrote the "Memphis Blues" he builded [*sic*] better than he knew. He was censured by many for writing what they claimed was an inferior piece of music and greatly below his standard as a composer. It is a unique composition, having but twelve measures to a strain instead of sixteen. Its rapid increase in popularity everywhere makes it a psychological study and it is bound to become a classic of its kind just as the real compositions of Will Marion Cooke [sic], Scott Joplin, and other Negro composers are now considered to be the only real expression of Negro music and the only genuine American music.

Handy indeed had built better than he knew. At this commencement of his national career as a blues artist, he had learned three hard, constructive lessons. First, never sell a copyright. He now knew that the real money to be made in popular music was not in the performance of a blues song, or even in its recording, but in the ownership of the copyrights to these songs, which continued to accumulate money nationally long after an audience listening to a particular performance had gone home. Second, he had learned that even should he succeed in keeping the copyright and obtaining an honest publisher with national distribution for his sheet music, he needed his compositions to be identified with a white performer to gain national acceptance by retailers or audiences. Handy cannily observed how Theron Bennett had first marketed "The Memphis Blues" with an illustration on its reprinted covers of a "white fiddle player," and how Bennett had introduced the song nationally with the minstrel troupe led by Honey Boy Evans, well known to be white under the burnt cork makeup. Additional undisputable evidence was available to Handy on his need for a crossover. The African American stage venue alone had not provided sufficient national sales for the success of the blues tune, however enthusiastic had been the audiences of black vaudeville to performances by the Blanks sisters of "The Memphis Blues." Further national sales of this song had not occurred until after Vernon and Irene Castle had heard this tune and given it their endorsement by "fronting" it before James Europe's black orchestra.

The final, third lesson learned by the composer from the loss of "The Memphis Blues" was that he was in sore need of a trust-worthy partner with a greater business sense than his own. Prefer-ably, this person would be an educated African American male from the middle or upper classes in order to have Handy's full confidence and emotional kinship. Handy could not, for instance, have part-nered equitably and personally comfortably with an uneducated rural bluesman such as Charley Patton or even a highly articulate but definitely vulgar vaudevillian such as Franklin "Baby" Seals. And although Handy was thoughtful and protective toward the older, talented, alcoholic, and non-score-reading Jim Turner, their relation-ship definitely was one of Handy as employer toward an employee. An appreciation of popular music and the verbal skills required of lyrics would be welcome, but this future partner should necessarily possess a bookkeeping background, and, whether Handy was will-ing to admit it or not, a cautious personality to counterbalance Handy's own Micawberlike optimism and his impulsive vulnerabil-ity to song sharks and bad business decisions. He was lucky to find such a future partner already living in the city in the person of a for-mer student of W. E. B. Du Bois and a current employee at the Beale Avenue bank owned by Robert Church Sr. This future partner of Handy's was the bank's cashier, Harry H. Pace. Together, as the operators of the Pace & Handy Music Company, W. C. Handy and Harry Pace would make Memphis the capital of the nation's pub-lished blues music from 1914 to 1918.

—

CHAPTER EIGHT

Tempo à Blues

PACE & HANDY, BEALE AVENUE
MUSIC PUBLISHERS, 1913–1917

PACE & HANDY MUSIC CO.

"Home of the Blues"

H. H. PACE,

Formerly Cashier Solvent Savings Bank and Trust Co., Memphis, Tenn.,
Secretary Standard Life Insurance Co., Atlanta, Ga.,

PRESIDENT

W. C. HANDY,

Composer of *"The Memphis Blues,"*

MANAGER

> —Pace & Handy Company
> promotion, *Freeman*,
> November 15, 1913

W. C. Handy was not the only ambitious black businessman of the time who had moved to Memphis. When
W. E. B. Du Bois had obtained financial backing in 1905 to become
the publisher of a weekly newspaper for a national African American readership, he had not chosen his own city of Atlanta as the site
for his future editorial and business offices. Nor had he picked Birmingham or New Orleans, two other southern cities with large black
populations. Instead, Du Bois decided to locate his newspaper—its
masthead entitled the *Moon Illustrated Weekly,* in contradistinction to
the established black newspaper, the *Sun*, sponsored by Booker T.

Washington—in Memphis. Du Bois favored the upper Mississippi River city because one of his former students operated a print shop there on Beale Avenue, and another former student, Harry H. Pace, was willing to relocate from Georgia to Memphis in order to edit the newsweekly advocating Du Bois's views.

Pace accordingly had moved to Memphis in 1905, at about the time Handy had arrived with his family. Du Bois and Pace alike had entertained high hopes for the successful patronage of their planned newspaper, with subscriptions and advertisements to be placed in the *Moon* by the "Beale 400," that approximate number of prosperous and property-owning black families who lived in proximity to Beale Avenue. Indeed, Harry Pace had enjoyed much better prospects for acceptance among the Beale 400 than did W. C. Handy. Handy had possessed few assets upon arriving in Memphis other than his cornet, and few opportunities other than a part-time job with the Colored Knights of Pythias band and a reputation as a hot dance musician in the Mississippi Delta. Pace at least had been able to contribute a share to the $3,000 capitalization for the *Moon*.

Pace had met with a genteel reception. "Mr. Pace is a graduate of Atlanta University and a young man of rare scholarship," a Memphis newspaper for African Americans—which outlasted the *Moon*—consequently wrote of his arrival in the city. This same article also noted that he had been a success in black academia, "and could be there now if he had not elected to engage in business life, where the rewards and possibilities are greater than in school work." Pace had joined several church choirs in Memphis, and the local notice continued: "He is a charming singer and an up-to-date, courteous gentleman."

Pace labored throughout 1905–06 to make the *Moon* a commercial success, a worthy successor to the other local and national newspapers for blacks that once had been circulated from Memphis, most notably the *Memphis Free Speech,* published by the former Mississippi slave Ida B. Wells-Barnett. Initially, the Beale 400 supported the *Moon.* Thomas H. Haynes Sr., the same Beale Avenue undertaker who at times also referred Handy to jobs playing at funerals, paid for occasional lines of advertising in the newspaper: "Finest funeral cars of any colored man in the South." But despite the hopes of Du Bois and Pace, there simply were not yet enough paying advertisers or subscribers of color in Memphis to support the planned national circulation of the newspaper on the scale of the Indianapolis *Freeman* or the later *Chicago Defender.* George Lee well remembered how Pace, trained as a classicist scholar, struggled each week to put out the *Moon:*

> With no money to pay the salaries of an editorial staff, most of the work in getting out the paper fell upon the shoulders of Harry Pace, who not only solicited and edited the material, but set its type, made up the paper, put it on the press and ran it off. . . . Most of the time he was half-hungry and insufficiently clad. At four o'clock Saturday mornings the milkman would see him dragging a United States mail sack down the streets to the post office.

The *Moon* permanently ended publication in the summer of 1906. Du Bois went on to publish the *Crisis,* the official newspaper of the National Association for the Advancement of Colored People, the organization he founded in 1910 in part with the assistance of Ida Wells-Barnett. As for Pace, he left Memphis by mid-1906, intending to return to a career of teaching Latin and Greek at black colleges. But his industriousness had caught the eye of Robert Church Sr., and when a position opened in 1907 at the black-owned Solvent Savings Bank, at 392 Beale Avenue, of which Church was founder and chairman, the likable and hardworking Pace was invited to return to Memphis and fill this position. He accepted. There, in 1907, this young bank cashier made the acquaintance of W. C. Handy.

The business association between Pace and Handy, or at least their first commercial musical collaboration, began that same year. Together they ventured to write in 1907 the song "In the Cotton Fields of Dixie," a conventionally Foster-styled sentimental parlor tune with words by Pace and score by Handy. They pooled their funds and had the song published at their expense by the George Jaberg Music Company of Cincinnati, which failed to keep its promises to promote sales of the sheet music. Their maiden effort at music failed commercially.

Despite this disappointment, the personal friendship between Pace and Handy continued into the second decade of the new century. By 1913, when Handy had determined to recoup his revenue lost subsequent to his sale of "The Memphis Blues," the ambitious orchestra leader and the socially rising cashier again agreed to act in concert as business partners, this time in the music publishing business as well as artistic composition. They would control the copyrighting and marketing of the songs they would either buy from others or compose for themselves.

There was certainly popular music to be heard in the Memphis streets, saloons, theaters, and genteel parlors throughout 1913 that would have been both enticing and vexing to Handy as he planned to reenter the commercial market with his new compositions. Among the most popular American tunes that year were "Fifteen Cents" by that apparently indefatigable early bluesman and composer Chris Smith; "Mammy Jinny's Jubilee," by Lewis Muir and L. Wolfe Gilbert, a coon song scored in ragtime and with lyrics not quite as vitriolic as earlier examples of its genre; and, from Tin Pan Alley, "Snooky Ookums" and "That International Rag," both written by Irving Berlin.

Handy certainly would have been confident that he could compose as well, or better, in any of these genres as the songwriters named above. He even had a new composition at hand, which he had worked on from 1912 to 1913, and with which he hoped to duplicate the commercial success of the "The Memphis Blues." Like the lost song, his new effort also was a musical synthesis, in this instance a black folk blues melody in twelve bars combined with a little ragtime. Later generations would hear portions of this score in the "St. Louis Blues," but for the moment Handy was entitling his new song "The Memphis Itch" and, eventually, the "Jogo Blues." It would be the first published musical effort of the partnership of Pace & Handy. (These two well-educated men always used the ampersand to refer to their company.) They registered the copyright and themselves arranged for the printing and marketing of the score.

Exactly what were the agreements, personal and commercial, made between W. C. Handy and Harry Pace in 1913 as they divided their responsibilities and attempted to market the "Jogo Blues" is uncertain. Although he was more than a decade younger than

Handy (who turned forty that year), Pace's name was always listed first in the advertisements of their partnership. Handy, at least initially, was in charge of publicity for their firm. In mid-November 1913 the Indianapolis *Freeman* published this advertisement:

> The Jogo Blues Now ready for Orchestra Leaders and Pianists. Something original and good by the composer of "The Memphis Blues." Also a beautiful waltz song, "The Girl You Never Have Met," words by H. H. Pace: music by W. C. Handy. For Piano 10¢ Orchestra 25¢ One New Number Each Month Pace & Handy Music Co. Bank Building 392 Beale Ave, Memphis Tenn.

Here was W. C. Handy at his very best, both as a copywriter and as an optimistic Mr. Micawber. The "beautiful waltz song" was in fact another nonblues, sentimental tune composed by Pace and Handy that was instantly forgettable. The "new number every month" was much more of a future hope than a present reality for the new-fledged music publishing firm. Handy himself obviously knew, inferring from his chosen words of self-praise in the company's advertisement, that he was well known only as the composer of "The Memphis Blues," which was now legally another man's song. And the "Jogo Blues," despite a local popularity in Memphis and its composer's description as "new and good," came a cropper when it was published.

The Pace & Handy Company did energetically try to sell the vividly illustrated score of the "Jogo Blues," which had been printed by Otto Zimmerman & Son. (Handy continued to do business with this Kentucky firm in the following decades.) The score's cover was illustrated by an African American male seated in evening dress, an instance to those who understood it to be a signification of the traditionally named black "professor" playing his piano at a saloon or downstairs inside a bordello. "Jogo" was itself a popular colloquial term among African Americans to signify all things authentically of their race. The song was promoted as having been "played by Handy and his bands," and the tune was identified as formerly known as "The Memphis Itch."

The "Jogo Blues" failed in sheet music sales, at best limited to local blacks and as a novelty song performed occasionally for white audiences. Handy later attributed its commercial failure to this instrumental score's complexity and its lack of words. The score was marked "Temp dí Rag à la Memphis Blues," an indication either that even Handy was not yet making a clear artistic distinction between published blues and ragtime or that he wanted to remind the public that he was the original composer of this earlier and still popular song. In assessing his latest song's failure to match "The Memphis Blues" in sales, it also certainly would have been likely for Handy to have considered that this song may have been too "jogo" in its title and cover art for a crossover success. Whatever the reason, the "Jogo Blues" was not irretrievably lost. Its measures would be heard the following year in the chorus of Handy's next composition. He would entitle this new song, almost certainly with an eye toward a broader marketability, the "St. Louis Blues."

Although the latter was Handy's masterpiece, neither he nor anyone else knew that in 1914. The score did not have exceptional sales initially. Pace, meanwhile, had moved in 1913 from Memphis back to Atlanta to take a better-paying job at the Standard Life Insurance Company. While still maintaining his partnership with Handy, he certainly must have occasionally considered that Pace & Handy, like the short-lived *Moon,* was perhaps an admirable idea in theory but in financial practice he was simply putting his money into Handy's pocket, which had a large hole in it. Handy, to meet his household expenses or to keep his various bands on the road, sometimes was reduced to pawning his cornet at Morris Lippman's loan business on Beale.

But 1914 eventually became the year that Pace & Handy—in confirmation of Handy's constant optimism and Pace's intermittent hopes—first saw strong regional sales. Its immediate hit was a song copyrighted that year as the "Yellow Dog Rag," which became known later in the decade as the "Yellow Dog Blues." Handy originally had performed this composition as the "Pattona Rag." (Handy and his band continued to play for Jim Crow cruises on the riverboat, performing on Sunday nights for white passengers and on Monday nights for blacks.) In the initial publication Handy titled his song "Yellow Dog Rag," and, commercially, this dog did run. Its sales far surpassed the "St. Louis Blues."

Handy cleverly wrote the "Yellow Dog" as a musical answer to a popular vaudeville number of 1913, sung in the "coon shouting" style by the white performer Sophie Tucker, "I Wonder Where My Easy Rider's Gone?" (White female coon shouters had been popular onstage since May Irwin's nineteenth-century renditions of the ragtime "Bully of the Town.") Handy's lyrical answer in 1914 to the song's bereft lover, Susan Johnson—*You can hear her moaning night and morn / "Wonder where my Easy Rider's gone?"*—is that her easy-riding "jockey" has jumped aboard a train in Tennessee without paying and is headed for the Deeper South. Such is a genteel summation of this easy rider's exit. In his actual lines to the "Yellow Dog," Handy shows for the first time his remarkably confident grasp of contemporary white slang and of African American dialect as the right words to accompany his music. The rider "had to vamp it" aboard the railroad car, a "rattler," because "he was on the hog" (i.e., without funds). As Handy wrote

> *The smoke was broke,*
> *no joke, not a jitney on him.*

But he had good news for his song's ending. With an inspired use of his past memories of the Mississippi Delta, he wrote "Dear Sue" that she did not have to travel outside the South to find her man, that "the hike ain't far"—

> *He's gone where the Southern*
> *'cross the Yellow Dog.*

This last line was, of course, a reference to Moorhead, Mississippi, where late one night inside the railway station there where the Southern and the Yellow Dog rail lines meet, Handy claimed first to have heard the folk blues.

"Yellow Dog Rag" was quickly picked up as a featured tune by the black vaudevillian singer Estelle Harris, and copies of the sheet music, picturing two trains rushing toward a rural intersection, sold widely among African American buyers. Later editions of the sheet music were illustrated by a lean and libidinous male dog baying at the moon. "Where the Southern 'cross the Yellow Dog" became a kind of subterranean jogo phrase among blues-listening African Americans for the pleasures of the Deep South, in effect becoming the black "Get Your Kicks on Route 66" of the 1910s. Both the phrase's colloquial popularity and Handy's identity with it was evinced by the news item that a member of the traveling black Dreamland Exposition Show later thought worth dispatching to the *Freeman:* "After a successful week in Winona, Miss., we are now in Moorhead, Miss., and I am writing this column right on the spot where the 'Southern' crosses the 'Yellow Dog.'"

The improving sales for Pace & Handy continued into 1915. The firm registered the copyrights for four songs, three composed by Handy, that year—two hits, a racial uplift composition and one disguised coon song. One hit was the blues composed and arranged by Handy, his adaption of a folk blues tune into "The Hesitating Blues." Like the peripatetic "Joe Turner's done been here and gone," the floating blues phrase of "Can I get you now, or must I hesitate?" had been heard around rural areas and vaudeville theaters for years. Either by chance or intent, this song was copyrighted in Handy's name, rather than in the firm's name. The other was the now-forgotten but once-popular "Fuzzy Wuzzy Rag" by Al Morton.

The curiosity of that year was a symphonic march composed by Handy entitled "Hail to the Spirit of Freedom." Like Harry Pace, who had retained his fondness for sentimental songs of an earlier generation, Handy apparently still harbored some hopes of becoming a March King. He wrote the march for the occasion of the Lincoln Jubilee Exposition held that year in Chicago in celebration of Lincoln's signing the Emancipation Proclamation. In what certainly must have been a pleasing sight to Handy's ego, and useful national promotion for Pace & Handy, the cover of the "Freedom" march score distributed in Chicago was illustrated with portraits of Lincoln, Frederick Douglass, and Handy arranged around a drawing of a black "Lady of Justice." The score, in which Handy sought musically to express the history and upward strivings of African Americans, perhaps reveals his continuing insistence that his past work in colored minstrelsy was also part of a respectable and honorable episode in the contributions of African Americans to the nation's popular culture. Handy's march includes melodies from Foster's "My Old Kentucky Home" and "Old Black Joe," both longtime favorites in colored and blackface minstrelsy's first part and olio. A syncopated coon song reminiscent of the minstrel show's repertoire was also composed by Handy in 1915, although to his credit he did not use that word in the song's lyrics. This was his "Shoeboot's Serenade," a sophisticated musical parody of the familiar Schubert's "Serenade," albeit illustrated on the Pace & Handy cover with a blackened-face illustration of Tom Post, the white comedian who performed the song that year for the J. A. Coburn Greater Minstrels Company. Largely forgotten after its initial popularity, the song is of continuing interest only because of Handy's noticeable use in its lyrics of floating folk blues phrases: *I woke up this morning with the blues all 'round my bed.*

With their firm actually making some money from the two blues compositions, in 1915 Pace and Handy legally specified their partnership in writing, two years after they first had agreed to print and sell the "Jogo Blues." The terms were generous to Handy. He was to receive a $75 monthly salary to manage the day-to-day activities in Memphis of their company, such as mailing orders and seeking new customers, paid out of the revenue coming in and overseen in Atlanta by Pace. And, most important for Handy personally, he had what amounted to a strong control over the artistic and commercial uses of his compositions. By the agreed-upon terms, Handy would receive two cents in royalty from the sale of each score he composed singly. There was certainly a need for the money. Handy's family at his crowded Janette Street home had grown again, with the birth of his second son and fifth child, Wyer, in 1915, who was named in honor of his orchestra's first violinist, Ed Wyer. The presence of these five "lively and robust youngsters at home, all bent on using my legs for teeterboards," Handy later recalled, "warmed the heart." But he also noted that "it put a crimp in my work" as a composer. He began to spend more time away from his home, sometimes renting a furnished room on Beale, where he could compose without distractions.

The following year, Handy as a performer and the firm of Pace & Handy both received their widest exposure yet to a white audience. Pace had arranged a concert booking for Handy and his first-line musicians on May 12, 1916, before a white and black audience, with Jim Crow seating, at an auditorium in Atlanta. Competition for sales of tickets to other black-performed entertainment was brisk throughout the city that night. New acts were featured at the TOBA-booked theater, and the Tolliver company's minstrel show and circus had just arrived in Atlanta, advertising that Gertrude "Ma" Rainey would perform "the blues, and singing them as only Ma herself can sing them." Handy's band, however, won the night, receiving the largest audience and the most favorable notice in the next day's press. He performed his "Hail to the Spirit of Freedom" march, and his daughter Katharine, then aged twelve, sang solos of two of her father's compositions, "St. Louis Blues" and a new number of 1916, "Joe Turner Blues." Although seldom performed now, "Joe Turner Blues" enjoyed a remarkable popularity throughout the mid-1910s. The "Yellow Dog Rag" and the "Joe Turner Blues," rather than the more complex "St. Louis Blues," were the Handy compositions that most people in Memphis and the South heard in 1915 being played in saloons or theaters, being whistled on the street, or being performed by Handy's bands at parties. Katharine Handy's featured performance that night was consistent with Handy's promoting the stage careers of his children, but it also perhaps represents a deliberate toning down of his blues compositions for this mixed audience of a respectable gentility. The reaction of the Atlanta listeners likely would have been quite different, for example, if these blues had been sung with a mature female sexuality by Estelle Harris or a twenty-two-year-old Bessie Smith.

Pace's pride at his successful promotion of the songs of Pace & Handy was likely muted, however, when a few days after the concert he was reminded again of the ups and downs of having Handy as a business partner. Handy had returned from Atlanta to find that a foreclosure was to be filed against his Janette Street house. Pace helped Handy and family avoid losing their home by refinancing his partner's debt through Pace's employer, the Standard Life Insurance Company.

Handy certainly worked very hard. With the continuing success of his "Yellow Dog Rag" beginning to give him a wider regional reputation, he continued energetically throughout 1914–17 to travel and perform at smaller bookings with his various bands. With the exception of "The Memphis Blues," his blues songs were not yet national crossover successes, though they enjoyed considerable popularity among younger whites. The *Freeman* earlier had praised Handy and his bands, not totally hyperbolically, as "doing the dance work for the best people within a radius of 150 miles of Memphis." Handy by now employed his younger brother, Charles, to help with the increased bookings. The composer by his growing repute was also able to attract and hire talented black musicians to his bands from markets outside Memphis, such as drummer Jasper Taylor from St. Louis or clarinetist William King Phillips, from Jacksonville, Florida, the composer of the then-popular "Florida Blues."

Traveling down the river into Mississippi, Handy and his band obtained frequent bookings not only in the Delta counties, where his reputation was established, but also in the towns of the state's more northern counties, particularly at the small town of Oxford, where the University of Mississippi is located. Handy's band was officially booked by the university at least once to play accompaniment to a silent film shown on campus, and much more frequently by Ole Miss fraternities and sororities to play for their dances at the university's Gordon Hall.

One person who attended these dances—although usually without a date—was a standoffish, dandyish young man known to his few friends as Bill who lived in Oxford and who then spelled his last name as Falkner. "He would watch, standing there, while the musicians played on until the early hours of the morning," a biographer of William Faulkner later confirmed from interviews with the relatives and friends about this author's presence at the Handy performances. Both the music and the sexual expectations were at that time changing from the conservative mores of Faulkner's nineteenth-century rural Mississippi boyhood. It is intriguing to consider how these Gordon Hall soirees were later absorbed into Faulkner's fiction, particularly his subsequent novel *Sanctuary*. There the character Temple Drake, the socially rebellious University of Mississippi coed who becomes the kept woman of a gangster in Memphis, is first seen by the reader from outside a university social building dancing erotically inside to a orchestra into the early morning hours:

> Later, the music wailing beyond the glass, they would watch her through the windows as she passed in swift rotation from one pair of black sleeves to the next, her waist shaped slender and urgent in the interval, her feet filling the rhythmic gap with music. Stooping they would drink from flasks and light cigarettes.

So played Handy and his hot Memphis bands of 1914–17 for white college audiences. *You can hear her moaning night and morn*—his cornet and the other brassy instruments of his orchestra insistently playing along to the sexually charged words of his "Yellow Dog Rag."

The financial success of Handy's various orchestras and his music publishing partnership enabled the firm of Pace & Handy by 1917 to "put a carnation in its buttonhole and begin to hold up its head," in Handy's Micawberian phrase, among the legitimate, semilegitimate, and criminal businesses along Beale Avenue. Handy personally became well known along that block or so along Beale's intersections with Fourth and Hernando streets. This stretch included Pee Wee's Saloon, the Monarch Saloon, Hammitt Ashford's saloon, and lesser bars, gambling hells, or drug dens. Handy was neither totally of this demimonde section of Beale, nor totally of the more respectable end of Beale that was represented by the Robert Church family. He was forty-four years old in 1917, and the married father of now five children, his third daughter, named Elizabeth for her mother, having been born. He stepped in a world apart from the black easy riders, grifters, professional gamblers, prostitutes, and narcotics peddlers who claimed this western end of Beale Avenue toward the DeSoto Fish Market and the levees of the Mississippi River as their territory. But undeniably he took a raffish pleasure at this time in his life—and, much later, when he was writing his memoir—at his being accepted there by the Beale Avenue criminal habitués.

Handy made a good appearance along this section of Beale

Avenue, having always been fastidious in his clothing and barbering. It was at this time that apparently he also acquired his lasting reputation in Memphis for being both an enthusiastic drinker and not always sleeping overnight at his home. "Maggie, arms akimbo and rolling pin poised, was waiting for Jiggs at the door." He thus nonspecifically recalled in his memoir the inevitable morning-after encounters with his wife, Elizabeth, back at 659 Janette Street. This was an intentionally disarming reference by Handy, implying his marital lapses were more humorous than hurtful, to the popular newspaper daily comic strip *Bringing Up Father.* It entertainingly featured a harridan wife, Maggie, and her profligate husband, Jiggs. Elizabeth Handy, whatever her anger or remonstrance, kept her reactions to this family discord between her husband and herself, or expressed her feelings only to close relatives.

"'Pee Wee's', Pimps, and Politics," was the title Handy also blithely chose in his 1941 memoir to begin this chapter of his life, and, like the earlier two sections in the book narrating his minstrelsy career, these pages are among the most highly detailed and among the most morally and aesthetically ambiguous of Handy's reminiscences. There is little doubt that Handy, writing as a sixty-eight-year-old in 1941, diffused his memories of Beale Avenue with a sentimental glow of nostalgia. To him, the saloon district was the boulevard for African Americans where

> [s]cores of powerfully built roustabouts from riverboats sauntered along the pavement, elbowing fashionable browns in beautiful gowns. Pimps in box-back coats and un-dented Stetsons came out to get a breath of early evening air and to welcome the young night. . . . Glittering young devils in silk toppers and Prince Alberts drifted in and out with insolent self-assurance.

In such sentimentalizing, he had not even the excuse of reliving his youth. As noted above, Handy was middle-aged when he moved among these pimps, saloon keepers, cocaine-addicted "snowbirds," prostitutes, Boss Crump enforcers, and other criminals of Beale Avenue. (Since Prohibition had been required statewide by the Tennessee legislature from 1909, a law that the "reform" administration of Boss Crump chose not to enforce within the city limits of Memphis, Beale Avenue saloon keepers were also among the criminals.) In some defense of Handy, it must be remembered that the composer, born in 1873, was among the first generation of African Americans to have been born out of slavery. So even into a prudent middle age, it must have been both intellectually and carnally intoxicating for any male of color of his generation to have stepped freely and for the first time into the ornately appointed Monarch Saloon, at that time one of the few fine establishments of drinking and gambling built exclusively for African American patrons, and certainly one of the most famous of such establishments known among blacks of the lower South. The lesser Pee Wee's Saloon, which ran a numbers game upstairs, also had its carnal pleasures, as was well known among Memphis blacks. Handy specifically remembered its large oil painting mounted just inside the door and above the bar. It pictured a scene from a Shakespearean tragedy, a lascivious (and presumably insufficiently clad) white Desdemona desirously reaching out her two arms to a very dark-skinned Othello.

But even with the personal allowances, Beale Avenue probably was never as Handy-as-Micawber thought he saw it. The prostitution, casual murders, and drug traffic likely were just as dehumanizing on Beale Avenue in 1917 as in America's twenty-first-century inner cities. And despite his considerable skills as a raconteur, his memoir's tales of the violence he witnessed on Beale—how the retributive murder of the St. Louis saloon keeper Fatty Grimes was discussed in advance at Pee Wee's Saloon, or how the bar bouncer whose street name was Cousin Hog was shot dead one Saturday night by the gambler Cornelius Coleman for having disrespected him—are, despite Handy's romanticizing, ultimately banal and depressing in their repetition. In his later years, Handy apparently regretted his overromanticizing of Beale Avenue, and he likely also would have regretted the street's transformation later in the century into a type of blues nostalgia park. In a surprising instance of candor—like a black minstrel backstage wiping off the burnt cork and dropping his genial demeanor—he wrote privately in 1950 of his impatience at what he called the "Pee Wee Salon [*sic*] crap" promoted for tourist revenues by the Memphis corporate interests.

The "glittering young devils" of whom Handy once wrote were often able literally to get away with murder because so long as the violence on Beale was not directed at white citizens, and the bribes and votes from the black wards were delivered to city hall in a timely manner, the Crump city machine simply did not care. A ditty very popular at this time among white policemen and news reporters in Memphis well expresses the official viewpoint toward Beale:

> *Two niggers git to fightin'. They ain't no kin*
> *One kill t'other. 'T ain't no sin.*

At its best, the wide-open black criminality of some blocks of Beale provided incidents that even Handy, with all his superior artistic talents as a lyricist and a raconteur, never could have contrived. When the aforementioned Fatty Grimes—a "handsome brown man" like Handy, and who like the composer also "wore finely tailored clothes and expensive shoes"—ran a few steps from inside Hammitt Ashford's saloon where he had been shot five times and then fell down dead in the street, someone shouted "Call Haynes's ambulance!" This of course was a call for Thomas H. Haynes Sr., the Beale Avenue undertaker. But before the Haynes ambulance could arrive, according to Beale historian and Handy contemporary George Lee, a competing black undertaker promptly spread his coattails and sat himself down atop the bloodied corpse. "'I am going to sit here until my wagon comes,'" Lee quotes the man as having declared, "and he stayed with his quarry until his men came with stretchers and carried the lifeless body of Fatty Grimes into the morgue." *I am going to sit here until my wagon comes* practically calls out to become a blues lyric.

In truth, romanticizing Beale Avenue's criminals in 1914–1917 for their own sakes, which following the example of Handy's memoir too many blues journalists and enthusiasts have done, misses the point. It is the equivalent of concentrating exclusively upon the lawless local color in Chicago during the first two decades of the twentieth century, when Sherwood Anderson and Ring Lardner, respectively, labored in that city writing advertising copy and newspaper stories. Anecdotes are easy from all three settings. What is important is the fact that Handy as a lyricist learned on Beale Avenue the same artistry that Lardner and Anderson were learning simultaneously from their surroundings in Chicago: how to write in the way that real American people actually talk. This avenue continued the composer's education in lyrical realism beyond his early success in the words to "Yellow Dog Rag." Handy, for example, once settled himself into a barber's chair for a late-night shave inside a Beale Avenue shop and asked the owner when the barbershop closed. "We never close," the owner replied, "unless somebody gets killed." This response, slightly changed but not made more "literary," became one of the most famous lines in his most popular hit of 1917, "Beale Street": *You'll meet honest men and pickpockets skilled / You'll find that bus'ness never closes 'til somebody gets killed.*

Beale Avenue and the surrounding streets also provided one other musical opportunity for Handy—not directly related to the sad local color of prostitutes, drug traffic, Boss Crump corruption, or murders. The Memphis-based booking agency for African American vaudevillians, or TOBA, supplied a constant stream of black musicians traveling into the city to perform at its theaters. Handy as the "Father of the Blues" owes a large and unacknowledged debt in the creation of his music to these now-forgotten black vaudevillians who also sang their blues.

Oh sing 'em, sing 'em, / Sing them blues, / 'Cause they cert'ly sound good to me! Franklin "Baby" Seals had shouted thus while gyrating and playing his piano in performing "Baby Seals Blues," his loud voice unamplified but electrifying black crowds in the small theaters throughout the South with his signature blues call. Seals had partnered personally and professionally since 1910 with Miss Floyd Fisher, known onstage as "the Doll of Memphis," and the pair played TOBA theaters until Seals's death in 1915. Handy does not mention in his memoir whether he ever chose to see Baby Seals or other vaudeville blues singers, but, as he later intriguingly told a friend, Seals had "met Handy's band." The future classical composer William Grant Still, who worked between college sessions in 1916 at Pace & Handy's office on Beale, also remembered having been in the audience with Handy at these musical performances of the city's black vaudevillians. He recalled the theaters as having been located in "a somewhat disreputable section" of the city, and the general atmosphere as "sordid," but Still emphasized how the black vaudevillian blues melodies were both remembered and eventually useful to him in his classical compositions, and particularly to his employer in his compositions of popular music: "W. C. Handy listened and learned—and what he learned profited him financially and in other ways in the succeeding years."

Handy's assumed indifference in his memoir to the black vaudeville blues thus is even harder to credit when one considers how close at hand were these vaudeville performers and theaters during his two decades on Beale Avenue. The Lyric vaudeville theater had a brief but colorful operation at 313½ Beale, only a few steps away from Pee Wee's Saloon, where Handy and other musicians stored their instruments and received their telephone messages. Handy literally could have stepped outside the doorway of Pee Wee's, just beyond the cigar stand inside, tossed a copper Indian head penny, and it would have hit the marquee of the Lyric. The Lincoln Theater, capitalized by local black investors, was also located on Beale, in the heart of the saloon and entertainment blocks between Hernando and Fourth. And grandest of all local theaters for blacks was the Barrassos' Savoy, headquarters of TOBA, owned and operated by this family of theatrical entrepreneurs. Curiously, although Handy would have passed within sight of the Savoy Theatre almost daily on his rounds through the city, he makes no mention of its owners in his *Father of the Blues*. Handy in this memoir name-checks practically everyone he had ever met in show business, particularly in Memphis, with an almost Rotary Club thoroughness; but one looks in vain in the book's index for any mention of one of Memphis's most colorful theatrical families.

Handy's later reticence to acknowledge TOBA suggests that he might have considered the Barrasso family's booking agency to be underpaying African American performers or their composers, such as himself. He may forthrightly have given the Barrassos a piece of his mind in some unrecorded incident in Memphis. Or it may suggest a possible business quarrel over royalty payments or song steal-

A proud W. C. Handy circa 1893 at age nineteen wears the uniform of the Hampton Cornet Band of Evansville, Indiana. Marching brass bands offered Handy his first employment as a professional musician, and their musical style later influenced his blues. (SPECIAL COLLECTIONS, UNIVERSITY OF MEMPHIS)

The perennially elected Edward H. "Boss" Crump was the absolute political arbiter of Memphis throughout much of Handy's lifetime. The Crump political machine commissioned Handy in 1909 to compose a campaign song for its candidate. The resulting score, "Mr. Crump," subsequently became recognized as one of the first published blues songs and was later the basis of Handy's first crossover national success, "The Memphis Blues." (SPECIAL COLLECTIONS, UNIVERSITY OF MEMPHIS)

A sharply dressed Handy, with a briefcase full of blues scores, pauses for a mome circa 1917, before leaving Memphis to sell his blues songs from Chicago in the nort small towns farther south and into rural Mississippi along the "Yellow Dog" rail l
(SPECIAL COLLECTIONS, UNIVERSITY OF MEMPHIS)

le Avenue as it appeared circa 1910, where Handy later claimed he said his "best
day prayers" while hurrying to the Mississippi River docks at the street's end. If
ndy arrived at the docks in time, he would board the Memphis excursion boats and
y his music for passengers throughout the day and night for a badly needed fifty
ars plus tips. (SPECIAL COLLECTIONS, UNIVERSITY OF MEMPHIS)

The small shotgun house at 659
Janette Place in Memphis, where
Handy lived with his wife and
children, and where he composed
many of his famous blues. The
house has since been relocated to
the Beale Street tourist district.
(SPECIAL COLLECTIONS, UNIVERSITY
OF MEMPHIS)

The commercial intersection of Beale Avenue, "the Main Street of Negro Americ[
and the white commercial district of Memphis, as it appeared to Handy in 1912. T[
intersection marked the city's invisible Jim Crow line. The streetcars were stri[
segregated. (SPECIAL COLLECTIONS, UNIVERSITY OF MEMPHIS)

During his lifetime and
afterward, Handy, a lifelong
Republican, was honored
nationally for his music by
presidential administrations
of both parties. Here, Stew[
Udall, secretary of the inter[
to two Democratic presiden[
meets with Handy's widow[
Louise Logan Handy, in
commemoration of what
Bessie Smith always empha[
sized was "Handy's Park,"
on Beale Street in Memphis[
Tennessee. (SPECIAL COLLEC[
TIONS, UNIVERSITY OF MEMPH[

e stylishly dressed members of the Memphis Blues Band of 1918 were among
eral groups of musicians Handy employed that year throughout the city. A bass,
lins, and wind instruments were then typically included in a blues orchestra, or
d. Handy is in the top row, far left, holding his cornet. The saxophone, cradled by
member of the band in the bottom row, far right, was then considered a novel
trument for popular music. Another newly introduced novelty was the gramo-
one, for playing recorded music, seen at the far right. (SPECIAL COLLECTIONS, UNI-
RSITY OF MEMPHIS)

An avuncular W. C. Handy in 1946,
after recovering from his near-fatal
accident in 1943. Despite the resulting blindness, he resumed giving
public performances and supervis-
ing his music publishing business.
(SPECIAL COLLECTIONS, UNIVERSITY
OF MEMPHIS)

Handy, shown here in his eighties, delights a local crowd on one of his freque[nt] returns to Memphis by playing a few bars of the "St. Louis Blues." (SPECIAL COLL[EC]TIONS, UNIVERSITY OF MEMPHIS)

Having already been a widower for two years, after the death of his fir[st] wife, a determinedly cheerful and social Han[dy] gathers with his extend[ed] family in November 193[9] for the celebration of his sixty-sixth birthday. (SCHOMBURG CENTER/ NEW YORK PUBLIC LIBRA[RY])

e irrepressible W. C. Handy in the company of his second wife, Louise Logan, at ir wedding in 1954. (SCHOMBURG CENTER/NEW YORK PUBLIC LIBRARY)

The statue of W. C. Handy keeps a lonely vigil over the changed Beale Street at Hand[y?] Park in contemporary Memphis. (SPECIAL COLLECTIONS, UNIVERSITY OF MEMPHIS)

ing occurring between Handy and TOBA-represented talent. Two
industrious recent scholars of black vaudeville, Lynn Abbott and
Doug Seroff, gather suggestive evidence that the word on the street
from some Beale Avenue black vaudeville performers in the mid-
1910s was that Handy had plagiarized part of his "Mr. Crump don't
'low" melody in the "Memphis Blues" from the signature song,
"Mama Don't Allow No Easy Talking Here," performed by the
husband-and-wife vaudevillian team known as Willie and Lulu Too
Sweet, who had a long run from 1912 onward in Memphis. Show
business was business, however, and Willie Too Sweet performed
the "Jogo Blues" in 1913 as a popular number of his act at a Macon,
Georgia, theater.

Handy certainly would have strenuously countered any assertion
of melody theft, if in fact he ever were confronted with it, by argu-
ing that the "Mama don't 'low" melody was a folk blues snatch just
as freely available to him as it was to the Too Sweets. Black vaudeville's techniques can certainly be heard in his most successful composition that year. This was his wonderful "Beale Street," published
on March 23, 1917. Its measures were played brassy and up-tempo,
and Handy's lyrics provided the perfect stage entrance song—or
encore-vamping exit—for black female vaudevillian blues singers
contemporary to Handy, some now forgotten and some not, such as
Sarah Brown, Effie Moore, or Bessie Smith:

> If Beale Street could talk, if Beale Street could talk,
> Married men would have to take their beds and walk.

"Beale Street Blues," as the song was later retitled, was the best
seller for Pace & Handy in 1917. Along with "Yellow Dog Rag," this
song by Handy is second in mastery only to the "St. Louis Blues,"
and it deserves more frequent modern performances. Like the earlier "Yellow Dog," its lyrics demonstrate Handy's confident artistry
in combining colloquial speech with blue notes to celebrate the
pleasures of the Memphis avenue that, as the above lyrics imply,
Handy in his personal life perhaps loved too much. *You'll see hog-nose
restaurants and chitlin' cafes,* Handy, always an enthusiastic diner, exuberantly tells a stroller on Beale Avenue. And he promises—perhaps

referring to his own religious childhood in the AME Church in Alabama and his adult transactions pawning his cornet at Morris Lippman's loan company—*You'll see Golden Balls enough to pave the New Jerusalem. . . .*

He then offers visions of Beale Avenue's famed sexual diversions, criminals, and respectable businessmen:

> *You'll see pretty Browns in beautiful gowns*
> *You'll see tailor-mades and hand-me-downs,*
> *You'll meet honest men and pickpockets skilled,*
> *You'll find that bus'ness never closes until somebody gets killed.*
> *I'd rather be here than any place I know.*

The wistfulness of the final lyrics leads to the slowed measures that Handy uses to close the song. His blue notes combine a floating folk phrase about the transitory nature of carnal pleasure with the Memphis specifics of Crump's politics: *Goin' to the river, maybe, by and by . . . Because the river's wet / And Beale Street's done gone dry.* This last is a local reference to the temporary removal of Boss Crump from his mayoral office by the state of Tennessee in 1917 for his continued refusal to enforce a local prohibition law in his city. (Boss Crump soon returned to power, however, and the city's saloons soon reopened. "Beale Street" continued to sell very well.)

"Beale Street" came the closest to a white crossover success for Handy, long before the ascendancy of his "St. Louis Blues." It was recorded in August 1917 by the white Earl Fuller's Famous Jass [Jazz] Band, featuring the "laughing trombone" of Harry Raderman, and again that same month by the white Wadsworth's Novelty Orchestra for the Pathé company. The royalties from the Raderman recording alone amounted to an astonishing $2,857 paid to Pace & Handy.

The black Mister Micawber seemed vindicated at last, and cash was coming in to Pace & Handy apparently even faster than Handy was spending it. The national times were truly "Tempo à Blues" in what was later called the Blues and Jazz Spring of 1917, although increasingly played up-tempo and brassy à la "Beale Street." The popular songs of that year certainly included patriotic numbers, after President Woodrow Wilson asked Congress for a declaration of war on April 6, 1917. These numbers included George M. Cohan's "Over There" and Lew Brown and Albert Tilzer's "Au Revoir, But Not Good-bye, Soldier Boy." (Also among the popular songs of that year was Rida Johnson Young and Sigmund Romberg's new arrangement of "Jump Jim Crow.") But the widely played songs of 1917 included the recordings that year by the white Original Dixieland Jass Band of "Tiger Rag" and Spenser Williams's hot "Shim-me-sha-wabble." The sheet music for sale from Pace & Handy, although it included a few commercial disappointments, was perhaps at the height of the company's national popularity in 1917–18 with their winning combination of ragtime, folk blues tunes, and vaudeville melodies such as "Beale Street" and the "Yellow Dog."

Yet, as indicated by the royalties from the phonograph recording in 1917 of "Beale Street," the era of brightly illustrated sheet music sales as the prime distribution of popular music was coming to a close. Phonograph records, with cheaply manufactured discs having technologically replaced cylinders on affordable machines, were profoundly changing the market, a fact that Handy, a former minstrel performer and current dance room musician, seemed to have been slow in grasping. Indeed, a former Mahara minstrel acquaintance of Handy's, Wilbur "Sweat" Sweatman, had already stolen a march on Handy by becoming the first African American to record a Handy-composed song, the clarinetist's "fast-paced and bluesy" version of "Joe Turner Blues," for Pathé Records in March 1917.

Harry Pace, even at his distance in Atlanta, had always been more innovative in marketing their firm's songs in newer ways than Handy, and, as his career later reveals, he was interested in the possibilities of owning his own phonographic business. While on a trip for his insurance company to New York City, Pace made arrangements with Columbia Records for Handy and his orchestra to make their first phonographic recordings, contracted for September 1917. The orchestra would record Pace & Handy properties, and, with legal permissions, some other popular blues and rags the company did not own. ("The Memphis Blues" would not be among them.) But Handy's impecuniosity almost broke the Columbia deal before a first record had been pressed.

When he told his best Memphis musicians about the upcoming

session, their reactions were, bluntly summarized, *W. C., we don't think you're good for it.* Some objected because they would have to give up sure-playing local engagements for the financially uncertain trip to New York City; others were more forthright that they did not think Handy could fully pay their up-front expenses for train travel and hotel rooms. In the end, he was able to persuade only four Memphis musicians who knew him to take the risk, out of a total of twelve whom Pace had promised to record as "Handy's Orchestra of Memphis." Two of Handy's perhaps most talented former side-men, Ed Wyer on violin and William King Phillips on clarinet and saxophone, had moved to Chicago, and when Handy called upon these two for their services, they diplomatically pled Chicago union regulations as prohibiting them from playing in New York City. Handy filled out his needed number by hiring three other Chicago musicians, on cello, bass, and drums, who had once played for him in Memphis, and four other Chicago pickup musicians who had not worked with Handy for needed violins and saxophones. The twelfth, a clarinist, was apparently hired at the last moment in New York City. Financed in part by a loan that Handy previously had taken out secured by his household furnishings—and that may have occasioned another noncomical Maggie-and-Jiggs domestic scene at 659 Janette Street—the mixed group calling themselves Handy's Orchestra of Memphis barely caught an already-moving passenger train out of the Memphis station and headed toward their New York City recording session.

One who was not on this train was guitarist Charley Patton, later known as the "King of the Delta Blues." Patton enjoyed Handy's music, and a mutual friend earlier had praised Patton to Handy with some qualifications—"He can play what he *knows* to play." Handy generously had invited Patton to attend an engagement with his orchestra in Beulah, Mississippi, a crossroads town outside of Rosedale. Patton presumably got in free. But Handy's band were strictly score-reading musicians, and Patton soon realized that he "couldn't play no-how 'cause he couldn't read that music." He gave up any ambition to play with Handy's bands.

Despite being a skillful score reader, Handy always remembered his intimidated entrance into the "little airtight studios" at Columbia to make his first mass-produced recording. He and the other musicians were instructed for reasons of acoustics to sit down to play their instruments on wooden stools of various heights throughout the studio. (There was no vocalist for these sessions.) Recording horns dangling from the ceiling above the performers' heads were connected via mysterious-looking acoustical tubing to the studio's central recording machinery. Throughout four days, September 21 and 22, and again on September 24 and 25, this group who had not previously rehearsed with one another recorded fifteen songs while Handy led on cornet or trumpet. Ten eventually were released by Columbia early the next year, two to a disc.

As expected, the performances by what was essentially a group of musical strangers were a little stiff; Handy later commented that these recordings of 1917 were "not up to scratch." These were not songs played as he and his best Memphis orchestras had performed them aboard the *Pattona,* or atop the Alaskan Roof Garden, or at Gordon Hall. But the group does a credible performance of a Pace & Handy–owned property, "Snakey Blues," complete with tapped wood blocks, that with trombonist Sylvester Bevard and xylophonist Jasper Taylor, almost swings; one of the clarinetists tries hard, but doesn't quite succeed, to take a blues break. On one of the two Handy-composed songs subsequently released by Columbia, the "Ole Miss Rag," the playing is much more sedate; it is as if Handy, always what musicians called a "score eagle," had insisted that there would be *no* deviation from his score. Things loosen up a little on the second Handy-written number that was released, "Hooking Cow Blues." The trombone and wind instruments play a bluesy stride— one can imagine Temple Drake doing at least a slow "shimmy" to its rhythm—and the wood blocks played at the rear are audible through the acoustical tubes all the way throughout the performance. Handy in this song even throws in a few rattling cowbells—à la the white "Original Dixieland Jass Band" as used in their recordings. *Jogo that, you New Orleans musicians,* he seems to be saying.

Interestingly, these 1917 recordings did not include any issuances of the "St. Louis Blues," indicating perhaps that Columbia did not then consider it sufficiently popular for a national white audience. The Columbia issues sold reasonably well, nonetheless, and, as Pace had hoped, resulted in more national publicity for the Memphis firm. Yet for Handy both personally and historically, this New York City trip was most significant for his first meeting with James Reese Europe, the adapter of "The Memphis Blues." By the autumn of 1917, Europe had accomplished far more than W. C. Handy in bringing African American music and musicians to a national white audience.

Europe had organized the first significant union and booking agency for black musicians, the Clef Club, and the biennial performances by its members as the Clef Club Orchestra of the City of New York—featuring one hundred musicians and twelve pianos—had drawn praiseful reviews from the white press. He was now Lieutenant James Europe when he met Handy, having previously accepted a commission in the all-black 15th New York Infantry National Guard to organize its regimental band and to encourage recruitment among African Americans. Europe later would be the first black officer to lead African American troops into combat in France. He would contribute significantly to Handy's international fame as the "Father of the Blues" when, during his convalescence from combat injuries, he performed "The Memphis Blues" and other Handy songs with the 369th U.S. Infantry "Hell Fighters" band to wildly enthusiastic French civilians. They loved the Memphis composer's songs, as Europe played them, which they termed *le jazz hot*.

Handy and Europe were a study in contrast when they met that autumn of 1917. Handy, as illustrated in the promotional line drawings for the Columbia releases, appeared as an avuncular, round-shouldered, and professorial-looking middle-aged man, dressed in the uniform of the earlier century's local brass bands. Europe, eight years younger and looking even more so, was "a big, tall man," his friend and fellow musician Eubie Blake later recalled, and he habitually stood up very straight "like a West Point soldier." A pair of rimless glasses gave Europe, despite his solid build, a studious look, almost as if he were the graduate student to Handy's professor. Both had studied music formally. What these two Alabama-born composers and arrangers may have warily said to each other when they first met was not recalled by others, nor later in his memoir by

Handy. But their encounter in 1917 was a turning point in the history of the blues and would prove significant in deciding which of these two ambitious African American men later would be remembered as its most preeminent practitioner.

Tempo à blues was becoming faster. By 1918, Europe would be at the Western Front, and Handy would have permanently moved the firm of Pace & Handy to New York City. Europe, after returning safely from France and leading a triumphal return parade down the streets of Harlem, would be murdered in 1919 by a deranged member of his band. Handy was sincerely shaken by his younger rival's death. On hearing the news of the murder, he did not sleep that night. "Harlem did not seem the same," he recalled. Europe's tragically shortened life prevented what almost certainly would have been major accomplishments by this gifted arranger. The appreciative national audience for the blues therefore would be achieved by another artist, the older Handy. By 1920, his "St. Louis Blues" would be recorded by a white female vocalist and become an extraordinary American cultural phenomenon. And by the beginning of the decade, W. C. Handy would be on his way to being celebrated as the Father of the Blues.

CHAPTER NINE

——

New York City

NATIONAL SUCCESS, THE "ST. LOUIS BLUES," AND BLUES: AN ANTHOLOGY, 1918–1926

W. C. Handy, a Negro, enjoys the undisputed distinction of having, by dint of his individual genius, brought the "blues" from comparative obscurity as folk-songs to their present pitch of popularity.

—Edmund Wilson, *The New Republic*, July 14, 1926

Memphis had given much to W. C. Handy in appreciation of his commercial blues. Handy, however, had received his increased earnings as a performer and publisher with the extended hand of his audience, figuratively, half-closed. The Jim Crow codes, although usually enforced with discreet police coercion in Boss Crump's city, vexed a man of his ambition and pride. And, in moving himself and his family slightly northward from Mississippi, he had increased his earnings and reputation only from playing in a small market to a regional one. There still remained limits oppressive to him, commercially and socially, as to how far he would be allowed to advance in Memphis. He was forty-five years of age in 1918, and had lived in Tennessee for more than ten years, his longest residence in any one place since his childhood in Florence. Never had he lived where Jim Crow laws and customs did not govern business and social advancement.

"Highly race conscious, he realized he couldn't be an artist who happened to be dark-skinned or a colored gentleman, either in white or black Memphis." So wrote in retrospect a white Memphis observer and contemporary of Handy's, Shields McIlwaine. McIlwaine continued:

> In white Memphis he was the favorite musical servant, but he was also a Negro; in black Memphis he was "old Handy" with his gang of horn-blowers and string pickers traipsing all over the tri-States. . . . For despite all of Handy's orchestra jobs, he lived on the financial edge; black bands were paid Negro wages. Much of the time his instruments were hocked with pawnbrokers to keep his organization together. It didn't matter to the colored high and mighty on Beale that Handy was a man of education and genius.

Approaching the personal decade of his fifties, when affronts and professional setbacks were more difficult to shoulder with equanimity, even the ever-optimistic "old Handy" at times lost his nearly constant geniality. "Every man who has had his downs only too well knows the petty indignities the struggler suffers daily," he later diplomatically recalled of these times. By no later than very early 1918, he had a bitter quarrel via letter and telephone with Pace in Atlanta, occasioned by the Solvent Savings and Loan Bank's refusal to cash a check for Handy of forty dollars from the Woolworth company's sales of sheet music. In Handy's retelling, Pace when first contacted demanded that their partnership be dissolved and that Handy pay him for his interests. The two temporarily reconciled, however, when their company shortly thereafter received a royalty check for more than two thousand dollars from the Earl Fuller band's recording of "Beale Street." But hard feelings over money would resurface.

There were other worries in late 1917 and early 1918. His younger brother, Charles, who had helped in Memphis with booking bands, was now in the U.S. Army, and many local black musicians upon whom Handy had relied to fill out regional engagements either were conscripted or had volunteered. (During the "Preparedness

Parades" in Memphis preceding this nation's declaration of war, neither Handy's bands nor any other black musicians had been invited to march. This was a slight that, for both patriotic and professional reasons, Handy remembered with some bitterness.) And in a horrific recalling of the lynching and mutilation of his young minstrel companion Louis Wright, and Governor Vardaman's lawless rule the previous decade in Mississippi, Handy had been witness to the aftermath of a notorious lynching just outside Memphis.

On May 23, 1917, a young African American, Eli Persons, was burned alive by a white mob in a rural area near Memphis after accusations that he had raped and murdered a young white woman. Some of the charred remains were then thrown by a passing automobile onto Beale Avenue, on the block where the future Handy Park would be located. Handy was among those who found the grisly remains. As he passionately wrote more than a quarter of a century later, this sight forcefully brought back to him his memories of earlier "brutal, savage acts—particularly those in which the hapless one came close to being myself." It also had stirred familial memories. "I thought of Grandpa Handy's rebellion against his servitude," he wrote, recalling William Wise Handy's resistance to his own slavery. Handy began then to think about jumping Jim Crow, to north of the Mason-Dixon line. "Some day I would be gone," he first had determined that day in 1917. "They'd look for me on Beale Street, up and down the river, along the Yellow Dog and the Pea Vine, but I would not be there."

(It is interesting to speculate how Boss Crump, in temporary political exile because of his refusal to enforce prohibition, would have handled this outrage on Beale Avenue. Crump, for all his many faults and willingness to resort to political intimidation, was never heard, speaking either in public or private, to have used the word *nigger,* and he forbade his sons from speaking that word in his presence.)

Handy by late 1917 and early 1918 already was applying for copyrights at a Chicago address, indicating that he had opened a smaller office there and was possibly also living part-time in that city, with or without his family. In moving some of his publishing business to Chicago, Handy was but one among the larger number of black residents of Memphis, skilled and unskilled, who in the war years or the immediate postwar years emigrated to "Chi," as the city was known on Beale Avenue. The incomparable Chicago blues pianist Lovey Austin even later answered Handy's praise of "Beale Street" with her own hugely popular song in black vaudeville, "Rampart Street," which promised its black audiences even more pleasures and freedom to be found along that Chicago boulevard.

But it was to New York City, not Chicago, where Handy—and Harry Pace—decided to relocate their business and, eventually, both their private residences. Pace, as noted, was becoming increasingly interested in the recording business, which at that time was centered in New York, and in 1920 he resigned his position at the Atlanta insurance agency and moved there. Handy himself, always a believer in immediate good luck to be found farther up the road, by the autumn of 1918 had moved to Harlem, to be joined a year later by his family. "And what a Harlem it was!" he later recalled of his solitary arrival into this black neighborhood. "Big, old, good-looking, easy-going, proud-walking Harlem," he enthused. This was, he was certain, Beale Avenue on a grander, national scale.

Handy characteristically had hung his hopes high in New York City in 1918–19 on what he felt was a future surefire winner of a song that was a Pace & Handy property—"A Good Man Is Hard to Find," by Eddie Green. The Chicago blues singer Alberta Hunter had introduced this song by Handy's permission to great success at that city's Dreamland cabaret, and it had been an immediate crossover sensation when it was first performed by the white coon shouter Sophie Tucker. Handy, however, at first received not a penny of royalties from Tucker's use of the song onstage, as her pianist had memorized the score and played it without legal permission. Song stealers could jump over both sides of the Jim Crow fence. But not for nothing had Handy learned the opportunistic ways of Beale Avenue; he quickly published a large press run of a score featuring a photograph of Tucker (presumably also without her permission). Sales for the Pace & Handy score eventually totaled 500,000 copies, and the revenues to the firm, Handy later recalled, were "most gratifying." ("A Good Man Is Hard to Find," like many Handy-written or Handy-owned lyrics, originated in and then reentered into colloquial usage for years, sometimes with salacious variations. Flannery O'Connor would use this phrase in 1957 as the title for one of her most celebrated short stories.)

The sales success of "A Good Man Is Hard to Find" boosted spirits at 1547 Broadway, inside the Gaiety Theater Building office of Pace & Handy. Handy earlier had rented a desk inside the building, and then later a full office. Interestingly, he chose to locate his business not in Harlem but at an address that was at the center of Tin Pan Alley. His business would operate at or near this Broadway address, with some temporary moves, for decades. He plainly was cocking his hat to compete with the major national New York music publishers, such as the Consolidated Music Corporation, to which Irving Berlin was a contributor.

Handy's daughters Lucile and Katharine were among his first employees. From 1919 to 1920, Handy also reassembled at this office many of his closest and most talented employees and associates from Memphis and elsewhere whom he employed as arrangers, copyists, song demonstrators, or other office help. His brother, Charles, had been demobilized from the military and rejoined his family and their business in the city; also militarily discharged and reemployed at Pace & Handy's office on Broadway was William Grant Still, who worked in the office as an arranger and played with the touring New York–based group that was known as W. C. Handy's Memphis Blues Orchestra. Although Handy's business was now fully removed to New York City, the risk of the move and his as yet largely unestablished reputation in the city were revealed by Still's later memory that Handy's house band "traveled to a large extent in the South. Not altogether in the South, but more so than any other sections."

Among others then in New York City who were newly employed at the Gaiety Theater Building was Frederick Bryan, who left his conductor's job at the Clef Club after James Europe's murder to become a copyist for Pace & Handy. Working there also were John Barbour, formerly a black vaudeville performer and now a copyist who sometimes played with Handy's touring orchestra; the mysterious H. Qualli Clark (1880?–1950?), a former Mahara minstrel who had toured as far as Australia and who showed a blues talent with his composition for the firm in 1919, "Pee Gee's Blues: Foxtrot"; and, foremost to achieve later fame as a composer and arranger among the new employees, there was Fletcher Henderson, later a big-band leader throughout the 1930s, who after graduation from Atlanta University joined Pace & Handy in 1920.

"Uncle Tom's Cabin" was how the Pace & Handy office became known, not necessarily affectionately, by white tenants of the Gaiety Theater Building. Disparagingly described or not, Handy's office unquestionably was becoming a magnet for African American composers, musicians, and performers, some of whom were already established and others who would become masters of jazz. Bert Williams, the former colored minstrel and current vaudevillian comedian, who was perhaps the highest-paid black performer of the time, was a frequent visitor; he successfully performed a Pace & Handy–owned comic monologue onstage, "O Death, Where Is Thy Sting?" and he eventually also became an office tenant at 1547 Broadway. Clarence Williams, whose Blue Five combo of the 1920s would feature Louis Armstrong and Sidney Bechet, also made his way from New Orleans to New York to visit the Pace & Handy office; he and his wife became very close friends to Handy. And there were many other black performers for whom Handy's geniality—and his willingness to make small loans or buy a needed meal—attracted them to him. Earlier, he also had renewed his acquaintance in the city with his friend and former Mahara minstrel, the underappreciated early jazz man Wilbur "Sweat" Sweatman.

But whether called Uncle Tom's Cabin or not, Pace & Handy's office was not a place of exclusively black employees. Also working there was J. Russell Robinson, who as a young white man growing up in Memphis had heard Handy's bands, and who after working in Georgia as a pianist to accompany silent movies, moved to New York City and was hired by Pace & Handy in 1918 to work as a song demonstrator. More than a generation before Jerry Lee Lewis would play a piano in Memphis, Robinson was known professionally in the mid-1910s as "the White boy with the colored fingers." Robinson later wrote the lyrics to Handy's "Ole Miss Rag."

Robinson's most important duty for the firm was to promote the use of Pace & Handy song properties by white vaudevillians and performers. Handy and his partner without doubt still were looking for that elusive national crossover hit and for the white performer who could perform it under license from their company. In addition to "A Good Man Is Hard to Find," the two had come tantalizingly close in September 1919, when "Beale Street Blues," as Handy's song was now copyrighted, was included among the numbers in the Broadway musical revue *Shubert's Gaieties of 1919*. Attendance at New York shows was at first hampered by a labor walkout of Broadway performers, one of many labor strikes in that strife-filled year for America. The popular white performers George Jessel and Gilda Gray were among this revue's singers who did choose to appear on the stage, and Gray's introduction to Broadway audiences of "Beale Street Blues" noticeably won at least as much applause as did another of the revue's numbers, "You'd Be Surprised," by Irving Berlin. And the next year, in 1920, Pace & Handy at last found their new white performer and their great, legally owned crossover success. With this performer's recording of an earlier Handy composition of 1914, the "St. Louis Blues" shook off its torpor and began its magnificent rise to become an international best seller and classic of American popular music. On September 25, 1920, the *Freeman* carried the following notice:

> Lovers of Phonograph music will be delighted to know that Miss Marion Harris, who sang for the Victor Company, and now under contract for the Columbus [Columbia] Co., has made a wonderful record of the "ST. LOUIS BLUES," also PACE & HANDY's latest song hit, "LONG GONE."

Almost totally forgotten in this century, Marion Harris (1896–1944), the "Jazz Vampire," was once one of this nation's most popular female vocalists and a culturally stylistic model for young white women throughout the country. A small-town twenty-four-year-old who had dyed her hair to blond, bobbed it short, and gone to the big city, Harris had charmed audiences in New York City with her coquettish performances of sentimental tunes in musicals at the Globe and Knickerbocker theaters. But as a vaudeville performer she also could "sell it within an inch of her life" with her personally chosen renditions of "Hot Lips," "I'm Gonna Do It If I Like It," "You've Got to See Your Momma Every Night," and, most notoriously in 1920, "I'm a Jazz Vampire." This was no crude coon shouting. Harris as a vocalist sometimes was remarkably "modern" sounding, often using her phrasing for erotic effect, rather than forthrightly singing her blues from her diaphragm. *"There's something in the tone of a saxophone / That makes me do a little wiggle all my own,"* she had teased and vamped her audiences with "I'm a Jazz Baby" in 1919. (In an early flapper look, Harris wore flat-chested, very short dresses, creating an effect either of an androgynous independence or an advertisement that she was available and "fast." Her nearest competitors, Sophie Tucker and May "I'm Looking for the Bully of the Town" Irwin, were much more formidable and buxom women, in a pre–World War I image of female sexuality.) Harris's atmospheric rendition of "After You're Gone" for Victor in 1918 had helped establish that song as a perennial classic.

She was also very open to performing songs about or by African Americans. She had, in addition to her following by young white fans, a considerable black audience nationally for her records. The *Freeman* notice was as much about her as Handy. In 1918 Harris had done her patriotic bit by recording her own unconventional version of a Great War song, "Good-bye Alexander, Good-bye Honey Boy": *"Alexander Cooper was a colored trooper . . . Good-bye, Alexander, good-bye, Honey Boy, / In that uniform you fill my heart with joy."* That year Harris also recorded for Victor her version of "I Ain't Got Nobody Much." ("Nobody" was the signature song of the black vaudevillian Bert Williams, and Harris performed her song very much in his style.) And, in a perfect choice for this young woman known both as the "Jazz Baby" and the "Jazz Vampire" and who was half ingénue and half femme fatale, in 1919 she recorded "A Good Man Is Hard to Find."

The two partners at the Gaiety Building certainly noticed her exceptional rendition of their musical property and other blues. Harry Pace rather than Handy is believed to have been the one who in 1920 persuaded Harris to record the "St. Louis Blues" for Columbia Records after Victor refused her request to record it. (The Victor

Company presumably thought, not unreasonably, that no one would buy a record of a six-year-old blues song that in some measures sounds more like a tango. The Jazz Vampire, for her part, apparently did not like to be refused.)

Harris was the first white performer to record a romantic, atmospheric version of the "St. Louis Blues," and her part in making the song an enormous crossover success in the coming decades for Handy cannot be underestimated. From his composition of his song in 1914 until 1918, only two recordings of the "St. Louis Blues" had been released, both in a military-band style. Handy himself had not recorded it at his 1917 sessions. Incredibly, he appears to have arranged an "exclusive" soon after its copyright in 1914 for his song to be performed onstage only by the minstrelsy and vaudeville female impersonator, the soubrette Charles Anderson. Handy either had not then realized that his blues as a musical art had escaped the novelty act of the colored minstrel olio, or he needed whatever money his latest composition could bring him. Harris recorded the song singing the lyrics in standard English rather than Handy's African American dialect, and in one version changed Handy's original lyric to sing of a rival with "yellow hair." Subsequent to Harris's recording of this song for Columbia on April 16, 1920, the "St. Louis Blues" was recorded by three other white performers and bands between 1921 and 1922, including the Original Dixieland Jazz Band. This latter recording on its first release returned royalties to Pace & Handy on 179,440 records sold. Before the end of the decade, at least twenty-five other different recordings of "St. Louis Blues" would be issued, many by white performers. Earlier, Sophie Tucker had sung it coon-style, and Katharine Handy had performed it with more subtlety on the stage, at her father's wishes. But neither performer had the vocal expressiveness or the commercial marketing behind her as did this young white vocalist. It is as a haunting, erotic lament that the "St. Louis Blues" was first recorded and sung onstage by Marion Harris, which is how most people now recognize its melody and regard it as a masterpiece.

Like all romantic masterpieces, the "St. Louis Blues" is the lyrical objectification of deeply remembered subjective experiences—"powerful feelings from the emotions recalled in tranquility," as an earlier adapter of folk ballads had phrased it—and not simply an autobiography of the composer's hard times. Handy chose to write the lyrics in rural black dialect, a further emotional distancing by the highly literate and sophisticated composer. (And Marion Harris was perhaps the only white performer at the time who could sing these lines in "standard" English with credibility to both white and black audiences.) Handy's now-famous opening words and notes—*I hate to see de eve-nin' sun go down / Cause my baby, he done lef' this town*—certainly recall his nights spent in despair on the cobblestone levees of St. Louis in 1893, homeless and jobless. But the song's following measures also enclose a full lifetime of personal experiences and artistic responses by Handy as he had sympathetically moved through the lives of many others, black and nonblack, from the big cities on the Mississippi River, the turn-of-the-century tropical island of Cuba, and the small towns of the American South.

The majestic, almost funereal, marchlike strains of the chorus of his "St. Louis Blues"—*Got de blues / Got de St. Louis Blues / Jes as blue as Ah can be*—were inspired in him much earlier than his Missouri misfortunes. Handy recalled first hearing the beginnings of this musical passage years before as a teenager in the 1890s in the liturgical singing by a senior member of his father's African Methodist Episcopal church in Florence, exhorting the black congregation to step forward to the altar of the small church and to drop into the collection plate whatever they could—*Come a-long, Come a-long, Come a-long.* This passionate singing by a church elder, Lazarus Gardner, recollected in tranquility, was later fashioned by Handy into one of the most moving passages of a secular masterpiece. Generations of rhythm-and-blues audiences would recognize its effect when subsequent performers in their songs would be called upon by their audiences to *Testify, Testify,* to the emotive power of singing the blues.

In its full score, the "St. Louis Blues" also includes the combination of sixteen bars and the folk blues' twelve-bar strains that so had intrigued Handy since 1909 and his composition of "Mister Crump." He knew lyrically that in this new song he wanted something "of the wail of a lovesick woman," he recalled thinking as he composed—*Dat man of mine got a heart lak a rock cast in the sea / Or else he wouldn't gone so far from me.* These notes and lyrics, Handy later explained, would be written as of the "doloric rhythm of a rock cast into the sea and numerous repercussions along the shore." Also into this third strain of his song he incorporated, as he specified in the printed 1914 score, the "melody from 'Jogo Blues,'" which Handy first had overheard whistled by a black workman—melancholy, tired, but still hopeful—returning late at night to his home in the Greasy Plank neighborhood. These were not the intentions or the memories of a naïve folk composer.

Handy additionally wrote something else unique into the second strain to his "St. Louis Blues": a nonblues Hispanic-originated melody that distinguishes this blues song from many others and also makes it so memorable to generations of listeners. This is the tango melody that Handy had first heard with his wife in Havana in 1900. Just as in "Mister Crump" the twelve-bar blues is enclosed by the sixteen bars of ragtime, so the "St. Louis Blues" has its hidden gift of the tango, with its inevitably erotic associations, beginning with the appearance of the femme fatale of that *Saint Louie woman wid her diamon' rings / Pulls that man aroun' by her apron strings / 'Twant for powder an' store-bought hair / De man I love would not gone nowhere . . .*

In the early-twentieth-century recordings of this song, including by Marion Harris, the tango measures were usually played up-tempo with cymbals or other brass, and, as in Harris's later recording with the Brunswick label, the inclusion of libidinal-sounding saxophones and clarinets. Thus, in an artistic experiment for Handy and a daring intuitive move by Harris, the familiar structure of jaunty ragtime/teasing melancholy/jaunty ragtime of "Mister Crump" is replaced in the "St. Louis Blues"—musically and verbally—with its new structure of blues/flashing erotic image/dirge of blues. In its repetition of current regret and remembered eroticism it is irresistible to all audiences. Who has not, for good or ill, at some time in the past, known—or wished they had known—his St. Louis woman? The "St. Louis Blues" became one of the most frequently performed and recorded songs of the twentieth century.

And beginning in 1920, Handy's song became much more than just a highly profitable crossover success. It also joined that wonderfully ethnically mixed American heritage of popular music, including "Jump Jim Crow," "God Bless America," "Dixie," "Happy Days Are Here Again," and "Shake, Rattle, and Roll," that so many listeners in this nation have at times traditionally enjoyed to the point that the music seems never to have had an individual originator. To a large degree, Handy had fulfilled his announced intention to be an "*American* composer." His song is now part of the shared American experience.

One careful listener to Handy's song in the subsequent decade was William Faulkner, as he was now known. He additionally fashioned a piece of Handy's art into the canon of American literary fiction. Faulkner apparently had long remembered Handy's performances in Oxford and he later used part of the words from Handy's lyric as the ironic title of his 1931 short story, "That Evening Sun Go Down." It tells a more harrowing blues, wherein a young black woman in Mississippi dreads sundown, knowing her ex-lover will return to her cabin in darkness and cut her throat.

For their part, Harris and Handy continued their friendly and mutually profitable musical relationship throughout the mid-1920s. Her photograph as a young vamp illustrated several Pace & Handy printed scores. "Marion Harris was in rehearsing 'Beale Street Blues,'" Handy at the Broadway office breezily added to a letter sent to Pace from Handy's office in March 1921. Her release of "Beale Street Blues" sold very well that year for Columbia Records. (She had recorded the "Long Gone" blues composed by Handy with words by the indefatigable Chris Smith on the reverse side of the "St. Louis Blues" recording.) The following year Harris recorded "Aggravatin' Papa" for Brunswick, a composition coauthored by J. Russell Robinson. Brunswick subsequently released its own recording in 1923 of Harris singing the "St. Louis Blues," which returned a respectable royalty to Handy on 39,981 records sold by this small company. Handy's best song continued its growing popularity with white audiences and performers. By the end of the decade, the Paul Whiteman Orchestra recorded a very successful orchestrated version of the "St. Louis Blues," and, in perhaps the ultimate acknowledgment of a crossover success, Rudy Vallee and

His Connecticut Yankees also recorded their version, with the "Heigh-ho!" bandleader attempting to sing this song in its black dialect.

By the end of fiscal 1920, the firm of Pace & Handy held sales receipts and accounts receivable in royalties of at least $76,000. Much of this was the result of the "St. Louis Blues," "Beale Street Blues," and "A Good Man Is Hard to Find." The office of these two rising black entrepreneurs could no longer be disparaged as "Uncle Tom's Cabin." Enjoying its increased revenues, Pace & Handy moved its business and furnishings in 1920 to 232 West Forty-sixth Street, where it occupied an entire building.

Handy that year also made a down payment on a handsome house for his family on the exclusive Strivers' Row, at 232 West 139th Street in Harlem, where residences sold at the time for $8,000 to $10,000 and up. Such were the ups and downs of his career, and of Elizabeth Handy's life with her husband—from a threatened foreclosure in Memphis in 1916 to an expensive town house in 1920 in New York City within a neighborhood originally designed by famed architect Stanford White.

Of course, financial reversals soon came. Nationally, a serious recession began to take hold from 1919 to 1921, as the Woodrow Wilson administration abruptly canceled millions of dollars of contracts for war material just as hundreds of thousands of young men were reentering the civilian labor market at factories and farms after their military demobilizations. (Or, as Handy, a lifelong supporter of the Republican Party, optimistically would have put it, the nation was not yet fully entered into the GOP prosperity of the new presidential administration of Warren G. Harding.) There also occurred in these years what were then the worst incidents of racial rioting in the United States, in cities including Chicago (from which he was lucky to have removed his offices and residence), Washington, D.C., and Knoxville, Tennessee. Sales of sheet music temporarily declined for publishers, the firm of Pace & Handy not excepted. Woolworth's dime stores eliminated their music counters, a serious loss of sales to the music publishing company. "Some recording companies went out of business," Handy additionally recalled. "Others sent us promissory notes instead of checks with our royalty statements."

Even worse in consequences for Handy's financial and legal future, the name and presence of Pace soon would be removed from their business. In January 1921, Harry Pace announced to Handy that he was leaving their partnership. He made this decision, he explained, in order to form his own phonographic recording company, to be devoted exclusively to recording black performers.

Handy in his memoir expressed surprise at Pace's move. "He simply chose this time to sever connections with our firm," Handy later wrote. "No harsh words were expressed." This was true as far as it went. Pace's interest in the phonographic business—as well as a totally black-supported mass medium as evinced in W. E. B. Du Bois's short-lived *Moon*—had been a long time coming. And in attempting a black capitalization for a business featuring solely African American performers for an African American audience, Pace perhaps saw himself, more effectively than the more accommodating Handy, as putting into action the calls by Du Bois for a self-accomplished artistry and commerce among the "talented tenth" of the United States' citizens of color. However, Pace's decision certainly also was the result of his feeling unease in the current recession about his creative friend's skills in handling their shared practical matters. "He had disagreed with some of my business methods," Handy then added in his memoir, an expression at once both diplomatically vague and personally honest, perennial characteristics of Handy's. But at least initially in 1921, the commercial parting of ways between Pace and Handy was, as Handy later chose to remember it, mutually cordial and promisingly profitable.

Pace retained some stock ownership in the company that was eventually reorganized that year as the Handy Brothers Music Company. Handy appointed his beloved younger brother, Charles, as a partner, and Pace perhaps tactfully knew that Handy was in no position to buy out his interests. The shared passion for the blues between these two former Memphis musical entrepreneurs, Pace and Handy, promised an opportunity for what a later generation would call a synergy: Pace intended profitably to record popular Handy-owned properties exclusively with black performers, as well as songs from other publishing companies. Such recordings in turn would provide a steady flow of royalties to his former partner while

Handy independently pursued the white market. Handy, however, was soon hurt both emotionally and practically when fourteen of his employees, including Fletcher Henderson, chose to leave Handy Brothers and to work for Pace's new company as a surer employment. Handy retained a lifelong affection for the young William Grant Still because of the latter's decision to remain for a while with Handy Brothers. And quarrels between the two former partners soon began, as always, about Handy's haphazard management of what remained of their corporation's money.

Pace, as he struggled to establish his new company—initially known as the Pace Phonographic Company and then, more poetically, as Black Swan Records—was vexed, to put it mildly, at the number of bad checks and notes returned by banks and drawn on the account of Pace & Handy, for which he was still legally liable. "Your check #325 in favor of Mr. I. Price for $16.65 on the Solvent Savings Bank and Trust Co. of Memphis, Tenn., has been returned to us," the bookkeeper at the Pace Phonographic Company wrote, in one of many such incidents, to Handy Brothers on June 25, 1921. (Irving Price was Handy's relative.) One month later, Pace personally contacted Handy in regard to a debt of $89.95 owed to the Lyraphone Company that "was due July 1st and which has been charged to my account by the bank. . . . [W]ill you please let me have your check for this amount as it was charged to me personally by the bank where it was discounted?" Handy was personally honest, but he was hopeless as a money manager and too eager to say yes to vendors and to performers. Pace became further infuriated when he learned that soon after his departure either Handy or someone else at his company had agreed to an exclusive performance deal with Harry Raderman, the Laughing Trombone Man, to perform "Beale Street Blues" on the vaudeville stage with no royalty payments either to Pace or Handy.

Throughout the autumn of 1921 and into 1922, Pace continued to send increasingly impatient letters to Handy Brothers asking for payment or repayment of notes and returned checks drawn on Pace & Handy. ("You know, of course, that I have my own problems and that I must finance my business," Pace wrote again to Handy in a dunning letter of 1922. "You do not seem to realize it and I do not think you have ever thought along this line, but I am carrying a very heavy burden in this connection through the endorsement of these notes and through my collateral which is on deposit as security for them." By this time, irritatingly, another Irving Price debt had been presented for payment to Pace's bank account, for $61.48.) These worrying requests could not have come at a worse time for Handy. In 1922, an infected tooth caused severe neuralgia throughout Handy's face, making it difficult for him to focus upon musical notes or even to see his own reflection in a mirror. This was a continuation of his problem with his vision since childhood. By March of that year a botched operation for the pain left Handy temporarily blind. In darkness, Handy took to his bed at home. At that time he did not know if his blindness would be permanent and experienced what he later frankly described as fear. "Fear of what might happen to my business, my family and me. Fear of what people would think and say. Fear of what Pace might do."

After a second operation Handy eventually recovered his eyesight, but it would be two full years, into 1924, before he could see clearly, and his eyesight would continue to bother him for decades. Meanwhile, his serious problems with money continued. As well as his debts to Pace (who had been quite compassionate and forbearing during Handy's total blindness) sales of his own blues and other songs from the Handy Brothers catalog remained slack even after the recession ended and the nation entered into the expanding and speculative economy of the 1920s. Handy, who during his blindness had adopted a personal motto of "fight it out," tried manfully despite his financial worries and health problems to recover his productivity and creativity of 1914–19. His composition of 1921, "Loveless Love: Blues Novelty," was an excellent song but would not gain exceptional popularity until its adaption into swing more than two decades later. In 1922, he wrote and published his adaptation of a black folk blues that he titled "John Henry Blues," as well as published three other compositions, including another of his original compositions, "Ape Mister Eddie." None sold remarkably. Handy tried again in 1923 with his "Harlem Blues" and "Sundown Blues," to no better success. Earlier he had composed and published his lively and personal "Aunt Hagar's Children Blues," the last in a 1915–20 trilogy with "Yellow Dog Blues" and "Beale Street Blues" to become what are now regarded as Handy's classic blues, and which are certainly worthy, after the "St. Louis Blues," of modern performances. But despite its later recognized excellence, "Aunt Hagar's Children Blues" in the early 1920s did not have the success of Handy's earlier Memphis compositions.

The truth was that Handy, forty-nine years old, was becoming a little old-fashioned both in his musical compositions and catalog purchases for popular music consumers of 1922 and subsequent years. The best-selling songs of that year included "Chicago, That Toddling Town," "Hot Lips," and "I Wish I Could Shimmy Like My Sister Kate"—none of them Handy Brothers properties. The urban blues formula of the 1910s that included ragtime syncopation, black folk melodies, tango rhythms, and vaudeville strides, was being replaced in the early twenties by *le jazz hot*, as had been pioneered by the late James Europe. Handy's sure musical touch on the pulse of this nation's popular tastes waned during his years in Memphis and did not come back to him in New York City.

The years 1922–24 unquestionably became the worst of Handy's life since he had been homeless and jobless in St. Louis. In 1922, Handy Brothers grossed only $7,015 in phonographic royalties. His company's outstanding debts were approximately $25,000. Music printers' bills went unpaid. (Pace as a stockholder had forced the decision that royalty payments from Pace & Handy properties first be applied to outstanding loans he had made the company.) Friends advised him to declare bankruptcy. At times even unable to see, Handy was approaching the nightmarish circumstances of becoming what he always had insisted he was not: just another penniless, itinerant black street peddler of the folk blues. In perhaps an unwitting and terrible self-prophecy nine years earlier in Memphis he once had written

> *Married men would have to pick up their beds*
> *   and walk,*
> *Except one or two who never drink booze*
> *And the blind man on the corner who sings these*
> *   Beale Street blues.*

His troubles even worsened when Pace, finally out of patience, filed legal action as a stockholder against W. C. Handy and Charles Handy on April 30, 1924, to have a court-appointed trustee assigned to run the Handy Brothers business. Handy somehow found the funds for a lawyer to represent him in this action. Depositions were followed by counterdepositions. In an ironic reversal of roles, Pace now claimed through his attorney that Handy Brothers had large revenues that were mismanaged by Handy. (Or, with malfeasance, Handy was accused of using Pace & Handy money to pay expenses of the bands that toured under Handy's name exclusively for ready cash to Handy Brothers.) The usually ebullient Handy asserted in court documents that the value of his company was wildly overestimated. In truth, he was obviously borrowing from Peter to pay Paul, but also in truth Handy probably no longer could distinguish Peter's account from Paul's, so desperate was he to satisfy the urgent demands and legal threats of his other creditors. Sometimes with even more acrimony and occasionally with temporary attempts at reconciliations, their dispute would drag on for six more years.

Handy survived throughout 1922–24—by "dint of his individual genius," as Edmund Wilson later dispassionately observed of him— and also by his returning, unshakeable optimism that better days would soon turn up in his life. He sold his Strivers' Row town house and moved with his family into an apartment building at 400 Convent Avenue in Harlem; Handy Brothers also temporarily relocated its office to cheaper spaces; and, in an extremity, he made an arrangement in October 1922 with a friend who did business in the wholesale grocery district to "park" the copyrights Handy personally owned—that is, to sell them to his friend for ready cash at a reduced rate, perhaps even for groceries—with the understanding that Handy later could buy back the rights at a low price. These "parked" copyrights included "Yellow Dog Blues," "Beale Street Blues," and the "St. Louis Blues." Despite the mutual firm assurances that Handy could later reclaim the copyrights at a low price, this arrangement is strong evidence of just how broke he was in 1922. He knew by that year what he had with these songs, but he had reached the point of selling the "St. Louis Blues" possibly just to put food on the table for his family. And inescapable to Handy must have been his memories of how he also once had sold his rights to "The Memphis Blues"—when he was a decade younger and experiencing greater success—for a needed fifty dollars.

Some in the African American community of blues and jazz musicians in New York City did what they could to help "old Handy." A needful loan of one thousand dollars was made, unasked, to Handy by the jazz pianist and composer Clarence Williams and his wife, Eva. This was an act of generosity that Handy remembered with deep feelings of gratitude in his memoir nearly twenty years later.

Handy even briefly attempted to start his own recording company in 1922 with the aid of his daughter Lucile as business manager and his younger daughter Katharine as a performer, but the company apparently folded before releasing any records. He returned to the recording studios himself for two sessions in January and March 1922 for Paramount. The performers were advertised as "W. C. Handy's Memphis Blues Orchestra," but several are believed to have been pickup musicians brought in by Paramount to give Handy's recordings a more contemporary sound. There was one very familiar face to Handy among the session's musicians, however: Jim Turner is credited as playing among the violinists. At this first session, Handy also at last recorded the "St. Louis Blues," a workmanlike version with a particular emphasis by him with his cornet to the tango measures, which introduce his version. The latter recording session of March 1922 was a heroic act by Handy, who was blind by that time. As the lead cornet on this session's recordings of "She's a Mean Job Blues" and "Muscle Shoals Blues," he was playing under extraordinary circumstances.

The Paramount releases and two later releases of "Gulf Coast Blues" and "Farewell Blues," recorded for Okeh Records in May 1923, sold reasonably well. The masters from these Paramount and Okeh recording sessions were later leased for commercial use by other labels, and these songs sold and returned royalties under a variety of labels such as Puritan, Davega—and Black Swan. Handy Brothers remained open, if not exactly solvent, throughout 1924. And sometimes Mister Micawber is right. Better days did turn up, literally on Handy's doorstep in the early spring of 1924, in the unlikely white person of a New Hampshire–born, highly educated Wall Street lawyer named Edward Abbe Niles.

Niles was a practitioner at the prestigious law firm of Cadwalader, Wickersham & Taft and had been a passionate appreciator of blues music since his college years. Just as a generation earlier the composer Charles Ives had listened with fascination to colored minstrels "ragging" their songs at a theater in Connecticut, so Niles as an undergraduate at Trinity College in Hartford delightedly had read in 1913 the score of "The Memphis Blues," finding it to be an "olive among the marshmallows of that year's popular music," in his colorful description. Niles had briefly studied at Oxford University, after serving as an officer in the air corps in the U.S. military. He then took a law degree from Harvard. But his tastes in unconventional popular music continued. He subsequently had become known to his professional peers as "the Boswell of the blues," in their playful reference to the attorney-biographer of Samuel Johnson, as in his off-hours Niles sought out blues performances in the city and began publishing articles in the *Bookman* and other magazines about the still largely black music and its composers. Niles had called on Handy in the spring of 1924, probably in preparation for an article, to ask him questions about his early blues years.

These two men of such different economic and social backgrounds took an immediate liking to each other at their first meeting. Niles found "old Handy" to be, emotionally and intellectually, anything but old: "He is a poet, composer, musician, humorist, and natural born folklorist, and a lot of fun," he later enthused. Handy, for his part, must have been deeply gratified at encountering such an enthusiastic appreciator of his art who also was of an admired Republican Party respectability, which the blues composer himself always hoped to achieve. (The "Taft" in the name of Niles's law firm was Henry W. Taft, relative of the former U.S. president and a member of the Ohio family then recognized politically as having proconsular status within the Republican Party.) Handy and Niles continued to meet and correspond after their first meeting, and Niles became a frequent visitor to the Handy Brothers' office—now in 1925 "doing business back at the old stand," in Handy's somewhat overly optimistic phrase, at 1545 Broadway next to the Gaiety Theater Building.

With a kind of bemused horror, Niles witnessed there what passed for Handy's business management:

> Between storms he reigns supreme, solving old and insoluble difficulties by sheer force of charm and personality, laying the firm foundations of new and worse ones, doing justice, spending money, borrowing more, paying other people's debts, planning good works, buying songs in magnificent haste, repenting at leisure.

In an act of openhearted generosity, Niles shortly after their first meeting volunteered his extensive—and expensive—legal skills to put Handy's business affairs in order, at almost pro bono rates. Handy gratefully accepted. From 1925 onward, although Handy occasionally retained other attorneys, Niles was his most trusted legal advisor and, in some ways, his money manager. It was for Niles, at least at the beginning, a Herculean task. "Things were tough in the '20s and '30s," the attorney later recollected, "and I still have a Handy file entitled 'Sup. Pros and Garnishments' [subpoenas, prosecutions, and garnishments]."

But the friendship between the two, which lasted three decades until Handy's death, was never one between a wealthy white patron and his naïve black folk artist as retainer. Niles never showed off Handy as a novelty or sought to profit commercially from their friendship. He simply could handle money more skillfully than Handy, as most people black or white could, and he was generously willing to apply his education—and to advance his own literary reputation as a blues auteur—by negotiating with creditors and arranging repurchases of sold copyrights to let W. C. Handy continue to be the great artist of "creative and analytic powers" that Niles in print insisted Handy was. And, as F. Scott Fitzgerald wrote of the intuitive kindness of his fictional character Jay Gatsby, Abbe Niles also had a nice sense of when to *stop*. Niles never tried unasked to ingratiate himself or his wife into the racial intimacies of Harlem society. The one possible exception could also be seen as the gracious act of a gentleman. At a party once given at the Cotton Club, at which the Handy family were guests, couples began to dance. Niles noticed that Katharine Handy was left without a partner. He promptly asked her to join him, and he and Handy's daughter then moved elegantly among the other dancing couples. Even for an intellectual bohemian in the New York City of the 1920s, this was a socially daring—and very thoughtful—act.

Handy entered 1926 in much better condition financially, owing both to his own efforts and to Niles's counsel. He recovered the copyrights to his most popular songs, including "Yellow Dog Blues," "St. Louis Blues," and "Beale Street Blues," the latter described by Fitzgerald as so erotically fascinating in his great novel of 1925. Rearranged by other performers and bandleaders for the hot jazz taste of the times, songs in the Handy Brothers catalog again began to be called for. And, in 1926, Handy firmly secured his reputation artistically and historically as the Father of the Blues. This latter artistic accomplishment was literary as well as musical. It was entitled *Blues: An Anthology*, which Niles persuaded the Albert & Charles Boni publishing firm to issue as a book in 1926. "Edited by W. C. Handy" was displayed on its title page, with an introduction by Niles and illustrations by Miguel Covarrubias.

The book was largely written by Niles and expanded from his conversations with Handy to include early instances of blueslike folk songs, work chants, and spirituals "all drawn from the memory of W. C. Handy." Handy serves as witness, progenitor, and controlling influence of the blues, as Niles discusses fifty blues compositions, many with accompanying scores, by both white and African American composers, from Baby Seals to George Gershwin. They all return, in Niles's argument, to Handy's first employment of the blue note. Yet the contributions by Handy and Covarrubias in the making of this anthology were by no means passive. The musical and historical provenances of the selected songs provided to Niles by Handy (and his wife) were encyclopedic and are much cited by later scholars and critics. The lively caricatures drawn by Covarrubias of Harlem street scenes and blues performers (Handy was caricatured on the final page of the book as a paternal-looking, neatly attired walrus) have the excitement of contemporaneous paintings of African American life that by 1925 were also being created by rising Harlem artists such as Archibald Motley Jr., in such paintings as *Syncopation,* and, later, Palmer Hayden in *Midsummer Night in Harlem.*

This learned but passionate exposition in words and graphics of an African American popular composer and his New York milieu literarily raised *Blues: An Anthology* above earlier studies of folk blues by such scholars as Howard Odum. Abbe Niles was "outside the university tradition," Edmund Wilson approvingly wrote in a noticeably praiseful review of both the anthology and Handy's music in *The New Republic.* Indeed, after more than three-quarters of a century in print (the latest edition was published by Arno Press in 1990), *Blues: An Anthology* bids fair to be an unrecognized masterpiece of the Harlem Renaissance. (It certainly was an early example of multiculturalism. "My Lord, a Mexican, a Yankee, and a nigger!" one white lady from the Southwest was said to have exclaimed on seeing the three names of the contributors on the cover of the first edition.) Covarrubias himself was as much an artist of Harlem, which he took as the subject of his 1927 book, *Negro Drawings,* as he was of his native Mexico. And in his remarkable book Niles persuasively compares Handy's artistic achievements in his music and lyrics—including his use of African American colloquialisms—as at least equal in merit to the poetry of the Harlem Renaissance writer Langston Hughes. His first volume of poetry, *The Weary Blues,* also employed the tripartite lyrical structure pioneered by Handy and was published in 1926.

James Weldon Johnson was equally generous in a review of *Blues: An Anthology* for the *Amsterdam News* in the summer of 1926, praising Handy "as the very first musician to recognize the significance of the blues as music." And, in addition to Edmund Wilson, other white urban intellectuals such Carl Van Vechten took up a renewed interest in Handy as a major artist of American popular music as a result of the favorable reviews of the book in the white and black presses.

Blues: An Anthology was the first monumental accomplishment that explains why Handy is still remembered into the twenty-first century, and why such talented performers of his works in the 1920s such as "The Jazz Vampire," Marion Harris, or Wilbur "Sweat" Sweatman are not; or why other African American composers of the early blues in the 1910s such as Chris Smith, Baby Seals, or James Reese Europe are also near-forgotten. Handy, fifty-three years old in 1926, had come through the midpoint of this tumultuous decade with most of his copyrights, his business, and his national reputation intact, and with his eyesight partially restored. He had the physical energy, the economic security, and the personal ambition for one more encore. For the remainder of the 1920s and throughout the 1930s, he would again return to the stage and the bandstand, and even to the sound tracks of motion pictures, to begin a long farewell act to American culture.

CHAPTER TEN

———

Symphonies and Movies, Spirituals and Politics, and W. C. Handy as Perennial Performer, 1927–1941

W. C. Handy, who as everybody is supposed to know, wrote the 'St. Louis Blues' [is] playing around vaudeville theaters in the East now, in an act composed of old-timers.

— *The New Yorker,* August 26, 1933

Handy, as a composer of the blues, and Niles, as its celebrator, had but one artistic divergence during their friendship of three decades, over the symphonic possibilities of African American music. The published blues were for Niles—like the spirituals of black churches—a seemingly naïve but sophisticated American art that was in no way inferior to the symphonies by the nineteenth-century European Romantic composers. Not all American performers and arrangers of the blues with musical ambitions agreed with Niles. Paul Whiteman had enjoyed great success throughout the 1920s conducting highly orchestrated versions of the "St. Louis Blues" and other blues and spirituals. In promoting the orchestral performance by his musicians of what was titled a blues-based "rhapsody" in 1924 by its composer, George Gershwin, Whiteman had sent a letter to his supporters emphasizing his hope that "eventually our music will become a stepping-stone which will be helpful in giving the coming generation a much deeper appreciation of better music."

Such a deliberately provocative statement of the "better music" of classical compositions dismissed both the secular black folk songs and the religious spirituals that Niles had found so artful in Handy's creation of the blues. Niles published his rebuttal in a *New Republic* magazine article of the late summer of 1926, criticizing Whiteman by name, in which Niles argued for black folk music as no mere "stepping-stones" but equal in artistry to, for instance, Antonín Dvořák's celebrated romantic symphonies with their use of American folk melodies. "Dvořák's use of Negro themes doubtless helped the spirituals toward recognition," Niles conceded, but with lawyerly emphasis he then categorically argued that such songs in symphonies "invigorate the latter only at the expense of the former; it is by no means written that the *New World Symphony* will outlive 'Go Down Moses.'"

As always, Handy was more ambiguous artistically in his ambitions for African American–inspired music. On the one hand, he publicly dismissed most symphonic arrangements of the blues or spirituals. In an image that recalled Booker T. Washington's insistence upon the mechanical and agricultural skills, Handy declared that such arrangements reminded him of "a farmer plowing in evening dress." Yet, the idea of a symphonic arrangement of the blues was very much in the intellectual air of America throughout the 1920s. The well-received score in this nation by the French composer Darius Milhaud, of his 1923 ballet *La Création du Monde*—inspired by his earlier visit to Harlem and celebrating the creation of a new, presumably African American–influenced world—incorporated melodies from the "Livery Stable Blues" and King Oliver's Creole Jazz Band. A year later, the most popular American symphonic use of blues was heard in Gershwin's *Rhapsody in Blue,* first performed in concert on February 12, 1924. Handy attended this Aeolian Hall premier performance in New York City, and that night he heard his own blues compositions "glorified," as he put it, in Gershwin's score.

As noted earlier, Paul Whiteman conducted, and although the night's symphonic program prior to the performance of Gershwin's piece included a number of adaptations of earlier blues, none was Handy's. Whiteman led his Palais Royal Orchestra in introductory pieces of what he termed "true jazz" of the previous decade, but had selected such songs as "Livery Stable Blues" by the New Orleans–based Original Dixieland Jazz Band, and "Alexander's Ragtime Band" of 1911 by Irving Berlin instead of "The Memphis Blues" of 1912 for semisymphonic treatment. But when the time came for the final orchestral performance of this concert, and Gershwin took his place at the piano, the composer's new *Rhapsody* immediately became heard as the merging of the "genius of Handy" with the "genius of Gershwin," in the words of the later classical pianist and scholar Henry Levine. Levine finds at least one dozen of what Handy called melodic "snatches" of "Beale Street Blues," "St. Louis Blues," and "Memphis Blues" within Gershwin's score, including the score's celebrated grandioso finale. Handy at this time did not personally know Gershwin—they were introduced after the performance by Whiteman—but he did not begrudge this younger composer's use of his melodic and rhythmic blues material. In fact, family members remembered Handy as having been noticeably happy at Gershwin's success at orchestrating his blues. Gershwin for his part was forthright in acknowledging his musical debt to Handy. He later presented to Handy the score for a piano solo of *Rhapsody* upon which Gershwin had handwritten:

To Mr. Handy,

Whose early 'blues' songs are the forefathers of this work. With admiration & best wishes,

George Gershwin

The score became a prized possession of Handy's. Gershwin subsequently became an occasional and welcomed visitor among the musicians and composers, black and white, who enjoyed dropping by Handy's Broadway office. (It is interesting, however, that by the mid-1920s and the rise of improvisational jazz, Handy's compositions, even the currently popular and rearranged the "St. Louis Blues" and "Beale Street Blues," were being regarded by Gershwin and other young composers as among the "early" blues songs.)

Handy had his opportunities both to conduct a jazz symphony

and to hear his own symphonic adaption of his blues. This latter was the performance at Aeolian Hall on December 6, 1925, of the *Jazz America Symphony* by the classicist composer Albert Chiaffarelli. Musical motifs from the "St. Louis Blues" and "Beale Street Blues" were interspersed with variations on Tchaikovsky. Handy and Niles were in the audience, and after the concert Niles was harsh in his criticism. *The New York Times* was no kinder in its subsequent review, calling the score "glib" and "wholly unconvincing." After this evening's disappointment, Handy had a second chance in the spring of 1927 to conduct a jazz concert himself. The occasion that led to it, appropriate for this most convivial of blues composers, was a cocktail party earlier given by the publisher Donald Friede.

At this party, Aaron Copland had been a guest and had played for Friede a selection from a composition by the Philadelphia expatriate composer George Antheil. The exuberant Friede was so taken by this performance of Antheil's work at his party that he enthusiastically determined to finance a concert of this Paris-based composer's music at Carnegie Hall, including the blues-influenced *Jazz Symphony*. (The title "Jazz Symphony" seems to have been eponymous among some composers during the 1920s.) Antheil's jazz score was a complex arrangement to be played by three saxophones, an oboe, three trumpets and three trombones, one tuba, two banjos, three pianos, four violins, one cello, and one bass. (Also to be used in the evening's performance as specified in the scores for the other performances of Antheil's works were an airplane propeller, a fire-alarm siren, and electric bells. Antheil's aesthetic ideas came highly approved by Ezra Pound.) Paul Whiteman declined, perhaps wisely, to conduct the symphony. Friede then approved the "excellent idea" of inviting Handy to conduct. "Surely the man who wrote the 'St. Louis Blues' would be a welcome addition to our already exciting group of performers," this producer remembered telling himself, perhaps in an instance of hopefully whistling in the dark.

Surprisingly, Handy accepted, apparently intrigued by the symphonic possibilities of this idea. Strangely, he also seemed "the least disturbed," Friede later remembered, among all those musicians who read Antheil's highly intricate scores. As for the fire siren and the airplane propeller to be used in the other pieces, Handy probably had known much more unusual sound effects to have been called for during the olio or afterpiece of his minstrelsy years. He himself had not been above using cowbells in his blues performances.

Handy attempted five times at rehearsals to conduct the *Jazz Symphony* to a satisfactory musical conclusion before giving up. The multi-shifting tempos, the abrupt, sometimes improvisational changes from one instrument to another, and the deliberate dissonances of Antheil's score—jazz itself—were simply not in his musical repertoire as a conductor or performer. Any extended experimentation beyond the twelve-bar blues, Friede sadly concluded of Handy, was "beyond him." After these failed rehearsal attempts, Friede and Handy then mutually agreed as friends that Handy was not the man for the job. However much he was ambitious for the "better music" of the symphonic blues, Handy's version of his music by the mid-1920s had developed into a jazz that was beyond his skills.

He could consider himself lucky that he was not the conductor on the podium at the April 10, 1927, concert at Carnegie Hall. The *Jazz Symphony* under the direction of conductor Allie Ross was well received, but Antheil's accomplishment was lost in the debacle of the performance of his other scores that followed. The airplane propeller malfunctioned and blew the hats off the ladies in the eleventh row, until one gentleman began waving a white handkerchief in apparent surrender. The fire siren stuck at its full clarion volume and could not be turned off. The audience began to laugh at inappropriate places, and Friede was later forced to conclude that his ambitious musical presentation had been a "flop." In the spirit of the twenties, however, the postperformance party exceeded the concert. The music critic Carl Van Vechten was in the audience—"loved the din"—and later noted in his journal: "Afterwards Donald Friede gives a ball and supper at the Club Deauville, & nearly everybody was there. . . . Home at 5. *W. C. Handy conducts orchestra at club* [original italics]." The music Handy conducted at the Club Deauville presumably was more to his liking.

Other than Gershwin, the only American composer and conductor to have achieved lasting aesthetic or popular success with a blues symphony in this decade was Handy's former employee William Grant Still. The latter's *Afro-American Symphony*, completed in 1930 and frequently performed since, employs an original twelve-bar blues for its theme, introductorily played by the English horn. Despite the hopes of Handy and others, further attempts at the blues symphonies throughout the 1920s are largely forgotten and unperformed. Symphonic developments of the blues would come after 1930, not during the 1920s, and it would be Edward "Duke" Ellington who was remembered as their composer and conductor, not W. C. Handy.

The Modernist blues or jazz symphony of the 1920s, both in terms of Handy's individual talents and the decade's aesthetic attempts at the musical genre, seems to have come chronologically to a dead end. With the important exceptions of the compositions by Gershwin and Still, the concept appears dated as inextricably to the decade of the 1920s as the musical composition "Krazy Cat Ballet" by John A. Carpenter, inspired by the surrealistic comic strip *Krazy Kat*, or Ezra Pound's poem "Hugh Selwyn Mauberley," or many other near-forgotten Modernist attempts of that decade to combine high and low art. Or, it could be vigorously argued, the blues and jazz symphonies *did* succeed in the 1920s and beyond, in the new form of symphonic arrangements and sound tracks to this nation's movies. (Still himself later moved to California and composed cinema orchestrations for Columbia Pictures.) Here again, Handy was an innovator and creative influence.

Almost as soon as the cinema had a reliable sound track, the songs of W. C. Handy were being recorded to accompany the moving images. The score to the "St. Louis Blues" was featured in at least ten short films by Vitaphone Studios between 1927 and the end of the decade. The song was further rearranged symphonically to great effect for the powerful score accompanying Paul Muni's acting for the gripping drama *I Am a Fugitive from a Chain Gang*. And, in the third remake later in the century of *The Great Gatsby*, in 1974, a lively scene between actors Robert Redford and Mia Farrow is accompanied by a witty piano performance of "Beale Street Blues."

Handy also is listed in film credits as musical advisor for what is perhaps historically the most important film of the 1920s featuring the early blues, the RKO Studios 1929 production of *The St. Louis Blues*, in which Bessie Smith, the soon to be acclaimed "Empress of the Blues," makes the only cinematic appearance of her career. The film was shot in the month of June at RCA Photophone studios in

Astoria, New York. A short introductory scene brings Smith on camera as the scorned lover—her hated rival, the "St. Louis Woman," also makes an appearance played by Isabelle Washington, a former employee at Black Swan Records—and Smith delivers her blues in a stage setting reminiscent of a Beale Avenue saloon, in which she appears very much at home. Smith sings the title song like she owns it and puts Marion Harris's earlier version in the shade. Members of the Fletcher Henderson Orchestra, under Handy's direction, provided the recorded accompaniment. Bessie Smith's performance in this film is considered by many as her finest singing of Handy's song, and, once again as in 1909, Handy was present at this historical moment as the controlling musical director.

Handy genuinely enjoyed Bessie Smith's company and had recommended her for this film role after she recorded his "Yellow Dog Blues" and other of his most popular songs. Even before their cinematic collaboration, she had been a welcomed social visitor at his Broadway offices, where they naturally fell into the roles of the good-time girl and her easy-rider man. Handy delighted in later years in retelling to others a story first told to him by Smith of how, when a park had been dedicated in his name at Memphis, a black vagrant had been ordered by a city police officer to "move on" from the park. The man had stood his ground, indignantly protesting, in Smith's description, "Ya'll white folks ain't got nothin' to do with me sleeping here. *This is Handy's Park.*" Handy always laughed when retelling her story, and he subsequently grieved when his good friend Smith was killed in 1937 in an automobile accident outside Clarksdale, Mississippi.

In another cinematic work of the 1920s, Handy himself, or at least a representative persona of him, was presented in a short feature by Vitaphone, *Ill Wind.* The plot, such as it is, presents a genial-appearing, middle-aged black gentleman, played by an actor who closely resembled the composer and who suddenly receives a hand-delivered note from his fiancée. The screen shows its contents:

Dear Mr. Handy

Our engagement is off. You have been very kind but I don't love you anymore.

Emmy White, my best friend, will deliver this note and the
tickets for the dance we were supposed to attend tonight.

Goodbye—Georgine

The ever-optimistic Handy on the screen, momentarily crest-fallen, now notices the attractive Miss Emmy White, who returns his interested glances. The two then exit the frame, arm in arm for the dance. By the time of this film's release, "Mr. Handy" apparently had become a generic cultural name for any well-known, jovial African American blues patriarch of a certain age, an identity that in later decades would be assumed in public by Handy's younger successor, Louis Armstrong.

Handy ended the 1920s apparently reconciled to the fact that the musical tastes for improvisational or hot jazz had passed him by. He earlier had demonstrated his own unchanging tastes in his sole major stage performance of the 1920s, a Carnegie Hall concert organized by Handy Brothers and advertised as showing the evolution of African American music. "The business of jazz is so dressed up that it has lost whatever soul it once possessed," Handy declared in a newspaper advertisement for this concert. "There's more art in a simple spiritual than in all the technical jazz orchestrations put together."

At this concert, the songs selected by Handy for performances by himself and about ninety other black musicians on the evening of April 27, 1927, did not venture in evolution much beyond the compositions of about 1916. "Jazz as it is jazzed in the nightclubs seemed furthest from this bald and smiling leader's presentation of it," *The New York Times* wrote the next morning in a generally favorable review. "The Memphis Blues" and "Beale Street Blues" were performed, the latter most memorably by Thomas "Fats" Waller on organ, along with a solo rendition of the "St. Louis Blues" sung by Handy's daughter Katharine. Handy's program was "simple jazz at its source," the *Times* continued, with spirituals also included. And, in an instance of Handy's constant insistence that black minstrelsy was also a legitimate contributor to American music, the composer had booked aging minstrel performers to again jump Jim Crow, this time on the stage of Carnegie Hall. The evening's performance even had included several cakewalks and walk-arounds by the black singers and dancers in the custom of the nineteenth-century minstrel show's first piece and afterpiece. Or, as the writer for *The New York Times*, who apparently had been unacquainted with the previous century's black minstrelsy, put it, "At times the participants slowly circled around the stage."

This was a nostalgia act that with small variations Handy would repeat into the 1930s. His acceptance that the popular era of the twelve-bar published blues had passed—both for him personally and for the blues catalog of Handy Brothers Music—must have been reinforced to him by the definitive end of any business obligations to Harry Pace in 1930. Pace had written Handy that year offering, as he had earlier, to sell his remaining stock in their former company and end their legal dispute. Handy was now in a financial position to agree. His erstwhile partner was no longer actively in the music business. Pace had returned to insurance and a highly successful career there. Ironically, his Black Swan Records—although remembered admirably by later music historians as "the record label of the Harlem Renaissance" and as the innovative recorder of such black artists as Ethel Waters—had lasted but two years, while the enterprise of the more feckless Handy would continue to do business into the twenty-first century. Despite its failure, Black Swan Records had been the most popular black-owned distributor of African American music until the rise in the late 1950s of Motown Records; in many ways, Harry Pace had been ahead of his times in the 1920s, just as Handy by 1930 was falling behind his.

That year, the former partners met one evening in New York, Handy accompanied by Abbe Niles, to complete the transfer of stock. Niles discovered at the last moment that a notary public was needed to legally validate the stock sale and that it was after business hours to telephone for one. Only after a frantic search was a notary found working at a Harlem funeral parlor, and late at night the transaction was completed there.

Handy decided to return to Memphis for about a year after the final dissolution of Pace & Handy. He was invited by the city in 1931 to attend the formal opening of a park (*"Handy's"* park, as Bessie Smith laughingly told him) on Beale Avenue to be named in his honor. Boss Crump, very much alive and very much in power, initially had opposed the idea. He still remembered Handy's local reputation as a tippler and rounder among the Beale Avenue saloons (or maybe he had finally gotten the joke to "Mister Crump"). Rather sourly, the political boss observed that he would hate to name a city park after someone who might one morning be found sleeping off a bender in it. Local friends and associates of Handy's such as George Lee interceded, however, and reminded Crump both of the favorable national press such an act by him would bring to his city and of the esteem in which Handy was regarded by voters in the black wards. Crump listened to the better angels of his nature, and Handy got his park. He arrived in Memphis for the dedication on March 29, 1931, leading a two-mile parade down Beale before an estimated crowd of ten thousand cheering spectators. Black fraternal societies marched behind the smiling and waving Handy in the leading automobile, including members of the city's social clubs of African American chauffeurs and barbers. Among the musical performers also stepping in the parade was the brass band of the local Knights of Pythias lodge, his first employer in the city more than a quarter of a century earlier.

After the dedication, Handy remained in Memphis into 1932, fronting occasional blues and jazz bands. He may simply not have wanted to go back to New York. Although both Handy and Elizabeth were devoted parents to their now-grown children, it was an open secret in show business that by the early 1930s the two were living much of their lives, albeit cordially in public, emotionally and physically apart. It should be remembered for Elizabeth Handy's part how steadfast she had remained to him during his early blindness and how many years she had lived self-effacingly with a husband frequently absent. For his part, Handy was far more gregarious than his wife and was inexorably drawn to outspoken and strong-willed women. (He was, it should be remembered, the fascinated celebrator of the infamous "St. Louis Woman.") In the 1930s, he was often seen in the company of Louise Logan, a woman whom he introduced to others as his personal assistant. Beyond that, Handy and his family, and his descendants, have kept a discreet silence. Soon after his return from Memphis, he again left his home for another tour.

As breezily observed in *The New Yorker*, Handy was on the road in 1933, appearing in theaters nationally with Joe Laurie's *Memory Lane*. He was then sixty years of age, but he was the comparative young-ster of the troupe, as most of the acts predated the "Blues Spring" of 1917 and were once popular in prewar vaudeville. (And some of the entertainers dated to much before: included was the eighty-nine-year-old Tommy Harris, who claimed to have danced, possibly in a "Jump Jim Crow" performance, for Abraham Lincoln.) There were still paying audiences in 1931 to be found for these early songs in small and medium-sized towns, even during the worst year of the Depression. And, for Handy, the money was easy: there was usually no more than a brief stage appearance at each engagement, playing the "St. Louis Blues" on his cornet or trumpet. For more contempo-rary urban audiences, Benny Goodman, Tommy Dorsey, Cab Cal-loway, Django Reinhardt, and Paul Whiteman were all recording popular rearrangements of Handy's compositions throughout the 1930s, with subsequent good royalties to Handy Brothers.

He was no mere old trouper. Upon his return to New York City, Handy vigorously applied his energies from 1935 onward to his new interests of strengthening the catalog of Handy Brothers Music Company and applying his celebrity to advocate some surprisingly liberal political causes, such as the leftist cause in the Spanish Civil War. As showman throughout the 1930s, Handy would never pass up a profitable opportunity to briefly appear on the nightclub stage—a writer for *The New York Times* on the night of October 15, 1938, would find this "venerable composer" performing the "St. Louis Blues" at the Cotton Club in Harlem, where "he claps a tin mute onto his trumpet and silences the audiences for a few aston-ishing seconds before he vanishes behind the swirl of fifty dusky maidens." But neither was he predictably a nostalgia act nor was he finished with his ambitions for African American music. And he was willing to risk his public persona of venerable jollity in order to enter the political controversies of the 1930s.

In a major artistic shift in 1935–37, Handy changed the new catalog of his music company and his own compositional energies in order to promote another distinctively African American form of music, the spiritual. It was not that great a distance to travel, musically; Beale Avenue also had been the street address of a large number of Baptist and African Methodist Episcopal churches and of their singing black congregations, as well as the avenue's more celebrated blues-loving saloons and bordellos. As Handy affirmed in his memoir, "the blues and spirituals are first cousins." Like the African American folk blues, the religious songs of spirituals frequently share with their secular counterparts a call-and-response structure, a strong lyric narrative, and occasional syncopation and unexpected flatted notes, all sung in common time, that had so fascinated Handy since his Mississippi years.

Handy had, of course, grown up hearing spirituals in Alabama. He once recalled to William Grant Still how, sometime in the late 1880s, he had worked as a teenager as the janitor at a white Baptist church in Florence, and the pastor there subsequently had made a courtesy visit to worship services at the African Methodist Episcopal Church led by Handy's father. "Our congregation sang in unison 'That Love My Jesus Gave Me Shine Like a Morning Star.'" Handy continued his reminiscence: "After that, whenever we met I had to sing that Spiritual for the white minister, so he could teach it to his congregation. He said the words are convincing and reveal a sublime faith." This spiritual later became one of many that Handy rearranged for commercial publication. Throughout the decade of the 1930s, Handy personally composed or rearranged for Handy Brothers a total of twenty-eight spirituals (in contradistinction to his having composed eleven strictly blues songs for Pace & Handy in the decade of the 1910s), and his company published arrangements and original compositions of spirituals by Still and many others. Just as he had brought the black folk blues beyond a regional expression of racial melancholy or carnal pleasure and into the mainstream of American music, so he determined from 1935 onward to bring the religious songs of his youth to a national audience. More than moving expressions of black piety, the spirituals were, Handy determined, also a national music that under his compositional hand could take its place as great American art.

In 1937, Handy published *Twelve Negro Spirituals,* arranged for voice and piano by Still. The next year he assembled his own scored rearrangements and the traditional lyrics of twelve spirituals into his 1938 book, *W. C. Handy's Collection of Negro Spirituals.* In the book's "Author's Note," Handy both movingly recalled first hearing these spirituals in his Alabama boyhood and compared them favorably to subsequent symphonic arrangements, presumably including jazz and blues, of African American–influenced music:

> Masterful choral or symphonic arrangements may probe deep into my emotions, but none can supersede that happy feeling of possession which is mine when, closing my eyes, I can become transplanted again to my own native Florence, Alabama, and the African Methodist Episcopal Church, first to be built by my grandfather and from whose pulpit my father preached many a sermon.

In this introduction Handy then distinguishes by mention the two "all but forgotten" members of his father's Alabama church— Reverends Northcross and Cordy White—who first had taught him to sing spirituals. This mention by name of the early practitioners was intentional. As Handy later wrote to Still about his own renewed interest in spirituals, his 1938 book was intended not only as an artistic statement but also as "a study for those engaged in research." His own research of spirituals, he told Still, "was not made in any archives or remote corners of the Southland, but from the recesses of my own mind." As with the published blues, Handy was attempting to bring to a national audience what he believed was a neglected African American art while he was personally trying to establish himself as a progenitor, or at least its earliest composer in formal scores.

Of course, as with the published blues, there were other "fathers" besides Handy born in the decade of the 1870s, in the first-generation African Americans not to grow up in slavery, who in the 1920s and 1930s also promoted the music of the spirituals to a national audience. These included James Weldon Johnson (1871–1938) and his brother, John Rosamond Johnson (1873–1954), who jointly edited and arranged *The Books of American Negro Spirituals* in 1925–26. Handy's artistic and personal ambitions for spirituals also were a historical consequence of the musical artistry of his fellow African American composer and arranger of spirituals who was the older friend of Handy's mature years, Harry T. Burleigh (1866–1949). Burleigh had studied in 1892 at the National Conservatory of Music in New York City, and there he sang the spirituals he had learned from his ex-slave grandfather in a private performance for the visiting Antonín Dvořák. So taken had been Dvořák by this performance of black folk music that he introduced spiritual melodies into his own "New World Symphony." Handy is second only to the now-neglected Burleigh as among the twentieth-century black arrangers and composers of spirituals who were formally trained and who had first heard spirituals sung in their nineteenth-century oral tradition, frequently by ex-slaves.

W. C. Handy's Collection of Negro Spirituals continues with a strong voice into the twenty-first century as both an expression of Handy's ambition for the book to be a primary source and also as a musical achievement. His twelve rearranged selections certainly include some old standards such as "Swing Low, Sweet Chariot" and "Nobody Knows the Trouble I Seen," already familiar to white audiences as sung by traveling jubilee singers of the nineteenth century; but Handy in the 1930s also rescued from undeserved obscurity such wonderful spirituals such as "Stand on That Sea of Glass," "Jesus Goin' Make Up My Dying Bed," and "The Bride Groom Has Done Come." This collection was followed the same year by *W. C. Handy's Second Collection of 37 Negro Spirituals*, thereby effecting an almost total change from blues to spirituals in the new publications of the Handy Brothers catalog. (The sole blues song of importance published by the company in the decade of the 1930s was Handy's own composition of 1931, "Chantez-les Bas: Creole Blues," written in the New Orleans style, as if he wished to demonstrate that he could also easily master that city's presumably more facile style of the blues.) The company ended the decade by publishing in 1939 Rosamond Johnson's latest collection, *Sixteen New Negro Spirituals*.

Handy's renewed interest in sacred music and the consolations of religion throughout 1937–39 may have been motivated by family loss. Even into the 1940s, he always remembered how his father had cried in his Florence church whenever the spiritual "March Along, I'll See You on Judgment Day" had been sung by the congregation. As the father had explained his tears to his young son, the family patriarch, William Wise Handy, had a second son also born into slavery, a brother to the Reverend Charles Handy. This son, Hanson Handy, as a young man had resisted being whipped and had been sold to another master, never to be seen by his family again. "That is what the slaves sang when the white folks sold Brother Hanson away," the composer's father had told him. "For me a reverence attaches to those old religious songs," Handy consequently wrote, and throughout his firm's publication of collected spirituals, Handy was insistent that "it would be inappropriate for anyone to adapt them to the requirements of the ballroom or cabaret." (In fact Paul Whiteman had adapted the spiritual "Deep River" for his dance orchestra in the 1920s.) Handy was by no means a regular church-goer, but his statements indicate that for him this change in his company's catalog was as much a devotional act as a commercial one. Later, perhaps only half-humorously, he commented: "Maybe there was still hope for me in my dying days."

A more immediate personal loss to the Handy family occurred in 1937, when the composer's wife, Elizabeth, died on March 26 at age sixty-five. Despite their earlier choice to live largely separated, Handy grieved the loss of his wife of thirty-nine years. Particularly painful to him emotionally were the circumstances of her last day. In an incident of Jim Crowism at its ugliest, the circumstances of her death were exacerbated by an act of racial prejudice grotesquely conflated in the press with the death of Bessie Smith. In reporting the death of the "Empress of Blues," *Down Beat* magazine and some black newspapers asserted that Smith after her automobile wreck in Mississippi had been left unattended to bleed to death at a whites-only hospital in Memphis, where she had been refused admittance. Subsequent research by *Down Beat* and by Smith's most recent biographers have determined that this story is untrue, and that she had been taken directly to the Afro-American Hospital in Clarksdale, where she died after about ten hours of treatment. But this erroneous story, appearing in publications Handy frequently read, must have been excruciating in their recalled memories of his wife's death six months earlier.

Elizabeth Handy, as reported by *The New York Times* the day after her death, had been kept in a parked ambulance outside of the Knickerbocker Hospital at Convent Avenue and 131st Street—the closest hospital to the Handy apartment—for forty-five minutes while Handy and his family's physician desperately pleaded for her immediate admittance. According to the news story, the two were told by the hospital's admitting supervisor that "[we] do not take colored patients in our private wards. Since you did not say she was colored when you made the arrangements, you misrepresented the case." Elizabeth Handy was eventually admitted (after Handy paid sixty-three dollars on the spot for a week's stay in a private room that he previously had been told would cost six dollars a day), and her death that night from a cerebral hemorrhage was, at least officially, not attributed to the delay. The admitting supervisor was later transferred but not fired by the hospital. In speaking to reporters the day after Elizabeth Handy's death, Mayor Fiorello La Guardia had been at pains to emphasize that the Knickerbocker was not a city-operated hospital, and thus its actions were not representative of the city.

Whatever rage Handy felt at the treatment of his dying wife he either tempered with the consolations of religion or work, or, more characteristically, silently internalized while maintaining a public persona of geniality. His 1941 memoir does not mention his wife's death or its circumstances. He kept his personal sorrows and joys for himself, and his art. After he became a widower at age sixty-four in 1937, Handy's most constant companions were his favorite daughter, Katharine, and Louise Logan. But, characteristically, there was seen the predictable reemergence in public of a seemingly optimistic and approachable "Mr. Handy" after 1937.

Handy became a highly visible attendee in the following years at the annual conventions in New York City of the American Society of Composers, Authors, and Publishers (ASCAP), a professional organization for the protection of composers' copyrights and performers' royalties that the membership-loving Handy earlier had joined. And much more controversially, in the autumn of 1938 he

willingly appeared in support of one of the greatest causes célèbres
of the American political left, the struggle of the Soviet-backed Loy-
alist government at war with German-supported fascist forces during the Spanish Civil War.

   This occasion was the belated celebration of his birthday and a
fund-raising concert on November 21 at Carnegie Hall at which
Handy was the honored guest of the Harlem Committee and the
Musicians' Committee to Aid Spanish Democracy. A brilliant gathering of other blues and jazz artists assembled that night both to pay
homage to Handy and to collect money for Spanish civilians injured
and malnourished in the fighting. Among those who performed
were Cab Calloway, Fats Waller, Lionel Hampton, Teddy Wilson,
Clarence Williams, and Eubie Blake. The "St. Louis Blues" was
played numerous times, of course, and there was additionally a special segment devoted to spirituals. Abbe Niles apparently had some
misgivings about Handy appearing at this event, sponsored by a
political committee that many considered to be simply "a bunch of
communists." But Handy was no aging or naïve public figure whose
well-known geniality was being taken advantage of, nor was he
being manipulated by the far left. Handy was there because he
wanted to be, and he knew what he was doing.

   Handy was proudly a lifelong backer of the Republican Party
(in his memoir he steadfastly refused to blame Herbert Hoover
for the economic depression of the 1930s). But he was a supporter
of the Theodore Roosevelt internationalist tradition, rather than of
Republican isolationists then prevalent in his party. He appears to
have genuinely felt sympathy for the Spanish civilians who had suffered horribly in their civil war—he knew firsthand about the after-
effects of a civil war—which in Spain had included mass executions
and the saturation bombing of civilians in the city of Guernica in
1937. Nor was this Carnegie Hall appearance the first time Handy
knowingly had lent his name to a politically controversial cause that
he considered just but that also was supported by groups far to the
left of him. In November 1932 he had performed, along with Duke
Ellington, at a fund-raising concert in New York City sponsored by
the Scottsboro Unity Defense Committee, to help pay for the legal
appeals of eight young black men sentenced to death on dubious

evidence for the rape of two white women in Scottsboro, Alabama. (The northern Alabama town of Scottsboro is located less than a day's drive from Florence.) After legal representation had been provided by the Communist Party of the United States to the Alabama defendants in January 1932, the Scottsboro Boys case, as the trials became known, was one of the nation's most divisive domestic incidents by the time of Handy's concert appearance in November. "I am no communist but I have taken part in their programs for the Scottsboro Boys and felt very good in doing so," Handy felt it necessary to assert in a letter to Niles in November 1938. "I also have taken part in benefits for the flood sufferers, Jews, Catholics, Negroes, white and everybody else and at the time I was sympathetic with the Loyalists of Spain."

In 1939, Handy as perennial showman also made many more, less controversial public appearances. He kept up his appearances at the Cotton Club, where he would briefly vamp the "St. Louis Blues" for delighted audiences, and that year he returned to the recording studio for the Variety label to record four of his compositions, including "Beale Street Blues" and "Loveless Love." Despite the backup on these recordings of musicians from Louis Armstrong's band, including Sidney Catlett on drums, the songs had an old-fashioned sound and did not sell particularly well. Apparently it was the public "Mr. Handy" as historical figure and blues patriarch that audiences now wanted to see, and not necessarily hear. Earlier, in the summer of 1938, Handy also had recorded ten songs for the Library of Congress, accompanying himself on guitar and singing in a light baritone. He performed none of his published blues but rather the folk songs on which he had based his published compositions. These folk tunes included "Careless Love," which Handy had adapted as "Loveless Love," and "Joe Turner," which he had adapted as "Joe Turner Blues."

In 1939, Handy also organized a giant showcase concert of African American musicians who were members of ASCAP. It was performed at Carnegie Hall the evening of October 1. He certainly knew how to put on a show. On stage that night were three choruses, a symphonic orchestra of seventy instruments, four swing bands, and, in Handy's constant insistence upon colored minstrelsy

having played a legitimate part in African American musical culture, a troupe of singing minstrel performers. The concert lived up
to its titled billing: the music Handy chose to be performed at this
concert extended far beyond his nineteenth-century and circa-1917
selections presented at the Carnegie Hall concert organized by
the Handy Brothers Music Company in 1927. At this ASCAP event
twelve years later, William Grant Still conducted two movements of
his *Afro-American Symphony* of 1930, swing bands performed lively
versions of Handy's blues, and Harry T. Burleigh sang "Deep River."
Critical reviews of this concert in both the white and black press
were highly favorable.

Handy also organized the entertainment given by African American musicians and performers on October 3 at the World's Fair exposition of 1939, "The World of Tomorrow," held in the borough of
Queens. In making the prior preparations as the music chairman of
the Harlem World's Fair committee, Handy had met and talked at
his Convent Avenue apartment with Arthur A. Schomburg, who
was then curator of the Negro Collection of Music and Art at the
135th Street branch of the New York Public Library. From the early
1930s, Schomburg had been urging Handy to write his memoir.
Intermittently, Handy had worked on this literary project throughout the decade, amid what Niles considered the controlled chaos at
the composer's Broadway offices. After his World's Fair committee
service and conversations with Schomburg, Handy for the next
two years concentrated on finishing his manuscript. His research
included visits to Maryland for genealogical expeditions on the slave
life of his lost paternal uncle, Hanson Handy. His efforts were published in May 1941 as *Father of the Blues,* by Macmillan.

Handy completed the decade-long project motivated by more
than his friends' encouragements. Earlier, his public reputation and
his right to present himself as a progenitor of the blues had been the
subjects of a remarkably ill-spirited attack in print. Handy did not
intend to let this criticism pass unchallenged. His antagonist was
Ferdinand Le Menthe, better known as Jelly Roll Morton, a jazz
pianist who had begun his career playing the blues in the Storyville
district of New Orleans. Long jealous of Handy's greater fame and
financial success, Morton had become particularly incensed on hear-

ing a *Ripley's Believe It or Not* radio program of March 26, 1938, identifying Handy as the undisputed "father of the blues." In letters written to Ripley and to the Baltimore *Afro-American,* and in a later
interview with an overly credulous folklorist, Alan Lomax, Morton
vehemently had protested awarding the honorific title to Handy. By
the summer of 1938 Morton's aspersions had become so widespread
in the music business (whenever he saw Handy on the street in New
York City he would attempt to draw a crowd and verbally berate
Handy's reputation) that Morton's letter to Ripley had been
reprinted in *Down Beat* magazine under the provocative quote, "I
Created Jazz in 1902, Not W. C. Handy." In this letter, Morton had
related his earlier success in performing New Orleans–styled blues
and early jazz throughout the South for half a decade before 1908,
before he had been invited "to Memphis by a small theater owner,
Fred Barasso [*sic*], as a feature attraction" and where he had first met
Handy. The latter was, in Morton's memory, no more than a preten-
tiously styled former "Professor" of music whose undistinguished
band performed several days a week at the Jim Crow amusement
pavilion of Dixie Park in the city. Handy's later composition "Jogo
Blues," Morton further asserted, had been stolen by Handy from
one of the guitarists in this band, and the subsequently successful
"St. Louis Blues" had also been nothing more than a stolen mélange
of stride piano tunes by other performers. "Mr. Handy cannot prove
anything is music that he has created," Morton emphatically concluded, calling attention to Handy's lack of success throughout the
1920s and 1930s in either composing or performing jazz. Instead, in
Morton's heated opinion, Handy's sole musical ability was in his
transcribing and competently performing "folk songs, hymns,
anthems, etc." As the spurious "Father of the Blues," W. C. Handy
simply had, in the dismissive words of Morton, "possibly taken
advantage of some unprotected material that sometimes floats
around."

Handy, usually one who at least pretended in public to be unper-
turbed by personal attacks or reversals, promptly had sent a reply to
Down Beat in answer to Morton's accusations. (Handy privately
believed that someone else, perhaps Lomax, had ghostwritten Morton's letter.) Handy's letter appeared in the subsequent September

1938 issue of the magazine. His tone, unusually for him, was indig-
nant. It was entitled "I Would Not Play Jazz If I Could." Handy
angrily had described the regional successes playing his originally
composed blues that his various bands had been enjoying at about
the time of Morton's arrival; Memphis was no sideshow to New
Orleans in the creation of the blues, he asserted, and he was no erstwhile music instructor. He also then indulged his scorn, masked in
irony, of what he considered the contribution of the Tough on Black
Asses circuit of vaudeville blues and its performers like Morton,
who in Handy's opinion could do no better for themselves:

> Handy's band was a household word throughout the
> Southland because he could play this music that we now
> call jazz better than any competitor. Yes, I remember
> when Jelly Roll played for Barasso [sic] in Memphis on
> what we call T.O.B.A. time. But we were too busy to take
> notice of his great musicianship.

Handy also noted that the Memphis guitarist Guy Williams, from
whom Morton claimed Handy had stolen "Jogo Blues," never had
contested Handy's copyright and had maintained a cordial friendship with Handy for more than a quarter of a century. And as for his
inability to play the current swing or improvisational versions of the
jazz that evolved from the blues, Handy answered Morton in words
that only can be described, inescapably, as paternal:

> Jelly Roll Morton says I cannot play "jazz." I am 65 years
> old and would not play it if I could, but I did have the good
> sense to write down the laws of jazz and the music that
> lends itself to jazz and had vision enough to copyright and
> publish all the music I wrote so I don't have to go around
> saying that I made up this piece and that piece in such and
> such a year like Jelly Roll and then say someone swiped it.

Handy's reply plainly had been intended to be both conclusive
and corrective. But the damage done by Morton's allegations that he
was at best a mere transcriber of the blues—and, at worst, a stealer

of others' songs—persisted throughout the late 1930s and beyond. Like the version of Bessie Smith's death, Morton's accusations have become exaggerated blues folklore. His charges at times subsequently have diminished Handy's reputation in the minds of those who, perhaps even unaware of the Handy-Morton contretemps of 1938 in *Down Beat*—or of Morton's other frequent and intemperate attacks on successful musicians such as Duke Ellington—simply have assumed as received knowledge that Handy was a figure of lesser importance and skill than other early-twentieth-century blues musicians from New Orleans. (As late as 1991, a distinguished historian of American culture, in a book detailing the events of the year of 1919, slightingly refers in a few lines to "W. C. Handy, the saloon piano player from Memphis's Beale Street.")

Father of the Blues was, upon its publication in 1941 at three-hundred-plus pages, Handy's attempt to have the last word. (Jelly Roll Morton died in 1941.) He retained the services of a journalist, Arna Bontemps, to help him complete the manuscript, and Niles provided a foreword and was instrumental in securing the book's initial publication by Macmillan. In a discursive twenty-three chapters, Handy related his early life in Alabama, his discovery of the rural blues in Delta Mississippi, and his anecdotes about other blues musicians who in Memphis, Chicago, and New York City had performed his songs—a statement, in effect, as to why he was entitled to his claim of being the patriarch of the blues. (Before the book's publication, the Harlem Renaissance writer James Weldon Johnson successfully had persuaded Handy to change the title of his memoir from the composer's originally combative title, *Fight It Out,* to the more preemptive *Father of the Blues.*) The style of the memoir very much represents what it must have been like to have actually encountered the public "Mr. Handy." His writing, indelibly fixed in the nineteenth-century rhetoric he learned in Florence, is florid, expansive, charming, very friendly, and a little dated.

And like all arguments, it is also selective. Not surprisingly, there is no mention in Handy's memoir of Jelly Roll Morton, King Oliver, or any other early New Orleans blues performers or composers. But for all these protective omissions, Handy *was* an equal among these other progenitors and he undeniably *made* the blues, his own and others, in the sense of his making them a national music. And he was surely the public's favorite as well, as the struggling, ever-optimistic "Mr. Handy." His memoir sold well. (Macmillan arranged for copies to be sold in movie lobbies to accompany the showing of the 1941 film *Birth of the Blues,* a New Orleans–set retelling that starred, incongruously, Bing Crosby.) Handy's honorific title was popularly accepted. "The Jovial Autobiography of W. C. Handy: The 'Father of the Blues' Tells His Story in a Rambling and Entertaining Fashion," was the headline chosen by *The New York Times* for its July 13, 1941, highly favorable review.

Subsequent generations should still find *Father of the Blues* worth a read. It has remained in print into the twenty-first century. With an awareness of the black mask of this once-practicing minstrel—or of the "two-soulness" necessary for the African American artist in W. E. B. Dubois's conviction—there also comes an appreciation of Handy as a skilled, discreet literary artist. Despite the surface jollity and the sincere moral uplift and patriotism expressed in its pages—Handy entitled his memoir's final chapter, written as war in Europe and the Pacific threatened this nation, with emphatic italics *"God Bless America"*—there is a deliberate subtext on the racism he had experienced in two centuries of American life.

The memoir's two chapters on minstrelsy, for example, are so entertainingly and ramblingly written that it is easy for a casual reader to overlook his briefer accounts of the lynching of Louis Wright, or his own near-lynchings in Texas, Mississippi, and Tennessee. Joy and sorrow intermix, as in the blues. Or consider a seemingly casual incident Handy relates late in his memoir, when he had been racially insulted by the white president of the Chicago musicians' union and, furious, had sought solace with a cigar in the smoking compartment of a train returning him to New York City: "Gradually the harmonious smoke rings curled into human beings and the 'Jim Crow' president went up in smoke," Handy wrote. Always, even when genially described, there is both his anger and his later insistence upon the evanescent nature of racism when compared to the "harmonious" possibilities of the American people and their best character. This is no "Uncle Tom-ism." With deliberate intent born of anger and characteristically public geniality, Handy places the reader and himself equally as two friends, both human beings, sharing a cigar.

Father of the Blues and *Blues: An Anthology* are the bookends, separated by his work of fifteen years, between which W. C. Handy's reputation as a beloved public figure and a significant artist in American culture remains firmly in place. His reputation and public respectability were now secure. Handy's memoir also was, in a sense, his final great nostalgic performance. Ahead were his private blues years, and a funeral in 1958.

CHAPTER ELEVEN

—

"St. Louis Blues"

THE FINAL PERFORMANCE, 1958

> Do you not see how necessary a World of Pains and troubles is
> to school an Intelligence and make it a soul?
>
> —The poet John Keats, in a letter
> of April 21, 1819, to his brother
> in America

On a Thursday afternoon, October 28, 1943, W. C. Handy suffered a near-fatal fall from a platform at the 147th Street and St. Nicholas Avenue subway station in New York City. The sixty-nine-year-old composer had been a passenger on a subway train, accompanied by his personal companion, Louise Logan, on his way to keep a four o'clock appointment at his office. He then realized he had left his trumpet behind at the apartment they shared in Yonkers. He suggested that Logan return for the instrument, and that he would get off the train and wait for her on the lower platform at the 147th Street stop. While he lingered, Handy went upstairs to the upper level and became disoriented. He fell off the platform and onto the subway tracks. Two bystanders bravely rescued Handy from the tracks, but he had fractured his skull in the fall and was taken to Harlem Hospital. His condition was listed as serious, and, as a result of the injury, his eyes, impaired since the 1920s, did not respond to light. He eventually recovered his mental lucidity, and some of his strength, but this time his blindness was permanent.

Handy recuperated at the Yonkers apartment where he lived in the company of Louise Logan following the death of his wife. ("Louise is taking splendid care of me," he dictated in a letter to William Grant Still three months after the accident. Handy and Logan would marry in 1954.) But even in his blindness, Handy's oft-expressed optimism did not fail him, nor did his appreciation of an audience. He was deeply gratified by the number of editorials in the national press, read to him, expressing concern about his injury and he was particularly pleased at hearing the praise published about him in the newspapers of his native state, in Florence and Birmingham. "I received so many beautiful testimonials, all races in all sections," he commented in another letter written for him to Still. Although he now required a physical guide as well as a stenographer and reader, Handy by mid-1944 attempted to resume his day-to-day supervision of business at his company, and, with extraordinary effort, he managed to complete a major publishing project he had begun earlier in that decade.

Handy had commenced the 1940s, three years before his injury, by accomplishing the long-desired legal consummation of an unfinished item of business. This was the recovery of his legal copyright to "The Memphis Blues." When the period of the original copyright, the rights to which Handy had sold for fifty dollars in 1912, had at last expired in 1940, he had been present at the Library of Congress accompanied by Abbe Niles to successfully assert his claim. Although the original score was now dated musically, Handy's first nationally popular song was nevertheless a profitable addition to his catalog, and its return brought more than just emotional satisfaction to its composer. Harry James recorded a big-band version of the song in July 1942, and Handy later recalled with pleasure that in that year he had received a royalty of $5,600 for the James recording. (The "St. Louis Blues" alone is estimated to have been returning about $10,000 annually in royalties during the 1940s.) Two other of Handy's earlier compositions, "Aunt Hagar's Children Blues" and "Loveless Love" of the early 1920s, also had been rearranged for jazz and big-band performances in the 1940s, and had been lucrative for Handy's company when recorded by Billie Holiday and Lena Horne. Holiday playfully had improvised upon one of Handy's lyrics in her recording of "Loveless Love," slyly referring to wartime rationing and singing of "silkless silk." Just months before his October accident, Handy had also been in the final preparations for publication by his firm in 1943 of a major anthology of black music and social accomplishment. After his injury and blindness, he completed his editing of this project, and in 1944 he published—but never saw as a book—*Unsung Americans Sung*.

This collection of short biographical essays and musical scores, composed by Handy and others, was both a promotion of African Americans whom he considered nationally underrecognized and a statement of African American contributions to the United States in the Second World War. (Handy's younger son, Wyer, currently was serving in the U.S. Medical Corps in Italy.) In prior war years, Handy apparently had made no public statements regarding the Roosevelt administration's attempt to secure equal employment and salaries for black defense workers through its Fair Employment Practices Committee (FEPC), and had not spoken out when one of the worst race riots of the war years occurred in his native state, when the FEPC had attempted in 1943 to enforce this job equality at the Mobile, Alabama, shipyards. But he *was* a racial spokesman, albeit a discreet and musically artistic one. Early in the war, Handy Brothers had published the patriotic and racially uplifting song "We Are Americans Too," and in 1942 the firm had issued "Go and Get the Enemy Blues," with lyrics by Langston Hughes and score by Handy and Clarence M. Jones. *Unsung Americans Sung* was a continuation into 1944 of this affirmative war-effort and racial-solidarity stance by Handy.

This book's multiple selections include a short biography and song in honor of Dorie Miller, the black sailor who, although previously considered by reasons of his race to be unqualified for gunnery training by the navy, voluntarily and effectively had manned an anti-aircraft gun in defense of his ship during the attack on Pearl Harbor. Other generations of Americans of color were also celebrated in words and song, such as the poet Paul Laurence Dunbar, and Arthur Schomburg, whose honorific song was entitled "The Curator." Intended in words and music to be the equivalent for black audiences of Frank Capra's wartime series of films *Why We Fight*, the book was also intended for white audiences as the statement "Why We Should Be *Allowed* to Fight." Handy could remember, and apparently wished to counteract, the popular coon songs of the previous world war in 1917–18, such as "Mammy's Little Chocolate Soldier." *Unsung Americans Sung* of 1944 was in the proud tradition of the combat-tested Jim Europe and his Hell Fighters band.

Handy's completion of editing this book in little more than six months after his skull fracture and permanent blindness was his bravest professional act since his appearing in the recording studio to perform "Muscle Shoals Blues" when he first had been blind in the 1920s. It was also bravery accomplished with considerable grace. However traumatic his latest injury, he complained very little about his loss of sight to his friends; his sole concern expressed privately to Still in 1944 was his fear because of his blindness of becoming a "do nothing." In public he was determined, with geniality and constant activity, to "fight it out" whatever the circumstances of his life. Within two months of his accident, he departed in the winter of 1944–45 for an extensive trip throughout the southern states, accompanied and physically led by his brother, Charles, and Louise Logan, playing what he called "the old Handy trumpet" for a war bond rally in Memphis, meeting with his family and admirers in Birmingham and Florence, and concluding—"train late and snow a-flying," in the blind composer's I'm-up-for-it description—in Kentucky.

In the remainder of the postwar decade, Handy, with all the energy of his sighted years, resumed his celebrated public and social appearances in New York City. In 1946, he was a prominent attendee at a political rally for the reelection of New York Governor Thomas E. Dewey. Handy later pointedly reminded his fellow African American voters that "New York under Governor Dewey is the first state in the Union to wipe out segregation and race discrimination by antidiscrimination laws." (It is interesting that in referring to Republican candidates, he instinctively used the language of the Civil War and the party of Lincoln, e.g., "the Union.") The composer's birthday parties held at the city's most prominent hotel ballrooms throughout the 1940s also became themselves report-worthy events for New York newspapers, with guest lists of a surprising show business eclecticism. Handy's fellow Alabamian Tallulah Bankhead was a very noticeable guest at one such birthday party. For a period in the late 1940s, he also appeared seven nights a week, playing his trumpet for Billy Rose's Diamond Horseshoe club on Broadway, and noted privately with satisfaction that "each night I am improving." Nor was he, despite his advancing age and lack of sight, predictably "old Handy." He made a brief and well-received televised appearance, in December 1949, on Ed Sullivan's *Talk of the Town* program. This was a remarkable performance for a man who could no longer see the stage or the position of the unfamiliar television cameras and lights, but he charmed his host and audience. Thus did W. C. Handy, who had been a boy when Ulysses S. Grant and Jefferson Davis were alive and active, participate at the beginnings of the American television age of the mid-twentieth century.

Handy and Niles in 1949 also completed their final literary collaboration, a revised edition of *Blues: An Anthology*, retitled and reissued that year as *A Treasury of the Blues*, once again published by the Boni firm. This reissue lacks the élan of the 1926 edition. (The version of 1949 reproduces some, but not all, of the wonderful caricatures by Miguel Covarrubias in the earlier edition. It does, however, include the score to "The Memphis Blues," which was legally unavailable to Handy in 1926.) The two authors were both more generous and more reserved to others in this later exposition of history of the blues. Handy was still given preeminence, but credit was given to Baby Seals as a significant blues progenitor for his "Baby Seals Blues," with the caveat that "its creator may, by 1912, have learned from *Mister Crump* or from folk music." Some credit for popularization of the early blues was also given to Artie Matthews's arrangement of Seals's signature tune and to Hart Wand's "Dallas Blues." Chris Smith and the Wyer brothers, Ed and Paul, who had contributed so much to the success of Handy's bands in Memphis, were also recalled with great affection.

The nettlesome Jelly Roll Morton was mentioned by Niles and Handy in one paragraph, with admirable grace and restraint by the authors, as both a "leader in the fields of blues and jazz" and "a talker of great fluency." Although *A Treasury of the Blues* did not revisit the New Orleans controversy, the pianist's accusations against Handy refused to go away in the year after its publication. In his 1950 biography of Morton, *Mister Jelly Roll,* Alan Lomax repeated

Morton's accusations. Handy, probably with the counsel of Niles, threatened legal action and publicly denounced this portion of the book.

A Treasury of the Blues was a slow but steady seller from 1949 onward, but with its emphasis on the published urban blues of the 1910s and 1920s, the book's text and scores would have appeared old-fashioned to the generation that had grown up listening to big bands and swing. To their children, who began listening to the blues as adolescents in the 1950s and 1960s and who identified blues solely with its rural performers, the book would be a puzzle. *A Treasury* included two boogie-woogie scores as derivatives of the blues, but this was as close to the emerging rhythm-and-blues as Handy and Niles got. The blues folk guitarist Huddie Ledbetter ("Leadbelly") is mentioned, but only in a swipe at Lomax, whose praise of Leadbelly "does not prove anything," in Niles's judgment. (Niles presumably shared Handy's suspicion that Lomax had ghostwritten Morton's letter to *Down Beat* in 1938.) Surprisingly for Handy, who knew the Delta's regional black musicians as well as anyone and who had returned frequently to Memphis in the prior years, there is no mention in his book of Robert Johnson or Charley Patton, nor of B. B. King, who by 1947 was making things shake at the old Barrasso theater and who was then known as the "Beale Street Blues Boy."

Age and his physical infirmity, as well as changing tastes in national popular music and entertainment, were conclusively beginning to catch up with Handy by the early 1950s. In 1951, he distributed a national press release announcing that "because of my blindness," Handy Brothers was no longer accepting unsolicited submissions of musical scores. "There was a time when we could take your song and get it on records, or sell enough copies to make it worthwhile," Handy dictated. He then added, with remarkable prescience: "Television is changing this." One of the last original musical publications was a campaign tune for the Republican presidential candidate of 1952, Dwight D. Eisenhower, composed by Jack Gould and published by Handy under the unfortunately euphonious title "Hike with Ike." The song was an underperformer, but Handy was rewarded for his unswerving loyalty to every Republican presidential administration since William McKinley's by being invited on October 25, 1952, to be an honored guest on the podium beside Eisenhower and Governor Dewey at a late campaign rally in Harlem. Mrs. Eisenhower, who apparently told the composer to call her "Mamie," expressed to Handy her personal fondness for the "St. Louis Blues."

That year Handy was also deeply pleased when the poem "I See Tho' My Eyes Are Closed," by Lazarus A. Aaronson, had been published and dedicated to him. The verse was later recited, with accompaniment by the New York Choral Ensemble, in a recording made for Audio Archives in 1952 on which Handy played the guitar and sang in a weak baritone "The Memphis Blues" and "Beale Street Blues."

A part of Handy still relished this showmanship and public adulation, but as he neared eighty years of age, he confessed to Still to wondering whether "the game was worth the candle." Partly he showed up for reasons of what he considered racial uplift. "In these empty honors our people share with some delight," he explained to Still. By this time, outside of his domestic life with Logan and his correspondence with Still and Niles, he had become almost totally the iconic "Father of the Blues," and there were few of his contemporaries alive with whom he could privately socialize or share his honors. In 1944, the "Jazz Vampire" of the 1920s, Marion Harris, who had made the "St. Louis Blues" a national hit before she faded from popularity, had died in a fire alone in her New York hotel bed. He also missed the company of Ed Wyer, for whom Handy had named his second son and who had died in 1943. This violinist for Handy's band in 1909 "sure could pull some bow," Handy sadly later reminisced in a letter to Still, in a quote of the lyrics to his own "The Memphis Blues." Another good friend of Handy's middle years, Harry T. Burleigh, with whom Handy had shared a deep love of spirituals, died in 1949, "almost forgotten," Handy regretted. He also lost to death in this decade a favorite Alabama cousin, Llewellyn Brewer. Before his elderly cousin's death, Handy had made it a point to tell Brewer, who had served in the nineteenth-century U.S. military, how "when I was a kid I looked up to him because he came back home dressed in a fine soldier's uniform and carried his guns on his sides in the town." The white citizens of Florence, Alabama, had seen few black soldiers since the end of the Civil War, but

Handy recalled how his kinsman had made clear to the townspeople "he does not take foolishness." In 1954, even Boss Crump died.

The year of 1954–55 continued to be a time both of great private loss and some gain for Handy. On New Year's Day 1954, the eighty-year-old Handy married Louise Logan. This marriage apparently raised eyebrows among some of Handy's friends and his grown children, but it is incontestable that Louise had been a loyal helpmate to him during his injury and blindness. Shortly after their first wedding anniversary, in February 1955, his oldest daughter, Lucile, who had been ill for the past two years, died. Handy himself that year began to be seriously troubled by high blood pressure, and he suffered a stroke, thereafter requiring a wheelchair. In early March 1955, Abbe Nile and his wife, attempting to cheer their old friend, invited Handy and his wife from the house they now shared in White Plains, New York, to the Niles's home for dinner on Long Island. Afterward the couples listened together with pleasure to the newly released Columbia Records album *Louis Armstrong Plays W. C. Handy*. Handy paid in ill health for this outing, however. He caught a bad cold during the rainy trip back to his home, and was forced to concede later to Still that "perhaps the traveling was a little too much for me, so now I am taking it easy."

Handy's last major musical appearance was at the July 15, 1956, symphonic concert at Lewisohn Stadium in New York City, during which Leonard Bernstein conducted the stadium orchestra to Alfredo Antonini's arrangement of the "St. Louis Blues." This performance, as well as several others offered that night, was recorded and released as *Bernstein on Jazz*. Louis Armstrong on trumpet was the featured soloist for Handy's masterpiece. Armstrong, who had just returned from a world tour, was a brilliant choice, given the popularity of his long-playing recording of eleven of Handy's songs the previous year. But, in a sign of the changed musical tastes, the "cool jazz" of the Dave Brubeck Quartet was also performed in a separate segment of this concert.

This symphonic arrangement of Handy's most famous song was a musical mélange by Antonini, with passages performed in the Dixieland and big-band styles, Gene Krupa–style drumming, vaudeville slides, and cinemalike usage of the stringed instruments. But Armstrong's trumpet solos lift through this background arrangement like a clarion golden light that even Handy, blind and in a wheelchair, could have experienced from where he sat. At the performance's conclusion, Armstrong was formally introduced by Bernstein to great applause by the audience of 21,000—Armstrong had played "with his whole soul," Bernstein announced—and this gravelly voiced trumpeter then movingly spoke of his own gratitude to the original composer of the "St. Louis Blues." His brief statement ended in Armstrong's joyful and near-wordless expression of his pure, libidinal pleasure at the music: "Thanks very much to Mr. Bernstein. . . . And thanks, Mr. Handy, for being our guest this evening, as I've been playing his music for a long time. . . . I just don't know what to say. . . . [*Happy laughter*] . . . A-yeah, yeah, yeah."

Handy entered his final physical decline soon after this concert, with the national press regularly reporting on his worsening health. However, he was still Mr. Micawber. He dictated a letter to Still in August 1957, expressing his pleasure at signing a contract with Paramount Pictures for a film version of his life, titled inevitably *The St. Louis Blues,* which the eighty-three-year-old composer boasted would be "the crowning glory" of his career. (The film was released in 1958 and starred the rising young African American nightclub and television performer Nat "King" Cole in the role of Handy. The script of this "biopic," in studio jargon, was no more historically accurate than most of the earlier birth-of-the-blues cinema productions, but Cole was perfectly cast physically as the sleekly urbane young W. C. Handy.) Handy enthusiastically boasted to Still that he was "improving in health, and my doctor says that if I keep improving, I will be able to come to Hollywood in October, when they begin shooting the works." Yet, in an uncharacteristically elegiac mood, perhaps suggested to him by the title of this film project, he also added: "All the men who were with me when I wrote the 'St. Louis Blues' are gone but you; and that is where the sadness comes in."

On March 7, 1958, Handy dictated a short letter to his friend Still, briefly asking him to remember their heady times together four decades earlier "in the Gaiety Theater building days," when the tempo was à la blues, and "Beale Street Blues," "A Good Man Is Hard to Find," and the "St. Louis Blues" were national best sellers. Fourteen days later, he was taken to Sydenham Hospital in Harlem, suffering from pneumonia and other ailments. His closest family—

Louise Logan Handy; his brother, Charles; his sons, Wyer and William; his daughter Katharine; and a grandson gathered at his hospital bed. On March 29, W. C. Handy died.

The funeral, on April 2, 1958, was one of the largest public occasions in the history of New York City to that decade. A crowd estimated by city police at over 150,000 gathered alongside West 138th Street in Harlem to watch as Handy's coffin was slowly carried inside the Abyssinian Baptist Church for the funeral service. A thirty-piece brass band of Handy's fellow Masons, recalling his first musical employment as a bandleader, played their accompaniment to his body's arrival.

Inside the church, approximately 2,500 friends and acquaintances gathered along with his family. Their numbers, black and white alike, represented that unique social combination of racial politics, money, mass media, and musical art that had constituted African American popular entertainment throughout the nineteenth and twentieth centuries. Mayor Robert Wagner and several borough presidents were in attendance; so also were Cab Calloway, Eubie Blake, Marian Anderson, Oscar Hammerstein, Langston Hughes, and Ed Sullivan.

The Reverend Adam Clayton Powell Jr., minister of the Abyssinian Church and then a member of Congress, delivered the eulogy. He spoke with all his celebrated powers of oratory. "Gabriel now has an understudy," Powell declared to the congregation. "And when the last trumpet shall sound, I am sure that W. C. Handy will be there to bury this world, as a sideman." Powell then declaimed in a rhetorical apostrophe the finale of Handy's life: "No more the problems of Beale Street. No more the irritations of Memphis. No more the vexation of the St. Louis woman." The hymn "Nearer My God to Thee" was played, and then the body, accompanied by the family and forty honorary pallbearers, was carried out of the church and into a maroon Cadillac hearse for its final trip, to Woodlawn Cemetery, in the Bronx. The brass band formed up in front of the hearse to lead the procession a few blocks up Lenox Avenue.

· · ·

The maroon Cadillac likely would have pleased him. The automobile was the finest model that money could buy in the United States in 1958, and it represented the respectability he had always sought for himself and his musical art. "Son," his father had told him decades earlier when he had announced his plans to become a professional musician, "I'd rather see you in a hearse. I'd rather follow you to the graveyard than to hear that you had become a musician." The son did grow up to become a musician, but he became one of the most revered figures in American public life, and his music significantly contributed to this nation's popular culture. His musical art also had provided the personal financial success for his final means of transport out of the world. And, perhaps importantly, it was *not* the traditional, New Orleans–styled, black-plumed and horse-drawn carriage of that city's funeral processions.

Handy doubtless also would have been pleased by the national and regional honors accorded to his reputation as the "Father of the Blues": a memorial statue raised in Memphis, a United States postage stamp bearing his likeness, a major blues and jazz festival named for him that into the twenty-first century annually draws several hundreds of thousands of visitors, and, in 1968, the restoration of the log cabin of his childhood from Handy's Hill as a museum by the city of Florence. In 2006 the novelist Edward P. Jones paid homage to one of Handy's most personal blues songs by selecting its title for his celebrated collection of stories of African American family life in the nation's capital, *All Aunt Hagar's Children*. But Handy was also spared by death from witnessing much that would have displeased him, or puzzled him.

Composing his sophisticated blues outside of the New Orleans tradition into a music made from two centuries of American entertainment he had heard in brass bands, minstrelsy ragtime, riverboat serenades, tango rhythms, vaudeville, Tin Pan Alley tunes, and Delta folk melodies, Handy was disregarded by later blues purists as a lesser figure in favor of that Louisiana city's early musical performers. Handy's unapologetic celebration of his own black minstrelsy career also gave political pause to those who after his death unfavorably considered his minstrel show performances, despite incontrovertible evidence of blackfaced minstrelsy having been both subversive as well as subservient to the nation's cultural views on race. His political and social efforts at resisting this nation's Jim Crow laws, made at some physical risk in Mississippi and other states, also have been forgotten. Most puzzling is the historical neglect of Handy as one of the most successful of this nation's black entrepreneurs, both in Tin Pan Alley and on Beale Avenue. He was fortunate not to live into the subsequent decades of his beloved Beale Avenue's economic and social decline, nor to have seen its racial rioting and partial demolition. "Blues in Tennessee: W. C. Handy's Beale Street, Dingy and Tuneless Now, Will Be Cleaned Up," a headline ominously appeared in *The New York Times* on March 4, 1966. Shortly thereafter, his most familiar landmarks on the avenue were razed.

And, of course, the popular music of the nation also was totally changed by the year of his death. So too was the subsequent appreciation of what he had accomplished from the Hispanic rhythms and black folk tunes he had heard at the turn of the twentieth century. The nineteenth-century hopes of Dvořák for a twentieth-century "great national music" were fulfilled and then, later in that century, discarded. In historical fact, W. C. Handy's own life and compositions, with his varying popularity, his national wanderings either for desperate employment or satisfaction of his personal ambitions, and his ready adaptation to commercial uses of the melodies and rhythms of other races demonstrate that for this nation there is no one, permanently defining music. Instead, there is a constantly changing medley of American *musics,* dependent upon the nation's immigration, economics, social restraints, changing landscapes, and aspirations of individuals. "They'd look for me on Beale Street, up and down the river," Handy with unknowing accuracy had declared at the beginning of his national career, "but I would not be there." In the decades following 1958, few cared to remember anymore where the Southern crossed the Yellow Dog, or that Beale Street once could talk, or even that the mythical, blues-making Joe Turner has done been here and gone.

The procession briefly stopped at 152nd Street and Seventh Avenue. There the members of the brass band, who had been playing Chopin's funeral march, left the head of the procession and regrouped on the sidewalk, dressing their lines and adjusting their blue uniforms trimmed with gold braid. They watched as the Cadillac and the following cars then resumed the journey, carrying Handy's body toward the bridge over the Harlem River, and to Woodlawn Cemetery. "All right, men," the band's leader told his musicians, and announced the next composition to be played. "A little faster this time." Together in the late-afternoon sunshine they raised their instruments and played one last time, melancholy but up-tempo, as W. C. Handy had insisted was the essence of the blues, their final musical farewell. The unsung lyrics were the composer's own words in celebration and good-bye to a unique time in American culture and music:

I hate to see that evening sun go down . . .

Acknowledgments

As biographers research and write, they attempt what Edmund Wilson called the "triple thinking" of literature. There is the studied life of the biographical subject, perceived with all its archetypal and historical episodes; there are also simultaneously the thoughts and incidents of the biographer's own solitary life; and there are, thirdly, the thoughts and actions of those who have chosen with generosity to help the biographer. It is this third group whom I most wish to acknowledge.

Foremost for my thanks are two outstanding librarians at public institutions in the South. These are Edwin Frank at the Mississippi Valley Collection at the University of Memphis, and Lee Freeman of the Genealogical Department at the public library of Florence and Lauderdale County, Alabama. Morgan Swan of the Beinecke Library at Yale University was also most kind. Gracious in their voluntary help to me also are a remarkable group of musicians, both jazz and classical, and other talented individuals in residence in Cincinnati, Ohio. These include Dan Arlen, Dan Baker, Andrew Balterman, Paul Burch, Beth Cooper, Thomas Klenk, Sallie Mock, Myron Neal, Bruce Sherwood, Kate Slater, and Janice Williams. And, as always, I wish to thank the three literary individuals who had both faith and practical expectations in my abilities as a biographer and novelist. These three are my experienced editors at Knopf, Ash Green and Andrew Miller, and my respected agent, John Ware.

Many in my native state of Alabama also have helped me with the research for this book or have shared with me their knowledge and their love of the blues: *I heard, could be, a Hey there from the wing / and I went on: Miss Bessie sounding good / . . . the house is giving hell / to Yellow Dog,* as John Berryman once so poetically remembered. These good friends of mine in that joyful and rueful state of Alabama in the Deep South include Ben and Susan Windham, Bruce Lowry, the late Cody and Barbara Hall; and, most especially, Genie Sparks. And, in my greatest acknowledgments, in respectful memory of Talmadge Robertson (1905–1930) and Franklin "Baby" Seals (d. 1915), both of whom vamped their final blues in Anniston, Alabama.

David Robertson

CINCINNATI, OHIO
SPRING 2008

Notes

PROLOGUE: A VIEW OF MR. HANDY

3   *Alaskan Roof Garden:* W. C. Handy, *Father of the Blues: An Autobiography* (New York: Da Capo Press, 1985), 101, 113. Hereafter cited as *Father.*

3   *"Beale Street":* The lyrics are excerpted from the graphic reproductions of historical scores and lyrics to "Beale Street" available at the website http://memory.loc.gov/ammem/collections/sheetmusic/brown. This site is maintained by the Library of Congress and is hereafter cited as *LOC.* The musicians named in the text are among those identified by Handy as playing in his "first string" orchestra in 1918, *Father,* 101, 172. Bevard is spelled in some secondary sources as Bernard.

4   *"The Main Street of Negro America":* George W. Lee, *Beale Street: Where the Blues Began* (New York: Robert O. Ballou, 1934), 13. Hereafter cited as *Street. Thirteenth Census of the United States Taken in the Year 1910, Abstract of the Census* (Government Printing Office, 1913), 94–95.

4   *"ebony hands": Father,* 97.

5   *"enjoyed by the Negroes"* to *"pickpockets skilled": Street,* 13; "Beale Street," LOC.

5   *"jogo"* to *"'Fess Handy": Father,* 117, 86.

6   *Pee Wee's Saloon: Father,* 91; *Beale Street USA* (Bexhill-on-Sea, England: Blues Unlimited Publications, 1970), "Pee Wee's Saloon," unpaged, hereafter cited as *USA.*

6   *Beale Avenue's vaudeville theaters* to *"unbleached American": USA,* "Negroes Found Theater," unpaged; Lynn Abbott and Doug Seroff, "'They Cert'ly Sound Good to Me': Sheet Music, Southern Vaudeville, and the Commercial Ascendancy of the Blues," *American Music,* vol. 14 (winter 1996), 430–33, hereafter cited as Abbott; H. Loring White, *Ragging It: Getting Ragtime into History (and Some History into Ragtime)* (New York: iUniverse, 2005), 62–63, 87–89, 99. Hereafter cited as *Ragging It.* For "unbleached American," see the review of the performance at the Keith Theatre by the African American vaudevillian Frank Hogan, in *The Boston Globe* newspaper, 15 April 1902, quoted in Henry T. Sampson, *The Ghost Walks:*

A Chronological History of Blacks in Show Business, 1865–1910. (Metuchen, NJ: Scarecrow, 1988), 250–51. Hereafter cited as *Ghost.*

7	"*Tough on Black Asses*": Margaret McKee and Fred Chisenhall, *Beale Black & Blue: Life and Music on Black America's Main Street* (Baton Rouge: Louisiana State University Press, 1981), 13–15. Hereafter cited as *Black and Blue.* Abbott, 435.

7	"*Early Every Morning*": Street, 151–52.

8	"*endure it cheerfully*": Father, 135.

8	"*weirdest music*" to "*the colored Sousa*": Father, 74, 76–77, 120; Florence (AL) *Times*, 30 January 1903. Handy is described thus in the newspaper article reviewing his performance in Alabama shortly before his move to Mississippi.

8	*sounded like a mistake* to "*primitive music*": Father, 76–77, 120–21.

9	"*American composer*" to "*Dvořák Manifesto*": Father, 77; Antonín Dvořák, "The Real Value of Negro Melodies," *New York Herald*, 21 May 1893, quoted in Lynn Abbott and Doug Seroff, *Out of Sight: The Rise of African American Popular Music 1889–1895* (Oxford: University Press of Mississippi, 2003), 145–46. Hereafter cited as *Out of Sight.*

9	"*no grass grow*" to "*took them by the heels*": Father, 78, 122.

10	*Harry Raderman* to "*Miss Bessie Smith*": Tim Brooks, *Lost Sounds: Blacks and the Birth of the Recording Industry, 1890–1919* (Urbana: University of Illinois Press, 2004), 436. Hereafter cited as *Lost Sounds.* (Indianapolis) *Freeman* newspaper, 1 January 1916. Hereafter cited as *Freeman.*

10	*Lippman's Loan Office: 1910 Memphis City Directory for the Year Commencing May 1st* (Memphis: R. L. Polk, 1910), unpaged; *Father*, 126.

11	"*rating artistic work*": Father, 129–30.

11	"*two souls*": W. E. B. Du Bois, *The Souls of Black Folk* (New York: Oxford University Press, 2007), 8–9. Hereafter cited as *Souls.*

12	*short-lived newspaper:* Paul G. Partington, "The Moon Illustrated Weekly: The Precursor of *The Crisis,*" *Journal of Negro History*, vol. 48 (July 1963), 210.

12	"*monkey business*": Father, 135.

13	*Solvent Savings Bank:* The bank was first located in a building at 392 Beale, and is pictured in the photograph facing page 144, *Street.* In 1914, however, the bank and Handy's office moved to a building at 386–388 Beale. See photograph and text in William S. Worley, *Beale Street: Crossroads of America's Music* (Kansas City, MO: Andrews McMeel, 1998), 61. Hereafter cited as Worley.

13	"*Handy's 'blues'*": Freeman, 9 June 1917.

13	*sixty cents* to *three cents:* This maximum amount is the price listed for the Pace & Handy retail score of "Beale Street," at the onset of the song's national popularity, in a promotional sheet of 1919 reproduced in Elliott S. Hurwitt, "W. C. Handy as Music Publisher: Career and Reputation" (PhD diss., 2000, the City University of New York), 188. Hereafter cited as "Publisher." The wartime postage rate of 1918 is available at www.prc.gov/rates/stamphistory.

14	"*St. Louis Blues*": Handy's most famous blues song was copyrighted as the "Saint Louis Blues," but the title with the abbreviation was used very frequently in the subsequently printed scores and very often by Handy himself. Such use is followed in the book's text.

14   *move in late 1918 to New York City:* "Publisher," 137. Hurwitt, the closest
     redactor of the dates of the copyright and corporate documents from
     Handy's career, places Handy in New York City by July 1918, with his
     family joining him there later.

15   *Father of the Blues:* Handy's informal title was most widely publicized on
     the March 26, 1938, national broadcast of Robert Ripley's *Believe It or Not*
     radio program during which Handy was described to the audience as
     the "Father of the Blues," and Handy subsequently chose this phrase as
     the title of his 1941 memoir. But this coinage was in use much earlier. The
     Chicago Defender, a black-owned newspaper, described W. C. Handy in an
     article published on 14 June 1919, as being "well known the world over as
     the 'Daddy of the Blues.'"

15   *bronze statue:* Author's visits to Beale Street, August 2005; Worley, 91, 94.

16   *top-selling single records: Billboard,* "Best Selling Pop Singles in Stores,"
     24 March 1958.

16   *"apparently dropped by the marchers":* The New York Times, "A Negro Is
     Killed in Memphis March: Looting and Violence Disrupt a Massive
     Protest in Memphis," 29 March 1968, 1. *The New York Times* hereafter
     cited as *NYT.*

17   *"urban development scheme"* to *teenaged Elvis Presley: USA,* "Introduction,"
     unpaged; Worley, 121; Peter Guralnick, *Last Train to Memphis: The Rise of
     Elvis Presley* (Boston: Little, Brown, 1994), 45–46, 206, 507; author's visits
     to Beale Street, August 2005.

19   *Carnegie Hall* to *television studios: NYT,* "Handy Honored at Concert,"
     22 November 1938, 28; *NYT,* "Negro Music Given at ASCAP Recital,"
     3 October 1939, 26; *NYT,* "On Television," 12 December 1949, X10.

ONE: SLAVERY, THE AME CHURCH, AND EMANCIPATION

20   *"acknowledging the abolition of slavery":* quoted in Lucille Griffith,
     Alabama: A Documentary History to 1900 (Tuscaloosa: University of
     Alabama Press, 1972), 450.

20   *"French horn concealed"* to *"after the surrender": Father,* 14, 1.

21   *hopeful frontier surveyor:* Jack Kytle, ed., et al., *Alabama: A Guide to the Deep
     South* (New York: Hastings House, 1941), 185.

22   *population enslaved:* Margaret M. Storey, *Loyalty and Loss: Alabama's Union-
     ists in the Civil War and Reconstruction* (Baton Rouge: Louisiana State Uni-
     versity Press, 2004), 44–45, 160–61, "Appendix 3: Demographic Tables,"
     254–55.

22   *Andrew Jackson* to *Dred Scott:* John S. Bassett, ed., *Correspondence of
     Andrew Jackson,* vol. 2 (Washington, DC: Carnegie Institute of Washing-
     ton, 1927), 412, 440; Lauderdale County Commission, et al., "Civil War
     Trail," *Follow the Trail to Florence* (City of Florence and Lauderdale
     County 2004), unpaged; "Dred Scott" Internet archival file in Missouri
     State Archives, www.sos.mo.gov/archives/resources/africanamerican/
     scott.

22   *Muscle Shoals* to *Nathan Bedford Forrest:* Donald Davidson, *Rivers of Amer-
     ica: The Tennessee,* vol. 1 (New York: Rinehart, 1946), 23, 245; vol. 2 (New
     York: Rinehart, 1948), 44–45, 165. See also the military report on 18 Febru-
     ary 1862 from Union forces in Florence to Flag Officer Foote, U.S. Navy,

on "strong" Union sentiment in the Florence area despite the presence of "marauding bands of guerrilla companies," reprinted in Jill K. Garrett, *A History of Florence, Alabama* (Columbia, TN: n.p., 1968), 29. Hereafter cited as Garrett.

23 *left for dead: Father,* 3–4. The violence of the Handy family's story is substantiated by an almost identical account of the murder of the Lauderdale County farmer John Wilson, in the Nashville *Union* newspaper, 18 May 1865, reprinted in Garrett, 51–52. See also the unpublished scholarly article by Lee Freeman, "John Campbell, Charles Oliver and the Wilson Murders," at the Florence-Lauderdale County Public Library.

23 *"spoil a field hand"* to *"shoe mechanic":* quoted from the Montgomery *Advertiser* newspaper, 2 December 1888, in Allen Johnson Going, *Bourbon Democracy in Alabama 1874–1890* (Tuscaloosa: University of Alabama Press, 1951), 157; Polly Warren, *Lauderdale County, Alabama, in the 1870s* (Birmingham: P-Vine Press, 1982); "U.S. Census for Lauderdale County," 171.

24 *Princess Anne, Maryland* to *sold farther south:* "Recordum Familia Handy," single-page document at the Florence-Lauderdale County Public Library, Florence, Alabama. The author is indebted to Lee Freeman, genealogist at this library, for a photocopy of this family tree and brief history. This document gives the year of W. W. Handy's birth as 1810; the U.S. Census of 1870 gives the year as 1811. The year 1811, as well as the more frequent spelling in primary documents of the name of Handy's owner as "McKiernan," is used in the text.

24 *"shot but not killed"* to *"plots among slaves":* Father, 3; Herbert Aptheker, *American Negro Slave Revolts* (New York: International Publishers, 1974), 336.

25 *Seth Concklin* to *blunt trauma:* William Still, *The Underground Rail Road: A Record of Facts, Authentic Narratives, Letters, &c.* (Philadelphia: Porter & Coates, 1872), "Seth Concklin," 23–34; Evansville (IN) *Daily Journal* newspaper, "Fugitive Slaves," 15 April 1851.

26 *the tract of land in Florence:* Deed "Asher to Handy" recorded 29 November 1868 in Lauderdale County Deed Record, Vol. 17, 680–81; "Recordum Familia Handy."

26 *used as a cowshed:* Charlotte B. Johnson, "St. Paul African Methodist Episcopal Church in Retrospection," *Heritage of Lauderdale County, Alabama* (Columbia, TN: Heritage Publishing Consultants, 1999), 31–32; William L. McDonald, *History of the First United Methodist Church, Florence, Alabama* (Birmingham: Birmingham Printing and Publishing Company, 1983), 41.

26 *"missionaries to Alabama":* W. H. Mixon, *History of the African Methodist Episcopal Church in Alabama* (Nashville: Publishing House of the A.M.E. Sunday-School Union, 1902), 29. Hereafter cited as Mixon.

26 *James T. Rapier* to *"my father has told me":* Loren Schweninger, *James T. Rapier and Reconstruction* (Chicago: University of Chicago Press, 1978), 44–46, 71; Eileen Southern, ed., "In Retrospect: Letters from W. C. Handy to William Grant Still: Part 2," *Black Perspective in Music,* vol. 8 (spring 1980), 21 November 1952, 102. Hereafter cited as "Retrospect 2," and unless otherwise noted all letters are written by Handy to William G. Still.

27 *"a good teacher":* Mixon, 130.

28 *the* Watcher: Unpublished scholarly study by Lee Freeman, "Organized Religion of the African-American Community of Lauderdale County," unpaged.

28 *"social suicide"* to *"matter of guns"*: T. S. Stribling, *The Store* (New York: Literary Guild, 1932), 16; T. S. Stribling, *The Unfinished Cathedral* (Garden City, NY: Doubleday, Doran, 1934), 59, 150–51. Stribling's trilogy was initiated by *The Forge* (Garden City, NY: Doubleday, Doran, 1931). *The Store* received the Pulitzer Prize for the novel in 1933.

29 *smooth-bore musket: Father,* 9.

30 *"humble" character: Florence Times-Journal,* 15 October 1873.

30 *Booker T. Washington:* Charles R. Wilson, et al., *Encyclopedia of Southern Culture* (Chapel Hill: University of North Carolina Press, 1989), 228–29. Hereafter cited as *Southern Culture.*

31 *"fight my way": Father,* 4.

TWO: W. C. HANDY AND THE MUSIC OF BLACK AND WHITE AMERICA

32 *"confusion and doubt": Souls,* 8–9.

32 *"remained buried": Father,* 5.

33 *ash cakes:* letter, W. C. Handy to Karl Tyree, 4 June 1956, Florence-Lauderdale County Public Library.

33 *"pulled fodder"* to *Young A. Wallace* (page 34): *Father,* 8, 162, 4–5, 12–14. See also the photograph and brief biography of Wallace available at the Florence-Lauderdale County Public Library. Wallace was the county chairman of the "black-and-tan" Republicans in Lauderdale County; see the *Florence Standard Journal* newspaper, 6 May 1898.

33 *"Weary Traveler"* to *"Train's a-Comin'"*: W. C. Handy, ed., *Blues: An Anthology* (New York: Albert & Charles Boni, 1926), 25. Hereafter cited as *Blues Anthology.*

34 Gospel Hymns: Author's examination of *Gospel Hymns Consolidated: Embracing Volumes 1, 2, 3, and 4, Without Duplicates, for Use in Gospel Meetings and Other Religious Services* (Cincinnati: J. Church, 1883).

36 *"too far south": Father,* 137–38.

36 *"uneducated nigger"* to *Populist and explicitly racist: Father,* 80–81. Sheldon Hackney, *Populism to Progressivism in Alabama* (Princeton, NJ: Princeton University Press, 1969), 180–81, 204–05; William Rodgers, *The One-Gallused Rebellion: Agrarianism in Alabama, 1865–1896* (Baton Rouge: Louisiana State University Press, 1970), 53. The speaker's words in Handy's memoir are quoted from a similar speech he later heard in Mississippi, but Handy emphasizes how he was "reminded of the first time I had heard oratory of this sort," at the incident in Florence.

37 *"Aunt Hagar's children": Father,* 149.

38 *Lock Number Seven* to Hello Central: *Blues Anthology,* 10, 4, 94; David A. Jasen, ed., "The Hesitating Blues," *Beale Street and Other Classic Blues, 38 Works 1901–1921* (Mineola, NY: Dover, 1998), 21. Hereafter cited as *Classic.* The late-nineteenth-century folk songs excerpted in this chapter are quoted at greater length in *Blues Anthology* and are described there as "all drawn from the memory of W. C. Handy," and hence likely contemporary to his adolescent work at the Muscle Shoals construction site.

38 *James "Jim" Turner: Father*, 15–16, 230.

39 *a personal exception:* Turner is listed as one of the three violinists in Handy's Memphis Blues Band, which recorded sessions for Paramount in January and March, 1922. See www.redhotjazz.com/handymbb. Handy does not mention Turner's presence at this 1922 session, but the composer does recall in his memoir (230) the prior "Terrell's band in Huntsville" as an example of a nineteenth-century, very early jazz band, which was given to novelty sounds in its performances. A "Professor James Turner" is listed in a newspaper account of 4 May 1893 as one of this band's performers, along with Bob and Alonzo Terrell. See *Out of Sight*, 297. The Terrell brothers were barbers, and possibly also active along with Turner in the musical experimentations of the "barbershop chord" of the Tennessee River Valley—the vogue among popular musicians there for deliberately flattening or distorting a note—that Abbott finds as a precursor to Handy's later use of the blue note. See *Out of Sight*, 357.

Unless new archival material is discovered in Florence, or elsewhere, it seems that the hard-luck Jim Turner, although a significant figure in the development of the early blues along the Tennessee River Valley equal in his importance and musical talent to such blues pioneers in the Mississippi Delta as Henry Sloan and Charley Patton, is fated personally to an undeserved obscurity.

39 *"prototype of all blues":* Abbe Niles, "Notes to the Collection," *Blues Anthology*, 32; see also Abbe Niles, "Notes to the Collection," in W. C. Handy, ed., *A Treasury of the Blues: Complete Words and Music of 67 Great Songs from "Memphis Blues" to the Present Day* (New York: Charles Boni, 1949), 244.

40 *"long-chain man"* to never miss Joe Turner: Jerry Silverman, "Joe Turner," *Folk Blues: 110 American Folk Blues* (New York: Macmillan, 1958), 29. *Classic*, "Joe Turner Blues," 55–65. Handy's assertion that he learned "Joe Turner" in the oral folk tradition on the streets of Florence from Jim Turner can be heard on an archival Internet sound file maintained by National Public Radio, "Hearing Voices: W. C. Handy," www.npr.org.

40 *traveling circus:* Mark C. Gridley, *Jazz Styles* (New York: Prentice-Hall, 1978), 58–59; *Father*, 16–17.

40 *triple-tonguing:* Such a technique is, literally, more difficult than it sounds. To the nonmusician, Handy's physical versatility on his cornet can be appreciated by one's attempting to pronounce the *t-k-t* sounds in rapid succession as representative of three musical notes. Handy by analogy would be capable of articulating the frictive *t* sound, pronouncing the palatal *k* sound from lower in his mouth, and then quickly returning his tongue against the upper teeth to repeat the *t* sound, all in one brief exhalation. The author is indebted to two accomplished musicians and philologists, Dan Arlen and Bruce Sherwood of Cincinnati, Ohio, for this useful analogy.

41 *Brass bands:* Margaret Hazen, et al., *The Music Men: An Illustrated History of Brass Bands in America, 1800–1920* (Washington, D.C.: Smithsonian Institution Press, 1987), xviii, 140–41. Hereafter cited as Hazen.

41 *charismatic band directors:* Paul E. Bierley, *John Philip Sousa, American Phe-*

nomenon (Miami: Warner Brothers, 2001), 42–44, 54, 124. Hereafter cited as *Phenomenon*. Wilfrid Mellers, *Music in a New Found Land: Themes and Developments in the History of American Music* (New York: Alfred A. Knopf, 1965), 258–59; *Father*, 69.

42 *forbidden musical activities* to *"Old Hen Cackled"*: *Father*, 11, 17. Archival fiddle recordings on CD, including tunes performed in the 1920s and dating from the 1880s, in *Alabama Stringbands in Chronological Order of Dr. D. D. Hollis, Wyzee Hamilton, Short Creek Trio, Akino Birmingham Boys & Dixie Ramblers (1924–1937)*, Document Records DOCD-8032.

42 *"Run, Nigger, Run"*: Newman I. White, *American Negro Folk Songs* (Hatboro, PA: Folklore Associates, 1965), 168–69. White, who did much of his field research in Alabama during the 1910s, notes that this song was well known then by residents there "whose memories go back to the eighteen-sixties." The author of this biography, who grew up in Alabama during the middle decade of the twentieth century, can recall the song having been played by local white fiddlers.

43 *"change of heart"* to *"you niggers"*: *Father*, 11, 29, 162, 20–23.

44 *Columbian Exposition*: Dennis B. Downey, *A Season of Renewal: The Columbian Exposition and Victorian America* (New York: Praeger, 2002), 12, 8. Hereafter cited as Downey. Neil Harris, et al., *Grand Illusions: Chicago's World Fair of 1893* (Chicago: Chicago Historical Society, 1993), 156, map unpaged frontispiece, 144–48; Downey, 174–75.

45 *his optimistic assurances* to *"on our uppers"*: *Father*, 24–26.

45 *muddy construction* to *gilded telegraph key*: Downey, 28, 33–36, 3. Handy in his memoir dates his trip as a member of the quintet to Chicago as consequent to the economic panic "during Grover Cleveland's second administration" (23), that administration having been inaugurated in March 1893. Yet upon the group's arrival in Chicago, they found the fair "had been postponed for a year" in Handy's description (26), from its anticipated opening of October 1892, to October 1893. Handy and his friends therefore must have traveled to Chicago in late autumn of 1892, not 1893, and the year of their trip has been adjusted accordingly in the text.

46 *"professional idlers"* to *St. Louis police*: Carlos. C. Clossom, "The Unemployed in American Cities," *Quarterly Journal of Economics*, vol. 8, no. 2 (January 1894), 203–04.

46 *"blind baggage"*: *Father*, 26.

46 *his watch in pledge* to *"horse's stall"*: "Retrospect 2," 9 April 1952, 85–86; "Notes to the Collection," *Blues Anthology*, 29.

47 *particularly severe*: The average winter temperature in St. Louis during the winter of 1892–93 was 29.5 degrees F. See the National Oceanic and Atmospheric Administration Internet site, "Event Archives," at www.crh .noaa.gov/lsx.

48 *penniless*: *Father*, 30.

48 *mouthpieces for cornets* to *smart uniforms*: Hazen, xviii, 131; *Father*, 31–32.

48 *"King Cotton"* to *protégé of Sousa's*: *Phenomenon*, 233–34; *Father*, 31.

49 *uniform of the Hampton Cornet Band*: Photograph of W. C. Handy, Mississippi Valley Collection, University of Memphis, hereafter cited as MVC. This photograph is reproduced in *Father*, facing page 32, where it is iden-

tified by the author as "my picture at nineteen, in Hampton Cornet Band, Evansville, Indiana." Assuming the photograph was dated accurately by its subject, it was taken sometime between November 16, 1892, and November 15, 1893, when Handy was nineteen years of age. Allowing some time for him to remain in Chicago in the late autumn of 1892 and his traveling to St. Louis and sojourning there and in East St. Louis, his homelessness in Missouri is therefore dated in the text as the winter of 1892–93.

Handy's subsequent trip to Indiana riding the rails and his employment there with Hampton's band sufficiently long enough to justify purchasing a band uniform are therefore dated in the text as having occurred no later than summer or early fall of 1893. This dating is substantiated by Handy's noting in his memoir that he first did seasonal construction work in Indiana, where he sought out "a cooler spot in the shade," 30. See also the note on page 241 concerning internal dating of Handy's trip from Alabama to Illinois.

49 *ten dollars:* Hazen, 140.

50 F. W. Nesbitt to *"got paid for it":* Father, 163, 32.

50 *found a wife* to *his mother's funeral:* Father, 164–66. The obituary of Elizabeth Brewer Price was printed in the *Florence Herald,* 29 August 1895.

51 *"cakes"* to *"upper-crust Negroes":* Father, 32–33.

THREE: JUMPING JIM CROW

52 *COLORED TALENT:* Advertisement, late nineteenth century, with engravings of Jack and W. A. Mahara, reproduced in Henry T. Sampson, *The Ghost Walks: A Chronological History of Blacks in Show Business, 1865–1910* (Metuchen, NJ: Scarecrow Press, 1988), 95, hereafter cited as *Ghost.* The Mahara company billed itself under several names while on the road, including "Mahara's Colored Minstrels," "Mahara's Big City Minstrels," "Mahara's Mammoth Minstrels," "Mahara's Southern Minstrels," and "Mahara's Eastern Minstrels." All troupes were composed of African American performers and were under the ownership of the Mahara brothers. The "southern" and "eastern" minstrels may have been simply smaller troupes selected from the larger company of performers to travel shorter itineraries under contact to the Mahara brothers for tours where it would not have been profitable to pay traveling expenses of the entire troupe. The name most frequently used in playbills and advertisements appears to have been Mahara's Colored Minstrels, and this will be used herein to refer to the public name of the three Mahara brothers' minstrel troupe.

52 *"ambiguous":* Chicago Defender, 6 September 1919.

52 *"real Negro minstrel show":* Father, 34.

53 *burnt wine corks* to *"Daddy" Rice: Southern Culture,* 1018–20; Ken Emerson, *Doo-dah! Stephen Foster and the Rise of American Popular Culture* (New York: Simon & Schuster, 1997), 58–61; Dale Cockrell, *Demons of Disorder: Early Blackface Minstrels and Their World* (New York: Cambridge University Press, 1997), 62–63, 92–93, 99–100; *Southern Culture,* 213–14. Primary sources for the two U.S. states each proposed as a possible site where Rice first

witnessed the "Jim Crow" song and dance are found in Eric Lott, *Love and Theft: Blackface Minstrelsy and the American Working Class* (New York: Oxford University Press, 1993), 56, 59.

53 *"curious lurch"* to *"Ethiopian Mobility"*: John Strausbaugh, *Black Like You: Blackface, Whiteface, Insult & Imitation in American Popular Culture* (New York: Jeremy P. Tarcher/Penguin, 2006), 58, 61. Hereafter cited as *Black Like You*. W. T. Lhamon Jr., *Jump Jim Crow: Lost Plays, Lyrics, and Street Prose of the First Atlantic Popular Culture* (Cambridge, MA: Harvard University Press, 2003), 62–63, 19.

54 *"Sung by Mr. Rice"* to *"Camptown Races"*: Author's analysis of the 1832 score reproduced in Richard Jackson, ed., *Democratic Souvenirs: An Historical Anthology of 19th-Century American Music* (New York: C. F. Peters, 1988), 92, hereafter cited as *Souvenirs*. Robert C. Toll, *Blacking Up: The Minstrel Show in Nineteenth-Century America* (New York: Oxford University Press, 1974), 27, 58, hereafter cited as *Blacking Up*. See also the conclusion in Ken Emerson's *Doo-dah! Stephen Foster and the Rise of American Popular Music* (New York: Simon & Schuster, 1997), that "blackface borrowed more brazenly from African-American dance—that stablehand's gyrations, Juba's spectacular 'heelology' [see chapter four of this text for a discussion of "heelology" or "patting Juba"]—than from African-American music" (70); Dena J. Epstein, in *Sinful Tunes and Spirituals: Black Folk Music to the Civil War* (Urbana, IL: University of Illinois Press, 1977), 241–42, hereafter cited as *Sinful Tunes*.

Additionally examined by the author of this biography were antebellum scores in *George Christy & Wood's Melodies as Sung by Their Unique Companies, at Minstrel Hall* (Philadelphia: T. B. Peterson, 1854). The scores popular among minstrelsy companies during Handy's later nineteenth-century career before the advent of the 1890s coon songs were also examined in *Minstrel Songs, Old and New* (Chicago: Oliver Ditson, 1882). These popular songs, usually nonsyncopated and without "blue notes," include "Susan Jane: A Famous 'End Song' and Chorus," "Oh! Sam: A Famous Minstrel Song," "Old Dan Tucker," "In the Morning by the Bright Light: A Famous End Song," and "Old Black Joe." Of course, these scores indicate how the music *should* be played according to the composer's instructions, and it is possible that nineteenth-century minstrelsy orchestras occasionally would improvise to "swing" or "jazz" their performances, as twentieth-century musicians later would say. Intriguingly, the 1832 score of "Jim Crow" is marked *"Alla Nigaro."* But by the time of Handy's minstrelsy career, the orchestras in colored troupes were expected to be faithful score readers.

54 *folk songs of the African American slaves*: *Sinful Tunes*, 142–43, 241–42, 288, 340.

54 *this nation's laws*: C. Vann Woodward, *The Strange Career of Jim Crow* (New York: Oxford University Press, 1966), 7. Hereafter cited as *Strange Career*.

55 *"sleeping terror"*: James Baldwin, "In Search of a Majority," *Nobody Knows My Name: More Notes of a Native Son* (New York: Dial, 1961), 111–12.

55 *"schizoid"*: Rudi Blesh and Harriet Janis, *They All Played Ragtime*, 4th ed. (New York: Oak Publications, 1971), 84. Hereafter cited as *All Played*.

56 *going business* to *" 'Deed I Has to Laugh"*: Frank Costellow Davidson, "The

Rise, Development, Decline and Influence of the American Minstrel Show" (PhD diss., 1952, New York University), 92–93, 120. Hereafter cited as Davidson. See also *Phenomenon*, 39.

56 *all whiteface* to *actual people of color: Blackening Up*, 200–01, 203, 226–27; Le Roy Rice, *Monarchs of Minstrelsy from "Daddy" Rice to Date* (New York: Kenny Publishing, 1911), 363–64; hereafter cited as Rice. Stanley Sadie, et al., eds., *The New Grove Dictionary of Music and Musicians*, "Minstrelsy, American," 2nd ed., vol. 16 (New York: Grove, 2001), 738; *Out of Sight*, 65.

56 *had to turn away: Out of Sight*, 106. See also the press clipping dated 12 January 1898, reproduced in *Ghost*, 142, in regard to the performance of the Richards and Pringle's Colored Minstrels company in Dallas, Texas: "The two upper floors of the Opera House are reserved for colored people only, and are both packed to the doors."

57 *Belvidere, Illinois: Ghost*, 110.

57 *flamboyant members* to *specialty act: Father*, 33, 57, 37–42; *Out of Sight*, 66. In regard to male soubrettes in whiteface minstrelsy companies, see Dailey Paskman and Sigmund Spaeth, *"Gentlemen, Be Seated!": A Parade of the Old-Time Minstrels* (Garden City, NY: Doubleday, Doran, 1928), 87; hereafter cited as Paskman. See also Davidson, 109, and Rice, "Famed Favorites Who Favored Feminine Fancies," 201, 269, the former page illustrated with photogravures of nine popular white male minstrelsy female impersonators of the late nineteenth and early twentieth centuries, all but two pictured in theatrical drag.

58 *a grand parade:* Davidson, 103–04; *Ghost*, 110, 112, 190.

58 *"velvet knee pants"* to *"pickaninny band": Ghost*, 133, 138.

59 *"get them told"* to *the first part: Father*, 69; Davidson, 106. *Ghost*, 110, 190; *Father*, 34; Davidson, 103–04, 112; David Lee Joyner, "Southern Ragtime and Its Transition to Published Blues" (PhD diss., 1986, Memphis State University), 53–54, hereafter cited as "Southern Ragtime"; *Ghost*, 133; Davidson, 106.

59 *Los Angeles Theater:* The program is reprinted in *Ghost*, 143–44.

60 MISTER INTERLOCUTOR to *no-account Socialist:* Paskman, 122–24; *Ghost*, 143, 191; Davidson, 127–28; *Black Like You*, 116–18. Archival recordings of minstrelsy performances from the late nineteenth century are available on modern CD rerecordings. The "Minstrel First Part" by Quinn's Imperial Minstrels and others (circa 1894), and George W. Johnson's "The Laughing Coon" (1898) and "Listen to the Mocking Bird" (1896)—the latter tune a mainstay within minstrel shows since the lifetime of Daddy Rice—are preserved on *Lost Sounds: Blacks and the Birth of the Recording Industry, 1891–1922*, Archeophone Records 1005. A complete minstrel show, including olio and afterpiece, has been reassembled from archival recordings primarily of the early twentieth century and can be heard on the CD issued as *Monarchs of Minstrelsy: Historic Recordings by Stars of the Minstrel Stage*, Archeophone Records 1006.

61 *cakewalk:* Wilfrid Mellers, *Music in a New Land: Themes and Developments in the History of American Music* (New York: Alfred A. Knopf, 1965), 276–77; *Ragging It*, 101–2.

61 *"insult and imitation": Black Like You*, 32–34.

62 *"Farewell Ladies":* Score and lyrics for "Farewell Ladies: Written,

Composed, & Sung by E. P. Christy," 1847, reproduced in *Souvenirs*, 98. *Father*, 70.

63 "*disreputable*": *Father*, 33.

63 "*no avenue for the colored entertainer*": *Freeman*, 30 December 1899, 23 November 1907.

63 *in colored minstrelsy money was good*: *Father*, 33; the *New York Clipper* noted with approval on 16 February 1895 that in the Mahara brothers' company "the 'ghost' walks every Sunday"; the accommodations aboard the Maharaja are described in a *Clipper* article dated 7 September 1895; see also the explanation for the "ghost," or perambulating white paymaster, in *Ghost* (author Henry Sampson knew a good title when he found one), viii. Yet despite what the *Clipper* wrote, the Mahara brothers were not always good for the weekly salaries. Sampson elsewhere (193) excerpts an unidentified press clipping of 9 November 1899 that "Mahara's (Eastern) Minstrels disband after playing Girald's Theatre, Buffalo, N.Y., because of non-payment of salaries for two weeks. Some of the company join Smith's Comedy Co. (white) in Syracuse, N.Y. The band of ten members joins Moore's Uncle Tom's Cabin Company, where they receive two weeks' salary in advance."

The Mahara minstrels stranded in Buffalo apparently were not members of the company among whom Handy was traveling, as he makes no mention in his memoir of what would have been a remarkable incident in his show business career. The subsequent, fortuitous employment of the ten members of the band with a production of "Uncle Tom's Cabin" validates George Moxley's comment to a later generation of black performers that minstrel shows, spiritual or "jubilee" choirs, or the derivative Uncle Tom musical companies were practically all the employment available in the 1890s to African American musicians or singers.

64 *Broadway musical* to "*Coon! Coon! Coon!*": James Weldon Johnson, *Black Manhattan* (New York: Da Capo, 1991), 95; *All Played*, 84, 86–90; *Father*, 60; "Southern Ragtime," 50, 54; *Father*, 70; Julius Mattfeld, *Variety Music Cavalcade, 1620–1969: A Chronology of Vocal and Instrumental Music Popular in the United States*, 3d ed. (New York: Prentice-Hall, 1971), 223–24, 244, hereafter cited as *Cavalcade*; *All Played*, 88–89; Eileen Southern, ed., *Biographical Dictionary of Afro-American and African Musicians*, "Ernest Hogan" (Westport, CT: Greenwood, 1982), 185.

The lyrics to Ben Harney's "Mister Johnson" are quoted in John Edward Hasse, ed., *Ragtime: Its History, Composers, and Music* (New York: Schirmer, 1985), 72.

67 *first circuit in ten years* to "*his tongue cut out*": *Ghost*, 199; *Father*, 43–44. The veracity of Handy's account in his memoir of the horrific lynching of Louis Wright is corroborated by the news story of Wright's mutilation and murder published in the Indianapolis *Freeman*, 15 March 1902.

69 *endurance of smallpox* to "*nightmare of those minstrel days*": *Father*, 47–51; author's correspondence of 15 August 2006, with librarians at the Tyler Public Library, who searched professionally but in vain for any mention of news accounts of this 1899–1900 quarantine in the primary sources available in the archives at Tyler, Texas.

Cricket Smith can be heard playing along with other musicians of

Wilbur C. Sweatman's Original Jass [*sic*] Band on *Ragtime to Jazz I, 1912–1919,* Timeless CBC 1-035. "Jass" was Sweatman's usual spelling of the word in his band's name.

The "nightmare of minstrelsy," in Handy's memorable phrase, has perennially irradiated into American literature in books other than Handy's memoir. It was used in 1927 by T. S. Eliot in his "Fragment of an Agon," published in Eliot, *The Complete Poems and Plays: 1909–1950* (New York: Harcourt, Brace, 1952), 81:

"SONG BY WAUCHOPE AND HORSEFALL
SWARTS AS TAMBO. SNOW AS BONES."

Other examples include John Berryman's "Dream Songs" sequence of poems published from 1969 onward in which a jeering "Mr. Bones" addresses the poet's alter ego in an exaggeratedly black dialect similar to a routine spoken by an end-man from minstrelsy's first part, and the 1997 novel of Thomas Pynchon, *Mason & Dixon,* in which a fictional George Washington, apparently Jewish, speaks mysteriously to visitors in the theatrical dialect of a blackface minstrel.

W. T. Lhamon, in *Raising Cain: Blackface Performance from Jim Crow to Hip-Hop* (Cambridge, MA: Harvard University Press, 1998), persuasively argues that the Zip Coon of nineteenth-century minstrelsy survives as postironic performance art by hip-hop African Americans.

72   *"Minstrels—at Cuba"*: quoted in *Out of Sight,* 67.

72   *Key West, Florida: Father,* 51–54.

73   *"mainstream"* to *"ragtime coon songs"*: Lynn Abbott and Doug Seroff, *Ragged but Right: Black Traveling Shows, "Coon Songs," and the Dark Pathway to Blues and Jazz* (Jackson: University of Mississippi Press, 2007), 11–12. Hereafter cited as *Dark Pathway.*

73   *"odd new vogue": Father,* 58.

FOUR: AUNT HAGAR'S RAGTIME SON COMES HOME TO ALABAMA

74   *toured the towns of northern Alabama* to *"forgive you": Father,* 55; Huntsville (AL) *Weekly Mercury* newspaper, 7 March 1900, "Amusements" notice. I am grateful to Huntsville librarian Thomas Hutchins for this clipping.

75   *perennial fable* to *Al Jolson:* Michael Alexander, *Jazz Age Jews* (Princeton, NJ: Princeton University Press, 2001), 139, 212, note 7; Herbert G. Goldman, *Jolson: The Legend Comes to Life* (New York: Oxford University Press, 1988), 152.

75   *drew a pistol* to *small orchestra: Father,* 56–57.

76   *"trifle dull"* to *laws effectively disenfranchised: Father,* 56; *Strange Career,* 67.

77   *"was terrific"*: MVC, Paul Flowers interview with W. C. Handy, et al., 1 December 1954, Ms. 77, 4–5. Hereafter cited as Flowers interview.

78   *"Rastus on Parade"*: "Southern Ragtime," 54.

78   *tapping a pencil:* I am indebted to the Cincinnati musician Melinda Neal for this useful analogy.

78   *"patting Juba"*: quoted in *Sinful Tunes,* 142–43.

79   *"jig piano"* to *stanzaic architecture:* "Southern Ragtime," 23–24, 27–28, 46–47; *Southern Culture,* 1015–16; *All Played,* 210.

79   *"bad words"*: Scott Joplin, "Theatrical Comment," *New York Age,* 3 April

1913, quoted in Edward A. Berlin, *Ragtime: A Musical and Cultural History* (Berkeley: University of California Press, 1980), 36. Hereafter cited as Berlin.

79 *favorite of Handy's:* See the citation on page 249 about the Alan Lomax interview with former Handy band member S. L. "Stack" Mangham, in *Land Where the Blues Began.*

79 *paterfamilias of American music: Phenomenon,* 18.

80 *count the cows: Father,* 61.

80 *powerfully built man* to *"an enraged lion":* photograph of Councill and map of the itinerary for the Tour of Conquest and Melody reproduced in *Out of Sight,* 351, 355; Richard David Morrison, *History of Alabama Agricultural and Mechanical University 1875–1992* (Huntsville, AL: Liberal Arts Press, 1994), 26–27.

81 *"blackfaced comedians":* Charles E. Ives, *Memos,* ed. John Kirkpatrick (New York: W. W. Norton, 1972), 56.

82 *forty-three new ragtime songs:* Author's count from copyright notices for ragtime songs arranged chronologically in David A. Jasen and Gene Jones, *That American Rag: The Story of Ragtime from Coast to Coast* (New York: Schirmer, 2000), "Appendix D: A Checklist of 2,002 Published Rags," 342–405.

82 *"Real American Folk Song":* The lyrics are quoted in Ken Bloom, ed., *American Song: The Complete Musical Theatre Companion,* 2nd ed., vol. 1 (New York: Schirmer, 1996), 607.

82 *"our national music":* Moderwell is quoted in "The Great American Composer: Will He Speak in the Accent of Broadway?" *Current Opinion,* vol: 63 (November 1917), 316–17.

83 *"stickler for the classics"* to *"forty-dollar job": Father,* 59–61. Handy in the Flowers interview, 4–5, identifies this article as having been written by Sousa; it likely was Sousa's article, "What 'Rag Time' Means," published in the *New York World,* 7 April 1901. If Handy is correct as to the authorship, he was overstating the case in his memoir; although Sousa was not personally "fond" of ragtime (*Phenomenon,* 142), he included it in his band's performances.

83 *"almost vulgar words":* Joplin, cited in Berlin, above.

84 *Thomas Turpin:* David A. Jasen and Trebor Jay Tichenor, *Rags and Ragtime: A Musical History* (New York: Dover, 1978), 28–29. See also the discussion of genteel reaction to ragtime in Berlin, 38–44.

84 *"looking for that bully":* lyrics to "May Irwin's " 'Bully' Song" quoted in Berlin, 33–34.

84 *vagabonded there* to *oversized black seeds: Father,* 118–19, 61–63.

85 *"his band and orchestra"* to *replaced William Malone: Ghost,* 277.

    The 6 December 1902 roster, reproduced in *Ghost,* is the first extant notice of Handy's leading the stage orchestra as well as the marching band for the Maharas. Although this roster contains the names of some of the old troupers of the Mahara company, such as William Sweatman, the name of William Malone, the former orchestra leader, is absent.

    A "Professor William Malone" had been listed on 22 August 1897 as the director of the Mahara orchestra (*Ghost,* 133) and again on 18 June 1898 (*Ghost,* 152) and he therefore had been the conductor of Handy while the latter had played cornet onstage as a member of the orchestra during Handy's initial years as a minstrel. A "Wm. Malone" also had been listed as the "Orchestra Leader" on the Los Angeles Theater playbill for the Mahara company's performance of 31 January 1898, which lists "W. C. Handy" as "Leader of the Band." See *Ghost*, 144.

86 *C. G. Conn* to *George A. Swan: Father*, 33, 64; Richard I. Schwartz, *The Cornet Compendium: The History and Development of the Nineteenth-Century Cornet*, chapter 3, "Lesser-Known Cornet Soloists," 2000, Internet resource, http://www.angelfire.com/music2/thecornetcompendium/.

86 *"closed with Mahara's":* *Ghost*, 298.

86 *final performance in February:* Florence (AL) *Times*, 30 January 1903; Florence (AL) *Herald*, 2 February 1903.

87 *nostalgia act:* The last performing "authentic," or nonironist, southern African American minstrel died in 1993. Abner Jay, formerly a resident of a Stone Mountain, Georgia, plantation who had toured and performed on banjo for the Silas Green's Minstrel Show throughout the South in the early 1930s, continued his solo performances in the lower South into the early 1970s, working out of his eccentrically decorated automobile and adding songs such as "Cocaine Blues," comedy routines about collegiate hippies, and salacious jokes about his many wives to his performances of Stephen Foster tunes and his playing of banjo folk tunes. Some of these latter songs dated from the late nineteenth century. Jay recorded several LPs, now considered rare. See Tuscaloosa (AL) *News*, Ben Windham columnist, "Abner Jay a Real 'Outsider' Musician," 22 October 2006.

87 *"Old Stretch":* Ike Simond, *"Old Slack's" Reminiscences & Pocket History of the Colored Profession from 1865 to 1891* (Bowling Green, OH: Popular Press reprint, 1974), passim.

FIVE: WHERE THE SOUTHERN CROSSES THE YELLOW DOG

89 *"heavy on my mind"* to *Colored Knights of Pythias:* Son House, "Clarksdale Moan," in *The Stuff Dreams Are Made Of* (various artists), Yazoo Records B000E6Uk9Q; *Father*, 72; Theda Skopal and Ariane Liazos, et al., *What a Mighty Power We Can Be: African American Fraternal Groups and the Struggle for Racial Equality* (Princeton, NJ: Princeton University Press, 2006), 37–38; hereafter cited as Liazos.

90 *giant leaf:* The Delta extends across state lines to both sides of the Mississippi River, and, hence, one properly speaking should refer to the "Mississippi Delta," the "Tennessee Delta," the "Arkansas Delta," and so forth. Within this biography, "the Delta," unless otherwise specified, refers to that area within the state of Mississippi. The total square miles given for the Mississippi Delta is the sum of the areas contained by the fourteen counties accepted by both the state and federal governments as constituting the Mississippi Delta: Bolivar, Carroll, Coahoma, Holmes, Humphreys, Issaquena, Leflore, Quitman, Sharkey, Sunflower, Tallahatchie, Tunica, Washington, and Yazoo counties. This area's uniqueness in terms of geology, ecology, culture, economics, history, and practically all other categories is discussed at length in the National Park website entitled "Nile of the New World," accessible at www.cr.nps.gov/delta/.

90 *first gravel road* to *"leaving it still richer"*: John C. Willis, *Forgotten Time: The Yazoo-Mississippi Delta After the Civil War* (Charlottesville: University Press of Virginia, 2000), 11, hereafter cited as Willis; William Faulkner, *Sanctuary* (New York: Jonathan Cape, 1931), 16, "Delta Autumn," in *Go Down, Moses* (New York: Random House, 1955), 340; Stephen Calt and Gayle Wardlow, "The Delta," *King of the Delta Blues: The Life and Music of Charlie Patton* (Newton, NJ: Rock Chapel, 1988), 70–74, hereafter cited as Calt.

91 *four million acres* to *Yazoo & Mississippi Valley*: Clyde Woods, *Development Arrested: The Blues and Plantation Power in the Mississippi Delta* (New York: Verso, 1998), 90–91, hereafter cited as Woods; Max Haymes, *Railroadin' Some: Railroads in the Early Blues* (York, England: Music Mentor Books, 2006), 147–48, hereafter cited as Haymes.

92 *"whim of the mob"*: W. E. B. Du Bois, "The Economic Revolution in the South," in Du Bois and Booker T. Washington, *The Negro in the South: His Economic Progress Relative to His Moral and Religious Development; Being the William Levi Bull Lectures for the Year 1907* (Philadelphia: George W. Jacobs & Company, 1907), 93–94.

92 *Eighty-seven people* to *"the White Chief"*: Willis, 105; National Association for the Advancement of Colored People, *Thirty Years of Lynching in the United States, 1889–1918* (New York: Arno Press, 1969), Appendix I, Table No. 1: "Number of White and Colored People Lynched in the United States, 1889–1918"; Appendix II, "Chronological List of Persons Lynched in the United States, 1889–1918, Inclusive, Arranged by States," 29, 78, hereafter cited as *Thirty Years of Lynching*; William F. Holmes, *The White Chief: James Kimble Vardaman* (Baton Rouge: Louisiana State University Press, 1970), 108, 112, hereafter cited as Holmes.

93 *Clarksdale* to *yellow-colored canine*: *Father*, 72, 83; Robert S. McElvaine, ed., *Mississippi: The WPA Guide to the Magnolia State* (Jackson: University Press of Mississippi, 1988), 318, hereafter cited as *Mississippi*; Alan Lomax, *The Land Where the Blues Began* (New York: Pantheon, 1993), 166, hereafter cited as Lomax (Stack Mangham of this interview was the black bank teller mentioned in the text); *Street*, 138–39; Haymes, map, 149, 145; *Father*, 73–74; *Mississippi*, 319, 406–8; *Father*, 71; *Mississippi*, 405, 407.

   With the rise of blues tourism, the National Park Service has constructed an Internet site with blues biographies and current photographs of geographic sites in Clarksdale and other locations of importance to Handy's life, wonderfully titled "Trail of the Hellhound," *pace* a song by Robert Johnson, and located at www.cr.nps.gov/delta/blues.

95 *"weirdest music"* to *"shake any man's soul"*: *Father*, 74, 149; quoted in *Sinful Tunes*, 288, 295.

97 *"over-and-over strains"* to *"country black boys"*: *Father*, 76–77.

98 *"blue note"* to *"meaner the blues"*: Stanley Sadie, ed., *The New Grove Dictionary of Music and Musicians*, 2nd ed., vol. 3 (London: Macmillan, 2001), 727–28; *Blues Anthology*, 14.

98 *white sociologist* to *"stuff people wanted"*: Howard W. Odum, "Folk-Song and Folk-Poetry as Found in the Secular Songs of the Southern Negroes," *Journal of American Folklore*, vol. 24 (July–September 1911), 278–79, 293–94; Howard W. Odum, "Folk-Song and Folk-Poetry as Found in

the Secular Songs of the Southern Negroes," *Journal of American Folklore,* vol. 24 (October–December 1911), 396; author's analysis of "Atlanta Blues" in W. C. Handy, ed., *A Treasury of the Blues* (New York: Charles Boni, 1949), 208–9; Howard W. Odum, *Social and Mental Traits of the Negro* (New York: Columbia University Press, 1910), 13–19; *Father,* 78, 80–83, 77.

100 *"script"* to *"train time":* Lomax, 164; Calt, 105; Gayle Wardlow, *Chasin' That Devil Music: Searching for the Blues* (San Francisco: Miller Freeman, 1998), 42.

100 *"Mississippi problem":* Adam Gussow, "Racial Violence, 'Primitive' Music, and the Blues Entrepreneur: W. C. Handy's Mississippi Problem," *Southern Cultures,* vol. 8 (Fall 2002): 65–77; *Father,* 87.

101 *"black twice"* to *"Mr. Eddie":* King is quoted in Woods, 170; the authority for the contemporary black usage of "ape Mr. Eddy" is Abbe Niles in *Blues Anthology,* 12.

101 *frequently poor* to *"risky business":* Calt, 104; www.yazoo.org/website/famous/mcclenan.

   (The latter Internet site, entitled "Gateway to the Delta," is maintained by Triangle Research Center, Yazoo City, MS); www.cr.nps.gov/delta/blues/people/robert_johnson.htm; *Father,* 180–81, 70–80.

103 *jumped, vigorously, even in fraternal lodges:* Liazos, 142, 165.

103 *"talented tenth"* to *"had to kill somebody":* W. E. B. Du Bois, "The Talented Tenth," in *The Negro Problem: A Series of Articles by Burghardt Du Bois, Paul Laurence Dunbar, Charles W. Chesnutt, and Others* (New York: James Pott, 1903), 33; Antonín Dvořák, interview, "The Real Value of Negro Melodies," *New York Herald,* 21 May 1893, reprinted in *Out of Sight,* 273–74; Gussow, 74; Holmes, 198–99, 100–01; *Thirty Years of Lynching,* Appendix II, 78. Doddsville, Mississippi, plausibly may have been the town where Handy and his musicians were forced, as described in the book text, to perform "The Last Shot Got Him" and, after escaping, saw a black man being led away by a rope around his neck by a white man. *Father,* 179–80.

106 *"all-Negro train":* Shields McIlwaine, *Memphis Down in Dixie* (New York: E. P. Dutton, 1948), 254, hereafter cited as *Memphis.*

106 *winter of 1905:* The year of Handy's arrival with his family in Memphis is uncertain, with many casual biographers accepting 1909, the year mentioned in Handy's memoirs of his composing the song "Mr. Crump," as Handy's inaugural year in Memphis. This writer accepts the much earlier move of 1905 or 1906 as stated by Niles in *Blues Anthology,* 12, and proposed by a close student of internal dating from primary documents of Handy's life, Elliott Hurwitt, in "Publisher," 37. McIlwaine, an anecdotal historian but apparently one with good primary oral sources and social connections in Memphis, writes of "Handy's arrival in 1905" as if unaware there were ever any disagreements about the year of the composer's arrival, 338. Handy himself also writes, *Father,* 125, of his renting an office in the Solvent Savings Bank building of Memphis in 1907; it is possible that he did so while still retaining his private residence in Mississippi, although for practical reasons of expense this arrangement is unlikely.

108 *first adventurous steps:* MVC, Flowers interview, 8–9; MVC, Robert R.

Church papers, Box 12, File 16, letter, Handy to Annette Church, 19 December 1954.

SIX: MR. CRUMP DON'T 'LOW

109 *"ragtime syncopation"*: Father, 120.
109 *lobby of the Peabody* to *"uninviting place"*: David Cohn, *The Mississippi Delta and the World: The Memoirs of David L. Cohn*, ed. James C. Cobb (Baton Rouge: Louisiana State University Press, 1998), xi; William D. Miller, *Mr. Crump of Memphis* (Baton Rouge: Louisiana State University Press, 1964), 78, hereafter cited as Miller; Gerald Capers, *The Biography of a River Town: Memphis, Its Heroic Age* (Chapel Hill: University of North Carolina Press, 1939), 44. Hereafter cited as *River Town*.
110 *east-west venue of commerce:* James R. Aswell and William H. Bruce, eds., et al., *The WPA Guide to Tennessee* (Knoxville: University of Tennessee Press, 1986), 206; hereafter cited as *Tennessee*. *River Town*, 219.
110 *blueslike twelve measures* to *a different style:* "Southern Ragtime," 160.
110 *"ration sack":* Also believed derived from "donation sack." See Scott Ainslie and Dave Whitehill, *Robert Johnson* (Milwaukee: Hal Leonard, 1992), 28. Johnson in this song uses a melody that in this author's opinion is from the traditional white folk tune "Sitting on Top of the World," thereby demonstrating that black rural blues artists, as well as artists such as the more urban and educated Handy, also consciously incorporated elements from other musical genres into their songs.
110 *Jim Crow codes: Strange Career,* 97.
111 *"three o'clock"* to *city policeman: Street,* 104, 241.
111 *majority black city: Thirteenth Census of the United States Taken in the Year 1910, Abstract of the Census* (Washington, D.C.: Government Printing Office, 1913), 94–95.
111 *Church's Park: Street,* 27–28, 215; entry for "Robert R. Church Sr." in *The Tennessee Encyclopedia of History and Culture,* http://tennesseeencyclo pedia.net. This site, maintained by the Tennessee Historical Society, is hereafter cited as *Tennessee Encyclopedia*. MVC, Robert R. Church papers, Box 12, File 16, letter, Handy to Annette Church, 19 December 1954.
112 *murder capital:* "Explaining Our Homicide Record," *Literary Digest* (October 19, 1913), 656–57.
112 *lapel buttons* to *electric trolley cars:* Boyce House, "Memphis Memories of 50 Years Ago," *West Tennessee Historical Society,* vol. 14 (1960), 103, hereafter cited as House. Entry for "Street Car Era" in *Tennessee Encyclopedia*.
112 *skyscraper building:* William D. Miller, *Memphis During the Progressive Era, 1900–1917* (Memphis: Memphis State University Press, 1957), 181–82. Hereafter cited as *Progressive Era*.
112 *Greasy Plank* to *435 Beale:* "Publisher," 37–38, 40.
113 *"Main Street"* to *invisible boundary: Street,* 13. See also Lee's directions given in this same memoir to the Memphis neighborhoods for people of color: "East on Beale, beyond the white folks' Main Street." *Street,* 170.
114 *dead-ended into Beale:* Joseph Blotner, *Faulkner: A Biography,* vol. 1 (New York: Random House, 1974), 303; hereafter cited as *Faulkner*. Blotner, one of the most encyclopedic of biographers, based his description of early-

twentieth-century Mulberry Street, familiar to Faulkner, upon inter-views with Memphis historians and residents. See *Faulkner*, "Notes," for page 52 in this volume. Blotner also documents in this volume that in 1903, two years before Handy and his family moved to Memphis, this Tennessee city supported twice as many saloons as the cities of Birming-ham and Atlanta combined, *Faulkner*, 302.

     Gayoso Street, north of Beale Avenue, also was an infamous red-light district in the early decades of the twentieth century, as described by Lee and many others; but the Gayoso bordellos by repute catered more to a white, and a more well-heeled, clientele than the houses of prostitution located south of Beale. *Street*, 104–5.

114 *"Long before Handy's day"* to *fellow black Pythian: Street*, 127–28; *Father*, 94–95.

115 *able to recruit* to *"played the river": Father*, 95–96.

116 Majestic to Pattona: William Howland Kenney, *Jazz on the River* (Chicago: University of Chicago Press, 2005), 91, 102. Hereafter cited as Kenney.

116 *"Anything that's written":* quoted in *Father*, 96.

117 *source of income:* See representative entries in the untitled account book for July 1914. Handy's account book is an uncataloged but carefully pre-served item at the W. C. Handy Museum in Florence, Alabama, and I am very grateful to that institution for a photocopy of its sixty-four pages.

117 *hurrying down Beale* to *best Sunday prayers:* MVC, Flowers interview, 1–3.

117 *white society debutante:* unidentified quotation in Jesse W. Fox, "Beale Street and the Blues," *West Tennessee Historical Society*, vol. 14 (1960), 138.

117 *"Why not"* to *"that music":* MVC, Flowers interview, 13, 16.

118 *$20,000 in bets:* Miller, 75.

118 *concentrated along Beale Avenue: Ward Maps of United States Cities: A Selec-tive Checklist of Pre–1910 Maps in the Library of Congress* (Washington, D.C.: Library of Congress, 1974), 14; Miller, 73–74, 103, 212. See also "Tennessee: The Civil War and Mr. Crump," in V. O. Key, *Southern Politics in State and Nation* (New York: Alfred A. Knopf, 1949), 75: "In Shelby County [of which Memphis is the county seat] Negroes like whites have voted as Crump desired." Key is hereafter cited as *Southern Politics*. See also *Street*, 242–43: "As for the state, Tennessee has no voting prerequisites other than poll tax payment; nor has it a white primary rule. Hence, colored people play an important part in the primaries and general elections of both the Democratic and Republican parties."

118 *little difficulty for the Crump organization: Memphis*, 362. The author McIl-waine in this passage identifies Handy's employer, Jim Mulcahy, as among those serving as "heelers and clearing agents for [voter] registra-tion certificates" and maintains that at least "30,000 bogus registration certificates" were provided to friendly voters by the Crump political machine between 1910 and 1916.

118 *"beat the drum"* to *"weird melody": Father*, 93, 98–99.

119 *"people farthest down"* to *"Mr. Crump don't 'low": Street*, 133–34. The lyrics to "Mr. Crump" are quoted from Lee's recollection, *Street*, 134.

120 *city's courthouse square:* See *Tennessee*, 214–15, for a brief description of this city square and a map showing its location.

120   *Seated with Handy: Father*, 100. For the presence of Paul Wyer on the band-
      wagon, not named by Handy on this page or elsewhere in his memoir as
      having been present, see below, citations to *Street* and *Blues Anthology*.

120   *"Whiffenpoof Song": Cavalcade*, 293.

120   *remarkably cheerful sound*: Author's analysis of the score for "Memphis
      Blues or (Mr. Crump)" as printed in *Father*, 103–5.

121   *"went wild": Blues Anthology*, 17–18.

121   *may or may not have planned*: Despite the incontrovertible significance to
      popular music of Wyer's blues break, Handy by the time of his 1941
      memoir does not mention it; nor does he include Paul Wyer as among
      those on the bandwagon. However, George Lee, who consulted with
      Handy in the preparation of *Beale Street*, the 1934 history for which
      Handy wrote an introduction, writes that Ed Wyer's brother, Paul
      "Weir" [*sic*], also had been with Handy on the bandwagon that day. See
      Street, 134. Abbe Niles also places Paul Wyer there (spelling the last name
      correctly) and vividly describes the blues break played by Paul Wyer in
      the anthology published in 1926 and on which he collaborated in detail
      with Handy. See *Blues Anthology*, 17–18.

      The omission of Wyer's presence or his celebrated blues break may
      simply have been a lapse in memory by a sixty-eight-year-old memoirist
      in 1941, or be due to the fact that Handy seems to have been closer per-
      sonally and professionally to Ed Wyer, who is documented to have played
      more frequently with Handy and his bands than did his brother.
      (Handy's son Wyer Owens Handy was named to honor Ed Wyer.)

122   *"essence of instrumental jazz"*: "Southern Ragtime," 39–40.

123   *"Bull Dog Rag"*: The score for "Bull Dog Rag" and some biographical
      information about Dobyns is reprinted and briefly discussed in "South-
      ern Ragtime," 165–66 and 74–75. Interestingly, Hurwitt speculates ("Pub-
      lisher," 38–39) that Handy possibly may have been employed part-time at
      the O. K. Houck store circa 1909–10, although this is more of an inference
      than a documented fact.

123   *"'Mr. Crump' was mine": Father*, 99.

124   *"negro sunshine"* to *"catch himself some air"*: Gertrude Stein, in numbered
      paragraph eight, online edition of *Three Lives*, www.bartleby.com/
      74121.html; *Street*, 134.

124   *"good-time town": Memphis*, 346.

124   *still running for public office: Southern Politics*, 63–64.

124   *"Handy's sly joking": Memphis*, 344–45.

125   *"he never heard the song": Father*, 99.

125   *donate a dime*: Liazos, 37–38. The Court's decision was announced in
      Creswill et al. v. Grand Lodge Knights of Pythias of Georgia (1912).

126   *Taft arrived in town* to *blues combo*: Kenney, 91; *Father*, 107, 101; *Memphis*,
      347.

126   *"my esteemed friend"*: MVC, Robert R. Church Papers, photograph,
      "Handy's Memphis Blues Band,"

127   *"no matter where"*: W. C. Handy, "How I Came to Write the 'Memphis
      Blues,'" *New York Age*, 7 December 1916.

127   *"tender pathos"*: Hyram K. Moderwell, "Ragtime," *The New Republic*,
      vol. 4 (16 October 1915), 284–86.

127 *"polyphonic structure":* James Weldon Johnson, "The Negro's Contribution to American Art," *Literary Digest,* vol. 55 (20 October 1917), 27.

SEVEN: HANDY'S MEMPHIS COPYRIGHT BLUES

128 *"Darkies' sorrow song":* The lyrics are excerpted from the graphic reproduction of the sheet music to "The Memphis Blues," LOC.

128 *"Handy came"* to *"I told him":* Miller, 101–2, 73, 79–80; *Memphis,* 355–5, 360; *Southern Politics,* 68.

130 *"tired of writing":* W. C. Handy, "How I Came to Write the 'Memphis Blues,'" *New York Age,* 7 December 1916.

130 *659 Janette Street: Father,* 167–68. The spelling of this street varies within primary sources, and Handy's own spelling of the place-name is used in the text. The vital years for Handy's later children are: Katharine Handy (1902–1982), W. C. (William) Handy Jr. (1904–1972), and Wyer (1915–1995). The spellings of the names of these two Handy daughters vary even within their father's correspondence. (It must be remembered, however, that Handy in his blindness dictated personal letters to a stenographer who may have been unfamiliar with the family spellings.) "Lucile" rather then "Lucille" is used more frequently, and is spelled such in the text. "Katharine," rather than "Katherine," is spelled from Handy's most frequent usage and her obituary in the *NYT.* A photograph of Handy's former house, now relocated to the tourist district of Beale Street, is reproduced in *Black and Blue,* 12.

131 *record cylinder:* Randall Stross, *The Wizard of Menlo Park: How Thomas Edison Invented the Modern World* (New York: Crown, 2007), 218–20.

131 *"stack of sheet music":* House, 104.

131 *twelve-bar measures* to *"my customers don't": Father,* 107–8.

132 *the trade:* A commercial and cultural history of the O. K. Houck Piano Store, with references and links, is accessible at www.scottymoore.net/okhouck.html.

132 *Theron Catlin Bennett:* David A. Jasen and Trebor Jay Tichenor, "Theron Catlin Bennett," *Rags and Ragtime: A Musical History* (New York: Dover, 1978), 46–49.

133 *smart blue covers* to *September 28, 1912:* A first edition of the score of the original "Memphis Blues" is available for view through the Library of Congress at the entry for "American Memory: Today in History: September 28," http://memory.loc.gov/ammem/today/sep28.html.

133 *copies remained, seemingly unsold* to *fifty thousand copies: Father,* 108–11. Handy asserted in his memoir on the pages cited above that documents of the Zimmerman company regarding the printing of "Memphis Blues" were later made available to him and that these records confirmed the chicanery with the numbers. Apparently, however, there was no continuing ill will by Handy toward this firm, and the Otto Zimmerman Company remained an important vendor throughout Handy's career as a music publisher. (There may also have been little choice for him in choosing among vendors for this highly specialized printing.)

The Zimmerman Company also is identified by Handy in his memoir and later scholars such as Hurwitt as having been located in Cincinnati, but this venerable music printer only shipped its scores out of that city and in fact had its offices and presses in a substantial three-story brick building across the Ohio River in Newport, Kentucky. The building still stands, in what has now become a tourist bar district, although the family firm permanently closed its doors in 1998 after 123 years of continuous operation. Author's visits, 2006–07. See "Newport Printer Closing Doors," *Cincinnati Business Courier*, 3 December 1998.

135   *"down to Memphis town"*: "The Memphis Blues," LOC.
135   *"Honey Boy" Evans* to *Monette Moore:* See the biographical listing for Evans (written at least a year before he performed "The Memphis Blues" onstage) in Leroy Rice, *Monarchs of Minstrelsy from "Daddy" Rice to Date* (New York: Kenny Publishing, 1911), 339–40; Texas Trio, Monette Moore vocalist, performing as "Susan Smith," Ajax, 17127–B.
137   *"coon duo"* to *"Them Memphis blues"*: Tim Brooks, *Lost Sounds: Blacks and the Birth of the Recording Industry, 1890–1919* (Urbana: University of Illinois Press, 2004), 414–15, hereafter cited as *Lost Sounds*. William H. Kenney, *Recorded Music in American Life: The Phonograph and Popular Memory, 1890–1945* (New York: Oxford University Press, 1999), 38, hereafter cited as *Popular Memory. Freeman*, 13 September 1913.
137   *foxtrot* to *"negro dances"*: Reid Badger, *A Life in Ragtime: A Biography of James Reese Europe* (New York: Oxford University Press, 1995), 115–16.
138   *"Jim Europe recording of my song"*: Father, 113. This recollection by Handy in 1941, although subjectively accurate to him, shows the caution that must be used in employing his memoir as the sole source of chronology. Between the months of December 1913 and October 1914, Europe and his band in fact had three recording sessions at the Victor studio, but all but one of the songs recorded had been performed by the Castles before Europe's adaptation of "The Memphis Blues" for the foxtrot. At the last session, October 1, 1914, Europe and his orchestra did record a song titled "Fox Trot" (Victor 15231-1-2), but the two closest scholars of Europe's career, who have examined the Victor archives, agree that it was inexplicably rejected by Victor and never released. See Badger, 236, and *Lost Sounds*, 274.

Handy certainly would have been aware, for instance, from articles in African American newspapers such as the *Age*, and the white press, of Europe's success onstage and in ballrooms playing the adaptation of "The Memphis Blues" for the Castles' dance performances. Europe's released recordings for Victor in 1913–14, not including his adaptation of "The Memphis Blues," were also very successful nationally. It is certainly more than possible that O. K. Houck, as Handy remembered it, at some time in 1914 placed a photograph of Handy—perhaps without his permission—in the front window of the piano store arranged as if the composer were listening to a Europe recording that was not "The Memphis Blues." (Although Handy does not mention it, this placement also degradingly recalls the popular "His Master's Voice" advertisements of the time for the Victor company, in which the dog "Nipper" is illustrated listening attentively to a recording playing on a Victrola.) Handy apparently conflated in his memory this obnoxious promotional display for Europe with his knowledge of the latter's success with "my song," thus perhaps also unwittingly revealing in his 1941 memoir that Handy in the 1910s had considered Jim Europe as a major rival rather than the seldom-mentioned junior acquaintance as Handy chose to describe him in *Father of the Blues.*

139   *"I've Got de Blues"*: Classic: iv, 42–43.

139   *"Too Blamed Mean to Cry"*: The Library of Congress Catalogue of Copyright Entries, for the Year 1912, "part 3: Musical Compositions" (Government Printing Office, 1912), 9. This "New Series," as the Library named it, for copyright registrations began in 1906 and continued for consecutive years, and is hereafter cited as *Catalogue,* followed by the particular year and the "part" that contains registrations for musical compositions. This is followed by the page number within that part's volume or volumes for the particular registration of that musical composition. Although a "part" may, in some years, be of several volumes, pagination among volumes is consecutively numbered.

139   *"Dallas Blues"*: Catalogue 1912, Part 3, 1160.

139   *"Negro Blues"*: Ibid., 1372.

139   *"Baby Seals Blues"*: Ibid., 916.

140   *urban men such as Handy*: "Southern Ragtime," 90–91.

140   *"The Last Shot Got Him"*: Catalogue 1912, Part 3, 149.

141   *"Negro Blues" to "Dallas Blues"*: "Negro Blues" was recorded and released as "Nigger Blues." A recording of "Nigger Blues: A Fox Trot for Dancing" sung in 1916 by the white minstrel Leroy "'Lasses'" White, accompanied by the Victor Military Band, is available at the Institute of Jazz Studies at Rutgers University. The other side of the disc is a recording of Handy's arrangement of "Joe Turner Blues." The Rutgers library accession number is D000527.01. See Leroy "'Lasses' White, vocalist, "Nigger Blues," Columbia A2064.

141   *"common property" to "Apple Blossom Time"*: Blues Anthology, 2; Cavalcade, 316.

143   *"Oh, sing 'em"*: Lynn Abbott and Doug Seroff, "'They Cert'ly Sound Good to Me': Sheet Music, Southern Vaudeville, and the Commercial Ascendancy of the Blues," *American Music*, vol. 14 (winter 1996), 442–43. Hereafter cited as Abbott.

144   *"World Wide 'Blue' Note"*: See the graphically reproduced cover for the score in entry for "The Memphis Blues," LOC.

144   *"stood at the door"*: Street, 132.

145   *"headache and heartache"*: Father, 102.

145   *"meridian of life"*: Freeman, 26 September 1914.

EIGHT: TEMPO À BLUES

148   Moon Illustrated Weekly: Paul G. Partington, "The *Moon Illustrated Weekly*—The Precursor of *The Crisis*," *Journal of Negro History*, vol. 48 (July 1963), 206–16.

149   *"Beale 400"*: This Memphis colloquialism appears in print as quoted by Maude Greene, "The Background of the Beale Street Blues," *Tennessee Folklore Society Bulletin*, vol. 7 (1941), 5.

149   *"a charming singer"*: Partial newspaper clipping, circa 1907–08, tentatively

identified in "Publisher," 74, as from the African American newspaper the (Memphis) *Conservator*, MVC, Robert R. Church Family Papers, University of Memphis.

149 *worthy successor:* Street, 287–90.

150 *return to Memphis:* The year 1907 as Pace's return to the city is determined by internal dating within the text of *Street*, 290. Hurwitt, in "Publisher" (67), states the year, without citation, as having been 1908.

150 *"Cotton Fields of Dixie" to business partners:* Father, 125.

151 *"Fifteen Cents" to "That International Rag":* Cavalcade, 320–23.

151 *"The Memphis Itch":* Classic, 59.

152 *vividly illustrated to failure to match:* Classic, 59; Father, 117.

153 *better-paying job to Morris Lippman's:* Father, 126.

154 *"Yellow Dog Rag":* See entry for lyrics to "Yellow Dog Blues," as the song was retitled by 1919, in LOC.

154 *May Irwin's:* Dark Path, 16–17.

154 *Estelle Harris:* Father, 126.

155 *"now in Moorhead, Miss.":* Freeman, 11 March 1916.

155 *four songs . . . that year to olio:* Catalogue 1915, part 3, "First Half of 1915": "Shoeboot's Serenade," 402, "Fuzzy Wuzzy Rag," 468; *Catalogue 1915*, part 3, "Last Half of 1915": "The Hesitating Blues," 672, "Hail to the Spirit of Freedom," 795. The cover of this Handy march score and its borrowed melodies are further described in "Publisher," 102–3.

156 *monthly salary to "crimp in my work":* "Partnership Agreement of Pace & Handy Music Company," dated 29 October 1915, nonarchived document currently on display at the commercial Memphis Music Hall of Fame in the Beale Street entertainment district; *Father, 167, 118.

157 *May 12, 1916 to foreclosure:* Abbott, 442; *Catalogue 1916*, part 3, "First Half of 1916," 85; *Father*, 127–29; *Dark Pathway*, 149.

Pace & Handy had a banner year in the number of published scores in 1916. Other, less successful songs not composed exclusively by Handy but published by the firm were: *Catalogue 1916*, part 3, "First Half of 1916": "Down by the Chattahoochee River (I Wish I Was There Tonight)," 542; *Catalogue 1916*, part 3, "Last Half of 1916": "I Won't Stop Loving You Till You Stop the World from Turning," 653; "In the Land Where Cotton Is King," 892. This last was scored by Handy to words by Pace. As this inventory shows, Pace & Handy was by no means an exclusively blues publisher in 1916. The two other songs copyrighted that year, "Ole Miss Rag" and "Beale Street," are cited in notes below.

158 *"best people":* Freeman, 15 November 1913.

158 *younger brother to "Florida Blues":* Father, 132, 100.

158 *"He would watch" to "light cigarettes":* Faulkner, 175; William Faulkner, *Sanctuary* (New York: Jonathan Cape & Harrison Smith, 1931), 32.

159 *"put a carnation" to "Glittering young devils":* Father, 126, 167, 91. See the map of the era's Beale Avenue saloons in *Black and Blue*, 11.

160 *"Maggie, arms akimbo" to dark-skinned Othello:* Father, 91, 122.

161 *chose not to enforce:* Progressive Era, 175–77.

161 *Fatty Grimes to Cousin Hog:* Father, 92–93; Street, 85–87.

161 *"Pee Wee Salon [sic] crap":* "Retrospect 2," 30 November 1950, 83.

162 *"ain't no sin":* quoted in *Memphis*, 338.

162   "until my wagon comes": quoted in *Street*, 94.

163   cert'ly sound good to me!: ibid., 415–18.

163   *"met Handy's band"* to *"profited him financially"*: quoted in *Treasury*, 250. Still, quoted in Robert B. Haas, ed., *William Grant Still and the Fusion of Cultures in American Music* (Los Angeles: Black Sparrow, 1972), 114.

Handy's contemporary George Lee also diplomatically implies that Handy borrowed profitably from "colored stars of the stage." See *Street*, 151–52. For other non–Mississippi Delta, non-bordello district of New Orleans origins for the published blues, see Bruce Bastin, "From the Medicine Show to the Stage: Some Influences upon the Development of a Blues Tradition in the Southeastern United States," *American Music*, 2 (spring 1984), and "Blues for the Sideshow Tent," in *Dark Pathway*, 157ff.

164   *close at hand:* See map in *Black and Blue*, 11.

165   *Handy had plagiarized:* Abbott, 437–38.

165   *Willie Too Sweet: Freeman*, 2 September 1916.

165   Beale Street: *Catalogue 1916*, part three, "Last Half of 1916," 1195. The date of registration is 1 December 1916, and, as stated in the text, the song was commercially published in 1917. For lyrics, see entry in LOC.

166   *Raderman recording:* Earl Fuller's Famous Jazz Band, Victor 18369–B.

167   *popular songs: Cavalcade*, 351–56.

167   *commercial disappointments:* The Pace & Handy inventory registered in 1917 in *Catalogue, 1917*, part 3, included the popular "Hooking Cow Blues," 693, and the firm's purchased copyright of the "Florida Blues," 95. But the remainders, none composed by Handy, were unmemorable: "Lonesome Sal," 109; "The Song the Sunny Southland Sings," 125; "I'm So Glad My Daddy's Coming Home," 284; "Nightie Night, Kiss Yo' Mammy Nightie Night," 419, and "Preparedness Blues," 630. The latter score was illustrated by a buffoonish African American in uniform, happily stealing a chicken, with a playing card, a bottle of gin, and a Beale Street–style straight razor in his tunic pocket.

As the last two entries indicate, Handy as a song buyer was at times unwilling to forgo the once-popular coon songs of the 1890s, just as perhaps Pace was equally irresistibly attracted to the sentimental parlor songs of the 1900s. But in defense of Handy's attempts at flogging these now-objectionable, minstrel-olio-style songs of the nineteenth century in a hope for big sales, the reader is reminded that one of the most popular songs of 1917 was the rearranged tune from the Schirmer music publishing company, "Jump Jim Crow."

167   *"Joe Turner Blues":* William Sweatman and His Jass Band, "Joe Turner Blues," Pathé A20167.

167   *Pace made arrangements to passenger train: Father*, 131, 171–73.

168   *Charley Patton:* Calt, 108.

168   *"airtight studios": Father*, 173; *Lost Sounds*, 417–18.

169   *mass-produced recording:* The musicians playing with Handy on trumpet and cornet at these 1917 sessions were: Sylvester Bevard, trombone; Wilson Townes, Alex Poole, Charles Harris, and Nelson Kincaid on clarinets/saxophones; Edward Alexander, William Tyler, and Darnell Howard, violins; Henry Graves, cello; Charles Hillman, piano; Archie Walls, bass; and Jasper Taylor, drums and xylophone. See *Lost Sounds*, 417.

In 1897, while touring with Mahara's Minstrels, Handy and others of the troupe recorded the song "Cotton Blossoms" onto a recording cylinder at Helena, Montana. These individual cylinders were then placed inside stand-alone machines in saloons and other places of public entertainment, where patrons would pay a nickel, place rubber tubes in their ears, and then hear the recording. See *Father,* 173, and William Howard Kenney, *Recorded Music in American Life: The Phonograph and Popular Memory, 1890–1945* (New York: Oxford University Press, 1999), 24.

169 *a little stiff:* Archival recordings of some songs from this 1917 recording are available on the CD *W. C. Handy's Memphis Blues Band,* Memphis Archives MA 17006, and a modern performance of his early works is re-created on the CD *W. C. Handy's Beale Street: Where the Blues Began,* Inside Memphis ISC-0516.

169 *"not up to scratch":* Father, 174.

169 *"Ole Miss Rag":* Catalogue 1916, part 3, "Last Half of 1916," 778. According to the liner notes of the *Inside Memphis* CD of his works, "the Ole Miss" was the nickname of the fastest train from Memphis headed southward into Mississippi. The original sheet music was illustrated by a massive funnel-smoking railroad engine pulling a long line of cars onto a map of that state. Both the train and the song on this illustration are subtitled "The Fastest Thing Out of Memphis." See *Classic,* 94.

Although the University of Mississippi at Oxford is known affectionately by its alumni as "Ole Miss," there are no records in the university archives or the Handy archives indicating that he published this ragtime under any official commission with the administrators. (Author's correspondence with Blues Archive, University of Mississippi Libraries, 2006.) Of course, the musical connection with this university did not hurt sales of the song's scores for Pace & Handy, and, obversely, the Ole Miss football team, known as the Rebels, should consider themselves fortunate to have had such a preeminent composer for their adopted fight song of "Ole Miss Rag." The only other gridiron contenders with such a pedigree for their team song are the Louisiana State University footballers, who do violence to their opponents on the field to the early jazz tune of Nick LaRocca's "Tiger Rag" of 1917, also known as "Hold That Tiger!"

169 *cowbells:* Original Dixieland Jass (Jazz) Band, Vocalion 31206.

170 *his first meeting:* "Publisher," 138.

170 *Clef Club* to *murdered: Lost Sounds,* 268–69, 277–78, 287–88; *Father,* 228–29. For the enthusiastic response of French audiences to Europe's performance, see "Negro Jazz Music Rag Variety Taking Europe," *Freeman,* 24 August 1918.

Europe's performances in the United States in 1919—much more lively than Handy's released recordings of his own work in 1917—include his versions of Handy's "The Memphis Blues," "St. Louis Blues," and "Hesitating Blues." Europe's recording also that year of "On Patrol in No Man's Land," re-creating the sounds and fears of an American patrol on a trench raid, is arguably the first American attempt at a "jazz symphony." Europe's performances with his band in 1919 are available on the archival CD *Lieut. Jim Europe's 369th "Hell Fighters" Band,* Memphis Archives MA 7020.

NINE: NEW YORK CITY

172   *"Highly race conscious":* Memphis, 347–48.

173   *"petty indignities"* to *"Preparedness Parades":* Father, 133–34, 189.

174   *Eli Persons* to *"not be there":* Progressive Era, 194; Father, 178. Handy in his memoir, probably out of compassion for the victim's family, changes the family name from Persons to Smith.

174   *the word* nigger: Crump, 205.

174   *Chicago address* to *"Rampart Street":* "Publisher," 136; Lovey Austin and Her Blues Serenaders, "I've Got the Blues for Rampart Street," Paramount 12063-A. For the migration from Memphis to "Chi," see *Memphis,* passim.

175   *New York City* to *"what a Harlem":* Father, 187. Pace & Handy's arrival in the city is noted in *Billboard,* 14 September 1918. Some discographies list recordings Handy and his band had made in 1919 either in New York City or Newark for the Lyraphone Company (Lyric) label, numbered Lyric 4211 and 4212. If so, it is uncertain that these recordings ever were released, nor have any pressings been discovered, and the Lyric numbers subsequently were reassigned to other artists.

175   *Alberta Hunter* to *"most gratifying":* Street, 152; Father, 186.

176   *Broadway address* to *"Not altogether in the South":* "Publisher," 140; Father, 193, 197; Transcript, Oral History Program, California State University at Fullerton, "William Grant Still Interviewed by R. Donald Brown (13 November 1967 and 4 December 1967)," 4; Father, 228–29.

176   *mysterious H. Qualli Clark:* Blues Anthology, "Notes to the Collections," 37–38. Clark also chose to stay with Handy, his former minstrel companion, after the breakup of Pace & Handy.

177   *"Uncle Tom's Cabin":* Father, 198.

177   *"O Death, Where Is Thy Sting?":* Lost Sounds, 422.

177   *Clarence Williams* to *"Sweat" Sweatman:* Father, 208, 147.

177   *"colored fingers":* quoted in "Southern Ragtime," 103–4.

178   *Gaieties of 1919:* Lost Sounds, 423; "Retrospect 2," 29 July 1954, Handy to Charles Still, 104; Ann Hagedorn, *Savage Peace: Hope and Fear in America 1919* (New York: Simon & Schuster, 2007), 339. (Handy long remembered Gilda Gray's boost in 1919 to his song. In this 1954 letter the eighty-one-year-old Handy recounts having endured a cross-country airplane flight of more than eight hours to appear in Los Angeles on the television program *This Is Your Life,* honoring Gray.)

178   *Marion Harris* to *Victor refused:* Marion Harris, vocalist, "St. Louis Blues," Columbia A2944. Compilations of Harris's work, including her other recordings mentioned in the text, are available in *Marion Harris: The Complete Victor Recordings,* Archephone B0007WHAMC, and *Marion Harris: Look for the Silver Lining,* Asv Living Era B000BW9UMQ. Harris's recording popularity and her personal celebrity are discussed in *Popular Memory, 1890–1945* (New York: Oxford University Press, 1999), 102–4. (The "sell it" quote from these pages has been altered from author Kenney's preterit to the conditional subjunctive in this author's text.) Pace's marketing initiative in persuading Harris to record the "St. Louis Blues," as well as other biographical details of his post-Memphis career as included in the

book text, are discussed in John N. Ingram and Lynne B. Feldman, "Pace, Harry Herbert," *African-American Business Leaders: A Biographical Dictionary* (Westport, CT: Greenwood, 1994), 501–17.

Handy in his 1941 memoir, perhaps in residual quarrel with Pace, slighted Harris's contribution in popularizing his best song. Harris is discussed only as having occasioned the Victor promotional representative in New York angrily telephoning Pace and threatening to boycott the records of Pace & Handy songs in retaliation for Harris's signing with Columbia to record "St. Louis Blues." See *Father*, 199–200. Alfred (Al) Bernard, discussed with more praise by Handy in his memoir (196–97), was a white vocalist and a minstrelsy and vaudeville comedian who performed in blackface and had recorded "St. Louis Blues" in 1919; but Bernard in his most widely distributed releases of the song had chosen to give a minstrelsy recitation of the lyrics. See *Lost Sounds*, 423–24. The importance of Harris as a precedent-breaking performer in creating a crossover market success for the blues was to be affirmed in print a few years later by Handy's friend and fellow lover of the blues, Abbe Niles: "As to the singing of blues, it would seem necessary, first, to be a colored contralto—except for the fact that Marion Harris is white." See *Blues Anthology*, 31.

180 *female impersonator:* This arrangement, uncited, is described in "Publisher," 185.

180 *three other white performers:* The subsequent recordings of the "St. Louis Blues" are by Ted Lewis and His Band, Columbia A3790, released on 7 December 1922; Lanin's Southern Serenaders, Bell 97, released in July 1921; and the Original Dixieland Jass (Jazz) Band, Victor 18772A, released on 25 May 1921. This latter included the minstrel-style recitation by Bernard.

180 *179,440 records sold:* Frank Alkyer, ed., *Down Beat: 60 Years of Jazz* (Milwaukee: Hal Leonard, 1996), 37.

180 *"St. Louis Blues":* The uses of lyrics in their original dialectic form within the text are quoted from the sheet music and words for "The St. Louis Blues," circa 1920–22, in the sheet music collection of the Public Library of Cincinnati and Hamilton County. The sheet music is partially and descriptively cataloged as "Cover page: skyline of St. Louis; photograph of Marion Harris; in blue and orange."

182 *"doloric rhythm":* W. C. Handy, "Foreword," *Unsung Americans Sung* (New York: Handy Brothers Music Company, 1944), 7.

183 *"Shake, Rattle, and Roll":* Various songs of this title have been a musical perennial of American popular culture long before it became a rhythm-and-blues hit for Big Joe Turner and a rock-and-roll hit for Bill Haley and His Comets, both in 1954. Al Bernard recorded his song with this title in 1919, and Handy Brothers later bought his composition (*Father*, 197). Earlier, Baby Seals had a big hit in black vaudeville with his song entitled "Shake, Rattle, and Roll" in 1910 (Abbott, 415). Bernard at the very least was influenced by Seals's song. These two earlier songs both celebrate crap-shooting, but the sexual imagery and disregard for authority are common to all three.

183 *careful listener:* Faulkner, 565–66.

183   *"rehearsing 'Beale Street Blues'"*: W. C. Handy to Harry Pace, 3 March 1921,
      James Weldon Johnson Papers, MSS2, Yale Collection of American Liter-
      ature, Beinecke Rare Book and Manuscript Library. Hereafter cited as
      Beinecke MSS2.

183   *39,981 records sold:* Aylker, *Down Beat,* 37.

184   *fiscal 1920* to *"Strivers' Row":* The gross income for the company and the
      market value of Handy's house are taken from the Deposition of W. C.
      Handy in *Pace v. Handy,* 5 May 1924, "Publisher," 290. The extensive legal
      documents of the Handy-Pace dispute are reprinted or excerpted in this
      dissertation's chapter 5, 211ff., and citations will be to the dissertation
      page where the document is reproduced. For Handy's neighborhood, see
      "Strivers Row, A Historical Profile," at www.harlemlive.org.

184   *serious recession* to *"my business methods":* Mark Sullivan, *Our Times: The
      United States, 1900–1925,* vol. 6, "The Twenties" (New York: Charles Scrib-
      ner's Sons, 1935), 163–67; *Father,* 202.

186   *fourteen of his employees:* W. C. Handy to A. R. Tomlinson, 5 May 1948,
      Florence-Lauderdale County Public Library.

186   *bad checks* to *Laughing Trombone Man:* letters, Pace Phonographic Com-
      pany to W. C. Handy, 25 June 1921; Harry H. Pace to W. C. Handy, 26 July
      1921; Harry H. Pace to W. C. Handy, 6 May 1922, Beinecke MSS2.

186   *"my own problems":* Harry H. Pace to W. C. Handy, 4 May 1922, Beinecke
      MSS2.

187   *"Fear"* to *"fight it out": Father,* 205–7, 203; *Blues Anthology,* 14. Although
      Handy suggests a full recovery in his memoir, and speaks of such in his
      business correspondence of the early 1920s, the reference by Niles to two
      full years of his friend's visual impairment is evidence that the recovery
      was slow and partial. Handy's version reveals both his personal optimism
      and an understandable wariness not to appear frail to his creditors and
      professional competitors.

187   *"Loveless Love": Catalogue 1921,* part 3, "First Half of 1921," 204.

187   *"John Henry Blues"* to *"Ape Mister Eddie": Catalogue 1922,* part 3, "Last Half
      of 1922" and "Second Half of 1922," 744, 1547.

187   *"Aunt Hagar's Children": Catalogue 1920,* part 3, "Last Half of 1920," 965.

188   *"Chicago"* to *"Shimmy": Cavalcade,* 388–93.

188   *grossed only $7,015* to *filed legal action:* Deposition of W. C. Handy in *Pace v.
      Handy,* 5 May 1924, "Publisher," 290; *Father,* 207; Deposition of *Pace v.
      Handy,* 30 April 1924, "Publisher," 207, 286.

190   *once had sold* to *needful loan: Father,* 204; "Publisher," 300; *Father,* 208.

190   *company apparently folded* to *"Farewell Blues": Lost Sounds,* 426–28. Handy's
      own version of the "St. Louis Blues" is available on CD on the archival
      "W. C. Handy's Memphis Blues Band," Memphis Archives, MA 17006.
      Hurwitt asserts that the horn player at the March 1922 session, on this
      same CD, does not sound like Handy at his best and is an uncredited sub-
      stitution. See "Publisher," 244. Given the physical condition of Handy,
      the argument can be made either way.

191   *"olive among the marshmallows":* Abbe Niles, "Foreword," *Father,* v.

191   *"Boswell of the blues":* "Alumni Portraits," *Trinity College Bulletin,* March
      1954, archived at Abbe Niles Collection, Special Collections division of
      the Watkinson Library of Trinity College, Hartford, CT, hereafter cited
      as Trinity ANC.

191 *"a lot of fun"*: Abbe Niles, "William C. Handy," in *The Labellum News* [office newsletter of the Cadwalader, Wickersham, & Taft law firm], 7 November 1957, 270. Hereafter cited as *Labellum News*. This publication is archived in Box 7, Trinity ANC. In this reminiscence, Niles gives the year of their first meeting as 1924.

191 *former U.S. president:* See www.cadwalader.com. This prestigious law firm, like Handy Brothers Music Company, continues to do business into the twenty-first century.

192 *"business back at the old stand"*: Father, 208.

192 *"repenting at leisure"*: Abbe Niles, "Foreword," *Father*, vi.

192 *"Things were tough"*: Labellum News, 270, Trinity ANC.

192 *"creative and analytic powers"*: Abbe Niles, *Blues Anthology*, 1.

193 *other dancing couples:* Katherine Niles, "Notes on Abbe Niles and W. C. Handy," unpublished holographic and typewritten manuscript, ms. page 2, Box 7, Trinity ANC.

193 *"memory of W. C. Handy"*: Abbe Niles, "Notes to the Collection," *Blues Anthology*, 25.

193 *in Niles's argument:* Blues Anthology, 10–23.

194 *"outside the university tradition"*: Edmund Wilson, "Shanty-Boy Ballads and Blues," *The New Republic* (14 July 1926), 228. Wilson continues: "The career of Handy himself is particularly interesting as an example of the conscious use by a gifted ballad-writer of folk material."

194 *"Mexican, a Yankee, and a nigger!"* quoted by Abbe Niles, "Foreword," *Father*, ix.

194 *"the very first"*: James Weldon Johnson, "Now We Have the Blues," *New York Amsterdam News*, 7 July 1926, reprinted in Sondra K. Wilson, ed., *The Selected Writing of James Weldon Johnson*, vol. 2 (New York: Oxford University Press, 1995), 388–91.

194 *Van Vechten:* Bruce Keller, ed., *"Keep Inchin' Along": Selected Writing of Carl Van Vechten About Black Art and Letters* (Westport, CT: Greenwood Press, 1979), 28, 51, 148–51. Although some of his papers regarding Handy were donated by Van Vechten to Fisk University in Nashville, for future use by scholars, five queries by e-mail, telephone calls, and letters by the author to the university library's special collections department over a period of two years did not succeed in obtaining permission for their use.

TEN: SYMPHONIES AND MOVIES, SPIRITUALS AND POLITICS

196 *"better music"*: letter quoted in Harry O. Osgood, *So This Is Jazz* (Boston: Little, Brown, 1926), 144. Hereafter cited as Osgood.

197 "New World Symphony": Abbe Niles, "Rediscovering the Spirituals," *Nation*, vol. 123 (1 December 1926), 598–99.

197 *"farmer plowing"*: Father, 218.

197 *intellectual air* to *"Home at 5"* (page 200): Frank Salamone, "Jazz and Its Impact on European Classical Music," *Journal of Popular Culture* (May 2005), 739–40; *Father*, 218–19; Osgood, 158; *NYT*, "Music," 7 December 1925, 18; Donald Friede, *The Mechanical Angel: His Adventures and Enterprises in the Glittering 1920s* (New York: Alfred A. Knopf, 1948), 44–61; Carl Van Vechten, *The Splendid Drunken Twenties: Selections from the Daybooks, 1922–1930*, ed. Bruce Kellner (Urbana: University of Illinois Press, 2003), 160.

197 Rhapsody in Blue to *"best wishes"*: Osgood, 136–37; Henry Levine, "Gershwin, Handy and the Blues," *Clavier*, vol. 20 (October 1970), 10–20. The Gershwin letter is reproduced in holograph on the first page of this article.

200 Afro-American Symphony: Catherine Parsons Smith, *William Grant Still: A Study in Contradictions* (Berkeley: University of California Press, 2000), 114. Hereafter cited as Smith.

201 *Vitaphone Studios* to Ill Wind: See the forty-four entries under "Handy, W. C.," in the unpaginated index, David Meeker, *Jazz in the Movies* (New York: Da Capo Press, 1981); Chris Albertson, *Bessie* (New Haven, CT: Yale University Press, 2003), 193–96; hereafter cited as Albertson. "Still Interview," 24–25; *Father*, 258; "Publisher," 375. Smith's recordings in the 1920s of Handy-composed or Handy Brothers–owned songs include "A Good Man Is Hard to Find" (Columbia 14259-D, 1927), "Careless Love Blues" (Columbia 14083-D, 1925), "St. Louis Blues" (Columbia 14064-D, 1925), and "Yellow Dog Blues" (Columbia 14075-D, 1925).

203 *concert organized by Handy Brothers*: " 'Father of the Blues,' at 54, to Make Concert Debut," *New York World*, 22 April 1928, excerpted in "Publisher," 367; *NYT*, "Handy, Jazz Pioneer, Gives Famous 'Blues,' " 28 April 1928, 13.

204 *obligations to Harry Pace* to *notary public*: *Father*, 211. See also Helge Thygesen, et al., *Black Swan: The Record Label of the Harlem Renaissance* (Nottingham, England: Vintage Jazz Mart Publications, 1966).

205 *Crump listened*: David M. Tucker, *Lieutenant Lee of Beale Street* (Nashville: Vanderbilt University Press, 1971), 102–3.

205 *two-mile parade*: *Black and Blue*, 68.

205 *Louise Logan*: *Father*, 279.

206 *Joe Laurie's*: *Father*, 241–48; *NYT*, "Old Time Actors Pay Visit to Smith," 28 July 1933, 17.

206 *"fifty dusky maidens"*: *NYT*, "News Notes of the Night Clubs," 16 October 1938, 158.

207 *"first cousins"*: quoted from Harry T. Burleigh in *Father*, 157.

207 *call-and-response*: James Weldon Johnson, "Preface," *The Books of American Negro Spirituals* (New York: Da Capo Press, 1969), 23, 33.

207 *"sublime faith"*: Southern, Eileen, ed. "In Retrospect: Letters from W. C. Handy to William Grant Still: Part 1," *Black Perspective in Music*, vol. 7 (fall 1979), 23 October 1942, 210. Hereafter cited as "Retrospect 1." This reminiscence to Still is in the form of a quote from an earlier letter that Handy had written to his brother, Charles.

208 Twelve Negro Spirituals: Smith, 338. In addition to Handy's own collection of spirituals published that year, Handy Brothers also issued in 1938 a booklet edited by Handy, *Negro Authors and Composers of the United States*. It is an eclectic and by no means comprehensive twenty-four-page biographical listing of those lyricists and composers of color whom Handy thought worthy of distinction. Handy did, however, give some notice to the vaudevillian blues with his inclusion of Baby Seals, who is identified as a "pioneer blues composer" (23), and, in apparent gratitude to Clarence Williams and his wife for their kindness to him in the early 1920s, also included a multipage listing of the most popular artists in Williams's then-current catalog.

208   *"that happy feeling"* to *"all but forgotten"*: "Author's Note" (unpaged), *W. C. Handy's Collection of Negro Spirituals* (New York: Handy Brothers Music Company, 1938).

208   *"recesses of my own mind"*: "Retrospect 1," *op. cit.*

209   *Harry T. Burleigh: Lost Sounds*, 474.

209   *"Chantez-les Bas: Creole Blues"*: *Catalogue 1931*, part 3, "First Half of 1931," 159.

210   *"sold Brother Hanson"*: quoted in *Father*, 3.

210   *death of Bessie Smith*: Albertson, 256–67.

211   *"not take colored patients"*: *NYT*, "Hospital Accused by Negro Society," 27 March 1937, 30.

212   *causes célèbres*: *NYT*, "Handy Honored at Concert," 22 November 1938, 28.

212   *"bunch of communists"*: letter to Niles quoted in "Foreword," *Father*, ix.

212   *blame Herbert Hoover*: *Father*, 215.

212   *Scottsboro Unity Defense Committee*: *NYT*, "Music Notes," 4 October 1932, 26.

212   *eight young black men* to *Communist Party*: Dan T. Carter, *Scottsboro: A Tragedy of the American South* (Baton Rouge: Louisiana State University Press, 1969), 48, 54–56. There were nine defendants known as the Scottsboro Boys, but the ninth, Roy Wright, was spared the death penalty and sentenced to life imprisonment, as he was but thirteen years of age.

213   *"felt very good"*: "Foreword," *Father*, ix.

213   *Variety label: Lost Sounds*, 431–32.

213   *giant showcase*: *NYT*, "Negro Music Given at ASCAP Recital," 3 October 1939, 26.

214   *World's Fair: Father*, 275–77; "Author's Acknowledgments," *Father*, xiii; *New York Age*, "W. C. Handy Names Sub-Committee on Music and Entertainment for Harlem's World Fair Committee," 28 May 1938.

214   *visits to Maryland*: "Retrospect 1," 2 April 1941, 201.

215   *"I Created Jazz"* to *"someone swiped it"*: The letters in this exchange of August–September 1938 are reprinted in their entirety in Frank Alkyer, ed., *Down Beat: 60 Years of Jazz* (Milwaukee: Hal Leonard, 1996), 35–37. For Handy's suspicion that Morton's letter was ghostwritten, see "Retrospect 2," 9 April 1952, 87. As is evident, Handy had strong memories and opinions about this accusation of plagiarism even twelve years later. The spelling of "Barrasso" in this biography's text follows the spelling of the family name in the Memphis city directories for the years to which Morton and Handy refer.

217   *"saloon piano player"*: William D. Miller, *Pretty Bubbles in the Air: America in 1919* (Urbana: University of Illinois Press, 1991), 114. See also the earlier, historically inaccurate judgment in 1946 by Rudi Blesh, *Shining Trumpets* (New York: Da Capo, 1976), that Handy was "rather remote from the racial wellsprings from which the blues and jazz emerged" and "seems, from the time of his youth, to have been in the un-Negroid tradition that goes back to the Fisk Jubilee Singers or farther." (146).

217   *Fight It Out*: letter, Johnson to Handy, 15 March 1935, James Weldon Johnson Papers, MSS Johnson, Box and Folder 190, Yale Collection of American Literature, Beinecke Rare Book and Manuscript Library.

218   *movie lobbies*: "Retrospect 1," 7 November 1941, 206–7. After an extensive

public relations campaign by the city of Memphis, the "Birth of the Blues" nationally premiered in that Tennessee city. In this same letter, Handy complains, perhaps already vexed by the exclusively New Orleans origin of the blues presented in this film, of his underpayment of royalties from Paramount for their uses of the "St. Louis Blues." See also his complaints of underpayment in "Retrospect 1," 18 October 1943, 205.

218   "'Jim Crow' president": Father, 222.

ELEVEN: "ST. LOUIS BLUES"

220   *near-fatal* to *"beautiful testimonials": NYT,* "Blues Composer Injured," 29 October 1943, 21; "Retrospect 1," Charles Handy (brother) to Still, 2 November 1943, 213; "Retrospect 1," 20 September 1943, 212; "Retrospect 1," 5 January 1944, 220; "Retrospect 1," 21 January 1944, 221. Handy's future wife's full name was Irma Louise Logan, but following Handy's personal usage in his letters, she is referred to in the text by her middle name.

221   *"The Memphis Blues" to Lena Horne:* MVC, unnumbered file, Memphis *Press-Scimitar* newspaper, "Who Owns 'Memphis Blues'?" 1 July 1949. Along with a mention of the Harry James royalties, there is a discussion within this clipping that Handy was then facing a legal challenge to his copyright by the music publishing company founded by Jerry Vogel, which had copyrighted the lyrics originally composed by George Norton. This dispute was finally resolved in 1953 with Handy retaining legal ownership of his song, and the Jerry Vogel Music Company receiving compensation from Handy Brothers Music Company. See "Publisher," 466.

Holiday's performances of selected Handy songs are available on the CD *The Quintessential Billie Holiday,* vol. 9, 1940–42, Sony B0000027GP. Horne's versions are on the CD *Lena Horne: La Selection, 1936–1941,* L'Art Vocal B00000HU.

222   *FEPC to Mobile, Alabama:* David Robertson, *Sly and Able: A Political Biography of James F. Byrnes* (New York: W. W. Norton, 1994), 338.

222   *"We Are Americans Too" to "Go and Get the Enemy Blues": Catalogue 1941,* part 3, 1026; *Catalogue 1942,* part 3, 1573. (The Copyright Office of the Library of Congress apparently discontinued the more amply printed "First Half" and "Second Half" of each year's registrations during the war years.)

222   *Dorie Miller* to *"The Curator":* W. C. Handy, ed., *Unsung Americans Sung* (New York: Handy Brothers Music Company, 1944), 121, 157.

For the demeaning artwork of "Preparedness Blues," see the description of the cover of that sheet music in the endnotes to chapter seven.

223   *"do nothing"* to *"snow a-flying":* "Retrospect 1," 9 February 1944, 224; "Retrospect 2," 9 January 1945, 68.

223   *Thomas E. Dewey to Tallulah Bankhead: NYT,* "2000 on Citizens' Unit Support Dewey," 13 October 1946, 15; "Retrospect 2," 21 November 1952, 102; Katherine Niles, "Notes on Abbe Niles and W. C. Handy," 5, Box 7, Trinity ANC.

As an instance of what that decade's media frequently called "extravaganzas," a term borrowed from Italian music, see the reportage of

Handy's birthday celebrated at the Waldorf-Astoria Hotel, *NYT*, "W. C. Handy Hailed on 84th Birthday," 18 November 1957, 26.

224   *Ed Sullivan's*: *NYT*, "On Television," 12 December 1949, X10.

224   *"Baby Seals Blues" to B. B. King*: W. C. Handy, ed., *A Treasury of the Blues: Complete Words and Music of 67 Great Songs from Memphis Blues to Present Day* (New York: Charles Boni, 1949), 250, 241–42, 251, 25; Alan Lomax, *Mister Jelly Roll: The Fortunes of Jelly Roll Morton, New Orleans Creole, and "Inventor of Jazz"* (Berkeley: University of California Press, 1950), 140–41, 236–38; "Publisher," 466–67; *Southern Culture*, 1067.

The New Orleans controversy continued to dog Handy. Five years after the publication of the Morton biography, Still alerted Handy in 1955 that Antonio Maggio, the composer who while in residence in New Orleans in 1908 had published "I Got the Blues," had asserted in a Los Angeles publication that Handy had visited New Orleans in 1910 or 1911 and "took full advantage" of the blues there. See *Overture*, vol. 35 (December 1955), 13. Handy in an answering letter to Still emphatically stated, probably for Still's repetition in Los Angeles, that "I haven't been in New Orleans since 1900," when he was touring with the Mahara Minstrels, and "after going to Memphis to teach Thornton's K. of P. [Knights of Pythias] Band, I never did get to New Orleans." See "Retrospect 2," 20 December 1955, 107–8.

225   *"Television is changing"*: Handy Brothers Music Company press release, 3 August 1951, quoted in "Publisher," 469.

225   *"Hike with Ike" to rally in Harlem*: "Retrospect 2," 21 November 1952; *NYT*, "Eisenhower to Speak in Harlem Tomorrow," 24 October 1952, 18; Handy to Matthew Thornton, 15 November 1956, MVC, Robert R. Church papers, box 12, file 15.

226   *"Tho' My Eyes Are Closed" to "empty honors"*: "Retrospect 2," 16 April 1952, 98–99; "Retrospect 2," 27 August 1947, 76; *W. C. Handy, Father of the Blues*, Audio Archives Enterprises A-1200 (LP recording), available at archival Internet audio file at National Public Radio, "Hearing Voices: W. C. Handy," broadcast 16 January 2000; "Retrospect 1," 18 October 1941, 205.

226   *Ed Wyer to Boss Crump*: "Retrospect 1," 30 August 1943, 211; "Retrospect 2," 15 November 1945, 81; "Retrospect 2," 10 January 1945, 69; *Southern Culture*, 1185.

227   *married Louise Logan*: *NYT*, "W. C. Handy, 80, Weds," 3 January 1954, 70.

227   *Louis Armstrong Plays* to *"taking it easy"*: Armstrong's original LP recording is available on the CD *Louis Armstrong Plays W. C. Handy*, Columbia/Legacy CK64925; "Retrospect 2," 8 March 1955, 106–7.

227   *Leonard Bernstein*: *NYT*, "Music: Jazz Is Tested at Stadium," 16 July 1956, 70. This concert is available on the CD *Bernstein on Jazz*, Sony Music Entertainment SMK60560.

228   *"crowning glory"* to *"Gaiety Theater"*: "Retrospect 2," 12 August 1957, 113; "Retrospect 2," 7 March 1958, 118. To the composer's displeasure, the distribution of payments to the Handy family by Paramount apparently caused some dissension among his adult children. See "Retrospect 2," 23 August 1957, 115.

228   *Sydenham Hospital* to *"A little faster"*: *NYT*, "W. C. Handy Critically Ill," 25 March 1958, 30; *NYT*, "W. C. Handy, Composer, Is Dead; Author of

'St. Louis Blues,' 84," 29 March 1958, 17; *NYT*, "Handy's Funeral Attracts 150,000," 3 April 1958, 33; MVC, unnumbered file, "Memphis—People, W. C. Handy," photograph of statue; MVC, unnumbered file, postage stamp, dated "First Day of Issue," 17 May 1969; www.handyfest.com; Florence *Times* newspaper, 25 August 1968, 8 September 1968.

Selected Bibliography

BOOKS

Abbott, Lynn, and Douglas Seroff. *Out of Sight: The Rise of African-American Popular Music, 1889–1895.* Jackson: University of Mississippi Press, 2003.
———. *Ragged but Right: Black Traveling Shows, "Coon Songs," and the Dark Pathway to Blues and Jazz.* Jackson: University of Mississippi Press, 2007.
Berlin, Edward A. *Ragtime: A Musical and Cultural History.* Berkeley: University of California Press, 1980.
Brooks, Tim. *Lost Sounds: Blacks and the Birth of the Recording Industry, 1890–1919.* Urbana: University of Illinois Press, 2004.
Du Bois, W. E. B. *The Souls of Black Folk.* New York: Oxford University Press, 2007.
Epstein, Dena J. *Sinful Tunes and Spirituals: Black Folk Music to the Civil War.* Urbana: University of Illinois Press, 1977.
Handy, W. C. *Father of the Blues.* New York: Da Capo Press, 1985.
———, ed. *Blues: An Anthology.* New York: Albert & Charles Boni, 1926.
———, ed. *Unsung Americans Sung.* New York: Handy Brothers Music Company, 1944.
———, ed. *A Treasury of the Blues: Complete Words and Music of 67 Great Songs from Memphis Blues to Present Day.* New York: C. Boni, 1949.
Haymes, Max. *Railroadin' Some: Railroads in the Early Blues.* York, England: Music Mentor, 2006.
Hasse, John Edward. *Ragtime: Its History, Composers, and Music.* New York: Schirmer, 1985.
Jasen, David, ed. *Beale Street and Other Classic Blues: 38 Works, 1901–1921.* Mineola, NY: Dover Publications, 1998.
Kenney, William H. *Jazz on the River.* Chicago: University of Chicago Press, 2005.
———. *Recorded Music in American Life: The Phonograph and Popular Memory, 1890–1945.* New York: Oxford University Press, 1999.
Key, V. O. *Southern Politics in State and Nation.* New York: Alfred A. Knopf, 1949.
Lee, George W. *Beale Street: Where the Blues Began.* New York: Robert O. Ballou, 1934.

Lhamon, W. T., Jr. *Jump Jim Crow: Lost Plays, Lyrics, and Street Prose of the First Atlantic Popular Culture*. Cambridge, MA: Harvard University Press, 2003.

Lott, Eric. *Love and Theft: Blackface Minstrelsy and the American Working Class*. New York: Oxford University Press, 1993.

McKee, Margaret, and Fred Chisenhall. *Beale Black & Blue: Life and Music on Black America's Main Street*. Baton Rouge: Louisiana State University Press, 1981.

Mattfeld, Julius. *Variety Music Cavalcade, 1620–1969: A Chronology of Vocal and Instrumental Music Popular in the United States*. New York: Prentice-Hall, 1971.

Sampson, Henry T. *The Ghost Walks: A Chronological History of Blacks in Show Business, 1865–1910*. Metuchen, NJ: Scarecrow Press, 1988.

Strausbaugh, John. *Black Like You: Blackface, Whiteface, Insult & Imitation in American Popular Culture*. New York: Tarcher/Penguin, 2006.

Stribling, T. S. *The Store*. New York: Literary Guild, 1932.

———. *The Unfinished Cathedral*. Garden City, NY: Doubleday, Doran, 1934.

White, Loring H. *Ragging It: Getting Ragtime into History (and Some History into Ragtime)*. New York: iUniverse, 2005.

Willis, John C. *Forgotten Time: The Yazoo-Mississippi Delta After the Civil War*. Charlottesville: University of Virginia Press, 2000.

Wilson, Charles, et al., eds. *Encyclopedia of Southern Culture*. Chapel Hill: University of North Carolina Press, 1989.

Wilson, Sondra K., ed. *The Selected Writing of James Weldon Johnson*. Vols. 1 and 2. New York: Oxford University Press, 1995.

Woods, Clyde. *Development Arrested: The Blues and Plantation Power in the Mississippi Delta*. New York: Verso Press, 1998.

Woodward, C. Vann. *The Strange Career of Jim Crow*, 2nd ed., rev. New York: Oxford University Press, 1966.

SCHOLARLY ARTICLES

Abbott, Lynn, and Doug Seroff. " 'They Cert'ly Sound Good to Me': Sheet Music, Southern Vaudeville, and the Commercial Ascendancy of the Blues," *American Music* 14:4 (winter 1996), 402–54.

Gussow, Adam. "Racial Violence, 'Primitive' Music, and the Blues Entrepreneur: W. C. Handy's Mississippi Problem," *Southern Cultures* 7:3 (fall 2002), 65–77.

Levine, Harry. "Gershwin, Handy, and the Blues," *Clavier* 9:7 (October 1970), 11–20.

Southern, Eileen, ed. "In Retrospect: Letters from W. C. Handy to William Grant Still: Part 1," *Black Perspective in Music* 7:2 (fall 1979), 119–234.

———, ed. "In Retrospect: Letters from W. C. Handy to William Grant Still: Part 2," *Black Perspective in Music* 8:1 (spring 1980), 65–119.

DISSERTATIONS

Davidson, Frank C. "The Rise, Development, Decline and Influence of the American Minstrel Show" (PhD diss., New York University, 1952).

Hurwitt, Elliott S. "W. C. Handy as Music Publisher: Career and Reputation" (PhD diss., City University of New York, 2000).

Joyner, David L. "Southern Ragtime and Its Transition to Published Blues" (PhD diss., Memphis State University, 1986).

NEWSPAPERS

The *Freeman* (Indianapolis, IN) weekly, inclusive for 1896–1919.
The New York Times, inclusive for 1919–1958.

ARCHIVAL COLLECTIONS

Robert R. Church Family Papers, Mississippi Valley Collections, McWherter Library, University of Memphis.
Abbe Niles Papers, Special Collections of Watkinson Library, Trinity College, Hartford, CT.
James Weldon Johnson Papers, Yale Collection of American Literature, Beinecke Rare Book and Manuscript Library, Yale University, New Haven, CT.
History and Genealogy Department, Public Library of Florence and Lauderdale County, Florence, AL.

INTERNET SITES

http://memory.loc.gov/ammem/collections/sheetmusic/brown. Accessed in July 2008. Provides a link to the historical sheet music collection electronically maintained by the Library of Congress and physically archived at Brown University.
"Trail of the Hellhound" at www.nps.gov/history/delta/blues. Accessed in July 2008. Provides links to graphic files and descriptive text of geographic sites of importance to W. C. Handy's career in Mississippi and Tennessee.

CD DISCOLOGY

Armstrong, Louis. *Louis Armstrong Plays W. C. Handy.* Columbia/Legacy CK64925, 1997.
Handy, William Christopher. *W. C. Handy's Memphis Blues Band.* Memphis Archives MA 17006, 1994.
Wolfe, Carl, et al. *W. C. Handy's Beale Street: Where the Blues Began.* Inside Memphis ISC-0516, 2002.
Lost Sounds: Blacks and the Birth of the Recording Industry, 1891–1922 (various performers). Archeophone Records ARCH 1005, 2005.

Index

"She's a Mean Job Blues," 190

"Shim-me-sha-wabble" (Williams), 167

"Shoeboot's Serenade" (WCH), 156

Simond, "Old Stretch," 87

Sister Carrie (Dreiser), 123

"Sitting on Top of the World" (folk song), 251

Sixteen New Negro Spirituals (Johnson), 209

slaves, 11, 19, 21–6, 30, 42–3, 54, 67, 111, 208–10; emancipation of, 21, 24, 27, 29

Sloan, Henry, 101, 240n

Smith, Bessie, 10, 17, 157, 165, 201–2, 205, 210, 217

Smith, Chris, 139–42, 151, 183, 195, 224

Smith, William "Cricket," 69–70, 137, 245n

"Snakey Blues," 169

"Snooky Ookums" (Berlin), 151

Solvent Savings Bank (Memphis), 13, 150, 173, 186, 236n, 250n

"Some Blues (For You All)" (Bennett), 133

song sharking, 134

"Song the Sunny Southland Sings, The," 258n

Souls of Black Folk, The (Du Bois), 11, 32, 103

Sousa, John Philip, 8, 32, 48, 51, 86, 94, 98, 107; dance arrangements of marches of, 50; Marine Corps Band directed by, 41; ragtime incorporated by, 79, 247n; showmanship of, 41–2, 44

Southern Politics in State and Nation (Key), 124

Southern Railroad, 95

Spanish-American War, 72, 93

Spanish Civil War, 206, 212, 213

spirituals, 9, 35, 196, 197, 203, 207–10, 212, 226, 264n; *see also titles of specific songs*

Standard Life Insurance Company, 153, 157, 175

"Stand on That Sea of Glass" (spiritual), 209

"Stars and Stripes Forever, The" (Sousa), 48–9

Stein, Gertrude, 123–24

Stewart, Will, 114

Still, William Grant, 163–4, 176, 186, 207, 221, 223, 226–8, 267n; blues symphony by, 200–1, 214; spirituals arranged by, 208

Stone, Johnny ("Leroy Bland"), 57, 59, 75

Strausbaugh, John, 53

Stribling, Thomas S., 28–9

Strivers' Row (Harlem), 14, 184, 189

Sullivan, Ed, 224, 229

"Sundown Blues" (WCH), 187

Supreme Court, U.S., 22, 125

Swan, George A., 86

Sweatman, Wilbur C. "Sweat," 57, 167, 177, 195, 246n

"Sweetheart of Sigma Chi, The," 142

"Swing Low, Sweet Chariot" (spiritual), 209

swing, 187, 213, 214, 225

Sydenham Hospital (Harlem), 228

Syncopation (Motley), 194

Taft, Henry W., 191

Taft, William H., 117, 125, 126

Talk of the Town (television program), 224

"Tangana" (tango) rhythm, 3–4, 14, 182

Taylor, Jasper, 3, 158, 169, 258n

Tchaikovsky, Pyotr Ilyich, 199

Terrell, Bob and Alonzo, 240n

Texas Trio, 136

"That Evening Sun Go Down" (Faulkner), 183

"That International Rag" (Berlin), 151

Theater Owners Booking Association (TOBA), 7, 10, 17, 18, 137, 142, 157, 163–5, 216

This Is Your Life (television show), 260n

Thornton, Matthew, 106–8, 111, 267n

Thornton, Powers, 114

Three Lives (Stein), 123–24

"Tiger Rag" (LaRocca), 167, 259n

Wilson, Teddy, 212
Wilson, Woodrow, 167, 184
Woodlawn Cemetery (Bronx, New
York), 229, 232
Woolworth's stores, 13, 173, 184
Works Progress Administration, 95
World War I, 167, 170, 171, 173–5, 179,
184, 223
World War II, 222–3
World's Columbian Exposition
(Chicago, 1893), 44–6, 76, 241n
World's Fair (New York, 1939), 214
Wright, Louis, 68, 92, 174, 218
Wright, Roy, 265n
Wyer, Edward, 115, 116, 120–3, 126,
136, 156, 168, 224, 226, 253n
Wyer, Paul, 115, 116, 120–2, 136,
224, 253n

Yale University, 120
"Yankee Doodle Boy, The"
(Cohan), 65

Yazoo & Mississippi Valley (Y&MV)
Railroad, 92, 94–95, 99, 105–6, 143
Yellow Dog (Cleveland,
Mississippi), 97
"Yellow Dog Rag (later Blues)"
(WCH), 10, 13, 143, 145, 153–5, 157–
9, 163, 165, 167, 188, 189, 193, 202
"You'd Be Surprised" (Berlin), 178
Young, Billy, 60
Young, Rida Johnson, 167
Young, Robert, 120
"Young America" (minstrel
song), 59
"Your Clock Ain't Right" (blues), 98
"You're a Grand Old Flag"
(Cohan), 65
"You've Got to See Your Momma
Every Night," 179

Ziegfeld Follies, 66
Zimmerman & Son music printing
firm, 131, 134, 254n

David Robertson is the author of three prior biographies, of the slave rebel Denmark Vesey, former U.S. Secretary of State James F. Byrnes, and the bishop James A. Pike, and of a historical novel about John Wilkes Booth. His poetry has appeared in the *Sewanee Review* and other journals, he has lectured in American Studies at Princeton University, and he has provided political and literary commentary to ABC News and *The Washington Post*. He was educated in Alabama and lives in Ohio.

A NOTE ON THE TYPE

This book was set in Monotype Dante, a typeface designed by Giovanni Mardersteig (1892–1977). Conceived as a private type for the Officina Bodoni in Verona, Italy, Dante was originally cut only for hand composition by Charles Malin, the famous Parisian punch cutter, between 1946 and 1952. Although modeled on the Aldine type used for Pietro Cardinal Bembo's treatise *De Aetna* in 1495, Dante is a thoroughly modern interpretation of the venerable face.

Composed by North Market Street Graphics,
Lancaster, Pennsylvania
Printed and bound by Berryville Graphics,
Berryville, Virginia
Designed by Wesley Gott